Syncretism/Anti-syncretism

Syncretism refers to the synthesis of different religious forms. It is a contentious and contested term which has undergone many historical transformations in meaning. Some see it as a disparaging, ethnocentric label for religious traditions (such as independent African churches), which are deemed 'impure' or 'inauthentic' because they are permeated by local ideas and practices. Yet in other contexts religious synthesis may have positive connotations as a form of resistance to cultural dominance, as a link with a lost history, or as a means of establishing a national identity in a multicultural state. In the present era of displacement, migration, urbanization, global capitalism and generally increasing 'cultural compression', syncretic processes are multiplied and intensified. The appropriation of 'development' and 'modernization' is often accompanied by the syncretic appropriation of world religions.

These processes are examined by the contributors to *Syncretism/Anti-syncretism* across such topics as multiculturalism in India, new religious movements in Japan, interpretations of circumcision as crucifixion in Papua New Guinea and Turkish migrants' efforts to remain Muslims in Germany. In these studies, the politics of discourses *about* syncretism are treated as part of the politics of religious synthesis. Who has the authority to describe a particular religious tradition, including their own, as syncretic? What are the political consequences of such pronouncements in, for example, South Africa, India or the USA?

Syncretism/Anti-syncretism will be of interest to scholars and students of anthropology, religious studies, sociology, history and cultural studies.

Charles Stewart is Lecturer in Anthropology and Ancient History at University College, London. **Rosalind Shaw** is Assistant Professor of Sociocultural Anthropology, Tufts University, Massachusetts, USA.

European Association of Social Anthropologists

The European Association of Social Anthropologists (EASA) was inaugurated in January 1989, in response to a widely felt need for a professional association which would represent social anthropologists in Europe and foster co-operation and interchange in teaching and research. As Europe transforms itself in the nineties, the EASA is dedicated to the renewal of the distinctive European tradition in social anthropology.

Other titles in the series

Conceptualizing Society
Adam Kuper

Revitalizing European Rituals
Jeremy Boissevain

Other Histories
Kirsten Hastrup

Alcohol, Gender and Culture
Dimitra Gefou-Madianou

Understanding Rituals
Daniel de Coppet

Gendered Anthropology
Teresa del Valle

Social Experience and Anthropological Knowledge
Kirsten Hastrup and Peter Hervik

Fieldwork and Footnotes
Han F. Vermeulen and Arturo Alvarez Roldan

Syncretism/Anti-syncretism

The politics of religious synthesis

Edited by
Charles Stewart and Rosalind Shaw

London and New York

First published 1994
by Routledge
11 New Fetter Lane, London EC4P 4EE

Simultaneously published in the USA and Canada
by Routledge
29 West 35th Street, New York, NY 10001

Typeset in Times by J&L Composition Ltd, Filey, North Yorkshire
Printed and bound in Great Britain by
Mackays of Chatham PLC, Chatham, Kent

British Library Cataloguing in Publication Data
A catalogue record for this book is available from the British Library

Library of Congress Cataloging in Publication Data
A catalogue record for this book has been requested

ISBN 0–415–11116–1 (hbk)
ISBN 0–415–11117–X (pbk)

Contents

Contributors

Mariane Ferme received her PhD from the University of Chicago and is Assistant Professor of Anthropology at the University of California, Berkeley. She has conducted extensive field research among the Mende of Sierra Leone and is currently studying Sierra Leoneans in Egypt.

David M. Guss is currently a Senior Fellow at Harvard University as well as a member of the Department of Sociology and Anthropology at Tufts University. His most recent book is *To Weave and Sing: Art, Symbol and Narrative in the South American Rain Forest* (1989).

Wolfgang Kempf received his MA from Tübingen University and is currently a doctorand at the Department of Anthropology, University of Tübingen. He has conducted fieldwork for 22 months among the Ngaing in Madang Province, Papua New Guinea.

Jim Kiernan received his PhD from the University of Manchester and is Professor of Social Anthropology at the University of Natal, Durban, South Africa. His research on Zulu Zionists has produced numerous journal articles and a book, *The Production and Management of Therapeutic Power* (1990).

Klaus-Peter Koepping is Professor of Anthropology at the University of Heidelberg. His current interests are modernization and religious movements in Japan, but he has also conducted field research in Afghanistan, South Australia and Taiwan. He is the author of *Adolf Bastian and the Psychic Unity of Mankind* (1983).

Birgit Meyer studied pedagogy and comparative religion at the University of Bremen and cultural anthropology at the University of

Amsterdam. She is currently an associate of the Amsterdam School for Social Research where she is writing her doctoral thesis on local Christianity in Ghana.

David Mosse obtained his DPhil in social anthropology from Oxford University. He is currently Lecturer at the Centre for Development Studies, University of Wales, where he is working on social organization and environmental change in South India.

Rosalind Shaw is Assistant Professor of Sociocultural Anthropology at Tufts University. She co-edited *Dreaming, Religion and Society in Africa* (1992) and is Deputy Editor of the *Journal of Religion in Africa*. She is currently preparing a book on gender and divination among the Temne of Sierra Leone.

Charles Stewart is Lecturer in Anthropology and Ancient History at University College London. He is the author of *Demons and the Devil: Moral Imagination in Modern Greek Culture* (1991).

Peter van der Veer is Professor of Comparative Religion in the Faculty of Social Sciences at the University of Amsterdam. He is the author of *Gods on Earth* (1988) and *Religious Nationalism* (1994) and co-editor, with Carol A. Breckenridge, of *Orientalism and the Postcolonial Predicament* (1993).

Richard Werbner is Professor in African Anthropology at the University of Manchester. His most recent book is *Tears of the Dead: The Social Biography of an African Family* (1991), winner of the Amaury Talbot Prize of the Royal Anthropological Institute.

Lale Yalçın-Heckmann is Research Fellow at the University of Bamberg and works on Islam and migrants in Germany. She obtained her PhD in social anthropology at the London School of Economics. She is the author of *Tribe and Kinship among the Kurds in Turkey* (1991).

Acknowledgements

The editors would like to thank the following for their specialist suggestions and advice, which have enriched this volume: Louis Brenner, Tim Bryson, Kenneth George, Eric Hirsch, Adam Kuper, Ruth Mandel, D.P. Martinez, J. Lorand Matory, J.D.Y. Peel, Jonathan Spencer, Linda Thomas, A.R. Vasavi and Richard Werbner. They are also grateful to Daniel Stephanos for help with computers and e-mail and to the series editor, Marilyn Strathern, for her support. Rosalind Shaw gratefully acknowledges financial assistance from the Provost's Office, Tufts University.

Acknowledgments

Introduction: problematizing syncretism

Rosalind Shaw and Charles Stewart

'Syncretism' is a contentious term, often taken to imply 'inauthenticity' or 'contamination', the infiltration of a supposedly 'pure'
tradition by symbols and meanings seen as belonging to other,
incompatible traditions. Diverse local versions of notionally standard
'world religions' such as Christianity and Islam are often pointed to
as prime examples of syncretism in this critical sense, especially in
the writings of missionaries and theologians. Interestingly, a similarly
negative view of the concept of syncretism also holds sway over many
anthropologists and scholars in religious studies who work without
any particular religious affiliation or commitment. Yet within anthropology, where notions of the 'purity' of traditions have not had much
credibility for some time, syncretism has been ascribed a neutral, and
often positive, significance. Recently, the simmering scepticism about
perennial, stable 'traditions' has boiled over into a number of concise
statements by both anthropologists and historians (such as Wagner
1980; Hobsbawm and Ranger 1983; Handler and Linnekin 1984;
Marcus and Fisher 1986), which point to the 'invention of tradition'
while criticizing concepts such as cultural purity, wholeness or
'authenticity'. An optimistic view has thereby emerged in postmodern anthropology in which syncretic processes are considered
basic not only to religion and ritual but to 'the predicament of culture'
in general:

> Twentieth century identities no longer presuppose continuous
> cultures or traditions. Everywhere individuals and groups impro-
> vise local performances from (re)collected pasts, drawing on
> foreign media, symbols and languages. This existence among
> fragments has often been portrayed as a process of ruin and
> cultural decay, perhaps most eloquently by Claude Lévi-Strauss in
> *Tristes Tropiques* (1955) . . . But [this] . . . assumes a questionable

> Eurocentric position at the 'end' of a unified human history . . .
> Alongside this narrative of progressive monoculture a more
> ambiguous 'Caribbean' experience may be glimpsed . . . Aimé
> Césaire, a practitioner of 'neologistic' cultural politics, represents
> such a possibility – organic culture reconceived as inventive
> process or creolized 'interculture.'
>
> (Clifford 1988: 14–15)

Yet although syncretic processes currently loom large in such writings,
there seems to be an uneasiness about the term in postmodern
anthropology: we hear far less about culture as syncretic than about
culture as collage, as creolized, as fragmented, as 'interculture', as
subversive hybrid invention.

It is in particular the term 'creolization', borrowed from linguistics,
which currently enjoys 'favoured concept status' (for example,
Hannerz 1987) – which is ironic, given that prejudices about creole
languages in linguistics have often paralleled those about syncretism
in other disciplines. This uneasiness about 'syncretism' in contemporary
anthropology may be due to the term evoking for some of us the
existence of a 'purity' or 'authenticity' in contrast to which it is
defined. Perhaps, also, its very familiarity as a word is problematic,
suggesting modernity rather than postmodernity. But just as 'fetishism'
has been usefully reclaimed from its pejorative nineteenth-century
significance by current anthropological usage (for example, Taussig
1980), our aims in this volume are to recast syncretism.

Given the important place which processes of bricolage and
synthesis hold in our understanding of social and cultural practice, it
seems fruitful to re-examine an area in which such synthesis has long
been a subject of debate: religion and ritual. It also seems unneces-
sarily limiting to avoid a term which already exists to describe
religious synthesis because of some of the connotations it has been
given by (mostly) nineteenth-century scholars. On the contrary,
embracing a term which has acquired – in some quarters – pejorative
meanings can lead to a more challenging critique of the assumptions
on which those meanings are based than can its mere avoidance. In
contrast to the more 'neutralizing' terms favoured in postmodern
anthropology, the very contentiousness surrounding the concept of
syncretism puts us on the track of this volume's central concern: the
politics of religious synthesis and the competition between discourses
about syncretism.

IDIOSYNCRATIC ETYMOLOGY AND SYNCRETISTIC CONTROVERSY

Problems with syncretism do not seem to lie with any substantive objections to the semantics of the term – since hardly anyone would deny that different religious traditions have amalgamated in the past, and continue to interact and borrow from each other today – but with the very word itself and its history of application. A look at the etymology and historical usage of the word 'syncretism' is thus in order. It proves to be every bit as shifting and historically contingent as the religious boundaries to which it refers.

On semantic grounds the word could most plausibly derive from the Ancient Greek prefix *syn*, 'with', and *krasis*, 'mixture' which combined in words such as *syngkrasis*, 'a mixing together, compound', or *idiosyngkrasia*, meaning '(peculiar, individual) temperament'. Of course, the English word 'idiosyncrasy' derives directly from this Ancient Greek compound. The very first attestation of *syngkretismos*, the direct forerunner of 'syncretism', does not appear until relatively late, when Plutarch (AD 45–125) uses it in the *Moralia* (490b; in a chapter entitled 'On Brotherly Love' [*Peri Philadelphias*]). He makes the point that it is a necessity to be friendly with the friends of a brother, and inimical towards the enemies of a brother, 'imitating in this point, at least, the practice of the Cretans, who, though they often quarrelled with and warred against each other, made up their differences and united when outside enemies attacked; and this it was which they called "syncretism"'.

Plutarch clearly linked the word 'syncretism' to the word for 'Cretans', *kretoi*; it literally meant 'the coming together of Cretans, a combination of Cretans'. It is difficult to know whether Plutarch was earnestly communicating a widespread folk etymology, reporting and reviving an unattested earlier word, or simply making a pun on the familiar word *syngkrasis*. Whatever the case, Plutarch's 'syncretism' is highly idiosyncratic (in the modern sense of peculiar, but not uninteresting). As Kenneth George (1992) has commented, 'Plutarch's story should remind us that the arena of syncretism is a deeply politicized site of difference, contact and reconciliation',[1] and its application demands the consideration of past and present sociability. It is also noteworthy that the concept of syncretism begins its history with positive connotations, referring to a strategically practical, morally justified form of political allegiance – to a form of 'brotherly love'. Although its significance would change, especially for anthropologists, it is perhaps worth remarking in passing that Plutarch's

notion of syncretism anticipated Evans-Pritchard's concept of seg-
mentation among unilineal descent groups such as the Nuer.

Syncretism does not re-emerge as a topic of discussion until the
Renaissance, when the rediscovery of classical authors, especially the
Greek philosophers Plato and Aristotle, began to influence the
strictly ecclesiastical readings of Christian texts. Erasmus (1469–
1536), one of the most prominent Renaissance philologists, delighted
in the idea that Christian theology had absorbed classical influences
and viewed this as a positive achievement which strengthened and
enriched Christianity (Screech 1980: 21). This strain of thinking
continues in many quarters today, for example among modern Greek
nationalist folklorists and ideologues who seek to assert a continuity
with Ancient Greece without contradicting the Orthodox Christian
faith of most of the Greek populace (Stewart, this volume).

The next historical context of the term's usage – in the sixteenth
and seventeenth centuries – reversed its early positive associations.
During this period in Europe there was a movement among certain
Protestant theologians, led by George Calixtus, which called for the
reconciliation of the diverse Protestant denominations with each
other (Moffat 1922). These debates, which concerned issues not only
of doctrine but also of mutual access to each other's rituals of
communion and baptism, were known as the 'syncretistic controversies'. Opponents of this movement accused its proponents of
advancing an entirely unprincipled jumbling together of religions.
This critical view carried the day and since then 'syncretism' has
remained a term of disapprobation denoting the confused mixing of
religions.

In a fourth historical phase during the second half of the nineteenth
century this pejorative meaning again surfaces. Scholars of comparative religion at this time used it in their examinations of the religious
life of the Roman and Hellenistic world, characterizing it in terms of
'disorder', 'confusion' and reduction to a 'lowest common denominator'
(see Bryson 1992: 7–10). Interestingly, it was also regarded as an
imperialist strategy in which the Roman emperors, by appropriating
the foreign cults of those they conquered, 'would have all the
varieties of mankind called in and restamped at the Caesarian mint'
(anonymous review 1853, cited in Bryson 1992: 8). This reverses
Plutarch's meaning of solidarity in the face of a common enemy, since
syncretism now becomes an assimilative weapon of that enemy. Some
scholars also integrated syncretism into an evolutionary scheme,
viewing it as an intermediate stage prior to Christian monotheism
(ibid.). 'Syncretism' thus became an 'othering' term applied to

historically distant as well as geographically distant societies, in line with Tylorean evolutionist thinking (Fabian 1983).

Thereafter, the term has typically been heavily used but polemically loaded within the comparative study of religions. Although some historians and phenomenologists of religion observed long ago that syncretism is a feature of all religions (for example, Van der Leeuw 1938: 609), it has been difficult to develop this insight in a field in which authorized clerical perspectives are often implicitly adopted, giving rise to a view of traditions as 'given' entities which renders syncretic forms as 'ambiguous' or 'deviant' by definition (Droogers 1989). Many in religious studies now feel that the term is so tarnished that it is no longer usable. Droogers (1989) and Bryson (1992), however, advocate a recasting of the term in religious studies similar in many respects to that for which we are arguing in anthropology.

Within anthropology, syncretism has usually been given a more affirmative meaning. Studies of New World syncretic phenomena by American anthropologists were coloured by an optimism born in the heyday of America's melting-pot ideology. Herskovits (1941), for example, used the study of syncretized 'Africanisms' in the New World in pursuit of two interconnected research agendas: tracing the histories and cultures of peoples of African descent in the Americas, and developing the analysis of 'acculturation'. The first was explicitly addressed to issues of racism, since the white American stereotype of African-Americans as ahistorical and devoid of cultural ancestry – which he called 'the myth of the Negro past' – was (and often still is) 'one of the principal supports of race prejudice' and 'validates the concept of Negro inferiority' (1941: 1). Herskovits' language reflects this optimistic agenda, placing syncretism in conjunction with such words as 'importance', 'significance', 'fundamental', 'reconciliation', 'retrieval', 'survival', all of which suggest the transmutation and recovery of something inestimably valuable.

Herskovits' focus on 'acculturation' was a means of addressing issues of 'culture contact'. Here he perceived the concept of syncretism as an analytical tool:

> The very use of the term 'syncretism' helped to sharpen my analyses, and led me to a more precise formulation of problem and of theory . . . It was now evident that if we accepted the proposition that culture-contact produces cultural change, and that cultures of multiple origin do not represent a cultural mosaic, but rather become newly reintegrated, then the next essential step was to ascertain the degree to which these reconciliations had

actually been achieved, and where, on this acculturative continuum, a given manifestation of the process of reworking these elements might lie.

(1941: xxii–iii)

Herskovits' distinction between a cultural mosaic and an integrative syncretism is an important one. But his depiction of an 'acculturative continuum' entails a concept of change as an automatic mechanism analogous to the blending of elements in a chemical process. There is no sense of social actors who could have acted differently to produce alternative outcomes. Although Herskovits' vision of syncretism in terms of the survival of cultural meanings and identities stands in sharp contrast to the connotations of 'confusion' and 'deviance' which the term was given in the nineteenth century, the notion of a mechanical mixing remained.

What is especially problematic about the concept of 'acculturation' is its teleological and quantitative assumptions, such that if a person is placed in a new cultural setting he or she will acculturate progressively, proceeding along a continuum towards some ultimate completion. While people do 'acculturate' in the sense of picking up a dominant culture if they have to live in the midst of one for any length of time – they must do so, of course, in order to communicate – this does not happen in any necessarily logical, progressive way. As Peel observes in his critique of studies of syncretism and acculturation, '[t]he various ways in which . . . new syntheses relate to traditional culture vary not so much in degree or quantity of indebtedness as in kind or quality' (1968: 140). Such variation depends primarily upon how those involved *interpret* what they are doing rather than upon '[t]he mechanical assignation of cultural traits' (ibid.).

Whatever acculturative movement is made at any given point is, moreover, not irreversible: the shift from melting pot to fractious multiculturalism in the last twenty years of North American ideology is a case in point. Syntheses, adaptations, assemblages, incorporations or appropriations are renegotiated and sometimes denied and disassembled. Concepts of acculturation allowed only for a progressive adaptation. Herskovits did not foresee the possibility of 'anti-syncretism', to which we now turn.

AUTHENTICITY AND 'ANTI-SYNCRETISM', MULTICULTURALISM AND NATIONALISM

'Syncretism', then, is not a determinate term with a fixed meaning, but one which has been historically constituted and reconstituted. Of what use is it now? Simply identifying a ritual or tradition as 'syncretic' tells us very little and gets us practically nowhere, since all religions have composite origins and are continually reconstructed through ongoing processes of synthesis and erasure. Thus rather than treating syncretism as a category – an 'ism' – we wish to focus upon *processes* of religious synthesis and upon *discourses* of syncretism. This necessarily involves attending to the workings of power and agency.

If we recast the study of syncretism as the politics of religious synthesis, one of the first issues which needs to be confronted is what we have termed 'anti-syncretism': the antagonism to religious synthesis shown by agents concerned with the defence of religious boundaries. Anti-syncretism is frequently bound up with the construction of 'authenticity', which is in turn often linked to notions of 'purity'. In Western religious discourses and scholarship in particular, the implicit belief remains that assertions of purity speak out naturally and transcendentally as assertions of authenticity.

Yet 'authenticity' or 'originality' do not necessarily depend on purity. They are claimable as uniqueness, and both pure and mixed traditions can be unique. What makes them 'authentic' and valuable is a separate issue, a discursive matter involving power, rhetoric and persuasion. Thus both putatively pure *and* putatively syncretic traditions can be 'authentic' if people claim that these traditions are unique, and uniquely their (historical) possession. It could be argued, in fact, that syncretic blends are more unique because historically unrepeatable. An apt example of 'syncretism/mixing = authenticity' is that of Sri Lankan Buddhist nationalism which, in the hands of the ideologue Wickramasinghe, was cast as elastic and absorbent – a culture characterized by creative borrowing (Spencer 1990: 285). Interestingly, Wickramasinghe drew on Hocart's diffusionism and the writings of other anthropologists to reach his formulation. Despite viewing it as open and elastic, Wickramasinghe was none the less able to essentialize Sri Lankan Buddhist culture and view it as authentic and eternal.

A different understanding of syncretism as 'authenticity' is examined in Stewart's study (this volume) of the discourse of religious 'survivals' in modern Greek nationalism and folklore. In the nineteenth century, Greek intellectuals emphasized the presence of survivals from Ancient Greek ('pagan') religion in the practice of the contemporary Orthodox Christian population. This can be understood as a strategic interpretation based upon claims of cultural continuity with Ancient Greece – an effective one, in fact, since it was partly because of this connection with antiquity that European powers agreed to help the Greeks both during and after their struggle for independence. The assertion of syncretism (by both Greeks and their European patrons) also countered the charge that modern Greeks were 'racially impure', and hence not successors to the ancients: cultural determinism thus triumphed over nineteenth-century biological determinism. Claims of 'authenticity', then, may be disconnected from notions of purity. They depend instead on the political acumen and persuasiveness of cultural 'spin doctors' (the '*Multiplikatoren*' in Yalçın-Heckmann's contribution to this volume) who convert given historical particularities and contingencies to valued cultural resources.

The premise that 'pure = authentic', however, tends to be the dominant reading in discourses of nationalist, ethnic or regional identity, as well as those of religious movements which are categorized as 'fundamentalist' or 'nativist'. Such discourses are commonly anti-syncretic, involving the erasure of elements deemed alien from particular religious and ritual forms. Selected forms may be identified as foreign and extirpated, or alternatively recast and retained through claims that they have really always been 'ours', thereby deleting former religious syntheses from authorized cultural memory.

This latter form of erasure is the topic of Guss' chapter in this volume. The Day of the Monkey, a festival in the Venezuelan town of Caicara with heterogeneous cultural origins, has in the past few decades come to be viewed as a manifestation of indigenous 'Indian-ness', especially by younger male – and mostly Mestizo – participants. A large number of these young men are migrants who return to Caicara specifically for the Day of the Monkey. Caicara, formerly part of a prosperous agricultural region, was transformed through the arrival of the oil industry, whose subsequent mechanization led to unemployment. The young men displaced to the margins by this process return each year to find a centre.[2] Living lives of stranger-hood and alienation, they create this centre through tropes of indigenous belonging by celebrating 'Indianness' in a festival in which all readings of religious synthesis are denied.

The erasure of syncretism is also entailed by certain forms of multiculturalism in the USA. Previously, the invention of American identity through the image of different ethnicities united together in a melting pot, masked structures of political and economic domin-ance, social relations of racism and the hegemony of WASP cultural and linguistic practices. Resistance to this cultural colonialism entailed secesssion from the melting pot and the inscription of multiple ethnic, racial and cultural identities upon national institutions such as official holidays and school curricula (see van der Veer, this volume). It has also involved the construction of 'authentic' identities and the erasure of signs which signal the blurring and fluidity of such identities. Such erasure is at issue, for example, in Santeria, an Afro-Cuban religion brought to the USA by Cuban immigrants. It has now acquired a significant African-American membership, among whom a movement (the American Yoruba Movement) has developed which aims to delete traces of Spanish and Catholic provenance in order to create a re-Africanized religious practice (Palmié n.d.).

Multiculturalism is not necesarily anti-syncretic, however, either in the USA or elsewhere. In India, for example, modern Hindu nationalism is, according to van der Veer (this volume), based on encompassing claims about the inclusivist syncretism of Hinduism – claims which are now often combined with Western ideas of multiculturalism. Van der Veer argues, in fact, that debates on multiculturalism play a similar role in secular nation-states to that of debates over syncretism in societies in which identities are defined through religion: each 'refers to a politics of difference and identity'. Since India combines these by being a secular state in which religious affiliation partially defines cultural identity, it makes sense that syncretism and multiculturalism are often equated in Hindu political discourse.

That syncretism and anti-syncretism can both be paths to the construction of 'authenticity' and identity is underscored by instances in which both are used in the same cultural nationalist debate. Koepping (this volume) describes Japanese responses to the Westernizing transformations of the 1868 Meiji Reformation and to more recent forms of Western hegemony (and, we might add, devastating military power). One nineteenth-century response was that of the scholarly writings known as *Kokugaku* (National Learning), which involved the purging of foreign accretions from ancient Shinto sources. Such dispositions recur, Koepping argues, in contemporary *Nihonjinron* (theories of Japaneseness), quasi-scientific theories of Japanese uniqueness. Yet alternative syncretic standpoints have accompanied these, appropriating rather than excising the foreign, one example being certain of the 'new religions' in which the Japanese language and Shinto cosmology subsume foreign languages and religions in an integrative and universalizing exegesis.

SYNCRETISM, INCULTURATION AND FUNDAMENTALISM

In principle we agree with Richard Werbner who, in his capacity as discussant for our panel on syncretism at the 1992 American

Anthropological Association meetings, argued that the term 'syncretism' should be limited to the domain of religious or ritual phenomena, where elements of two different historical 'traditions' interact or combine. This would distinguish it from bricolage, the formation of new cultural forms from bits and pieces of cultural practice of diverse origins. While we generally support the view that syncretism be reserved for describing interactions in the sphere of religion, we recognize that this is only a provisional demarcation. One reason is that it rests upon a culturally constructed Western category – 'religion' – which may not be significant in other cultural and historical contexts. Where religious observance is inseparable from other social practices, we lose the ability to differentiate syncretism from other sorts of cultural bricolage and hybridization.

Furthermore, to the degree that a distinct sphere of religion is identifiable, whether in Western or non-Western societies, it is likely to be historically contingent and shifting. What appear to be important religious phenomena at a given point in time may later be reinterpreted as merely 'cultural' phenomena, and vice versa. During the nineteenth and early twentieth centuries the Catholic Church in Sri Lanka, for example, viewed the wearing of white as a colour of mourning and the use of drumming in religious ceremonies as 'Buddhist' and therefore antithetical to Christianity. After Independence in 1948, however, Buddhists came to comprise a powerful majority dominating and setting the tone of Sri Lankan national culture. Under these conditions it became politically expedient for Catholics to minimize their cultural difference. Drumming and the wearing of white were consequently reclassified as innocuous features of Sinhalese culture of no particular religious significance, thus opening the way for Catholics to adopt these in their ritual practices (Stirrat 1992: 46).

Mosse's analysis (this volume) of South Indian Christian–Hindu interactions offers a parallel case. In the last century the Catholic Church allowed the display of caste hierarchy in church in the form of seating precedence and differential participation in Church 'honours'. Now a number of factors militate against this. Caste has been reinterpreted as an incompatible expression of 'Hinduism'; the Church is increasingly concerned to promote social justice in the wake of Vatican II; and indigenous movements such as 'dalit theology' exist in their own right to oppose inequalities in the Indian socio-religious system.

These two South Asian examples indicate that students of syncretism cannot always specify their field of study in advance, but must remain sensitive to the ways in which people negotiate and redefine the boundaries of their ideas and practices. Importantly, the fluidity and political contingency of such boundaries as 'religion' and 'culture' become part of the very subject-matter of syncretism rather than impediments to its study.

The Catholic Church is, in fact, a recurring case in point. Especially since Vatican II, the Church has produced formulations of 'inculturation' and 'indigenization' (see Mosse, this volume). In Catholic theologians' notions of inculturation (Shorter 1988; Schreiter 1985; Luzbetak 1988), the Word of God, the message of the Gospel, is knowledge of a transcendental, timeless and transcultural Truth that is not tied to a particular human language or cultural form, but adaptable into local idioms and symbolic repertoires. Indeed the Church now contends that communities will apprehend the Christian message better if they do so in their own terms.[5] At an all-Africa symposium of Catholic clergy in Kampala in 1968, Pope Paul VI addressed the audience with these words:

> The expression [of the one faith], that is, the language and mode of manifesting it, may be manifold. Hence, it may be original, suited to the tongue, the style, the character, the genius, and the culture, of the one who professes this one faith. From this point of view, a certain pluralism is not only legitimate, but desirable . . . In this sense you may, and you must, have an African Christianity.
>
> (Cited in Burke 1992: 161)

As anthropologists we would probably label many instances of inculturation 'syncretism' in so far as they involve the combination of diverse traditions in the area of religion. Representatives of the Catholic Church would immediately dispute this usage, however, and reserve 'syncretism' for a narrower (and altogether negative) subset of such syntheses where they perceive that the Truth of the Christian message is distorted or lost. Yet given that Western distinctions between 'religion' and 'culture' may not translate elsewhere, Catholic clergy themselves often have great difficulty distinguishing 'proper inculturation' from 'illegitimate syncretism' (Hastings 1989), and at least one centre of research has been founded to probe just this problem (Barnes 1992: 171).

Some aspects of the above discourse of inculturation are also present in Protestant churches, though to different extents and in different ways (Pickering 1992; Howe 1992). Sanneh (1991) argues, in fact, that inculturation is an essential feature of Christianity in general due to its emphasis from its first beginnings on translatability into other languages (see Waldman and Yai's 1992 critiques). However, this ignores the fact that 'indigenizing' projects are often elite attempts, imposed from the top down, to control the direction of religious synthesis (Meyer 1992 and this volume).

Being global and possessing a centralized political and theological authority, the Catholic Church may approach syncretism, whether in Melanesia, Africa or Latin America, in broadly similar ways at any one time. Such global dispositions toward syncretism could, we might argue, impart a certain family resemblance to studies of syncretism where Catholicism is involved. Moreover, other religious traditions with universal claims and global dispersal, (such as Protestantism, Islam and Buddhism, may also to a certain degree standardize responses to syncretism, even without the centralized authority structure and bureaucracy of Catholicism. It is important to emphasize, however, that such family resemblances are not dictated by any essential qualities of particular religious traditions.

Islamic 'fundamentalist' developments, for example, may exhibit certain overlaps and parallels in their anti-syncretic dispositions in different parts of the world. But rather than being the manifestation of inherent tendencies within Islam, such dispositions may instead be seen as the intersection of hegemonic Islamic discourses with common global processes, in relation to which processes many Islamic communities are similarly situated. Reformations of Islam are, firstly, often responses to the integration of Islamic communities into a Western-dominated capitalist world economy (see Bernal 1994). Contemporary patterns of mobility through labour migration for working- and middle-class Muslims and of world travel for middle- and upper-class Muslims through education abroad and through pilgrimage to Mecca (Eickelman and Piscatori 1990) may, secondly, mean that dominant discourses – such as 'fundamentalist' anti-syncretism – can now achieve a significant global spread. And thirdly, financial and other forms of support from Middle Eastern nations often have important political consequences within recipient communities in different parts of the world, which may confer local hegemony upon 'foreign' anti-syncretic discourses of Islamic revision.

Yet such processes are not entirely determined by forces beyond the community: much depends upon 'local' appropriations of 'global' discourses. This localization and contestation of Islamic reform are explored in Ferme's contribution to this volume. She examines how the *imam* of a Mende village in Sierra Leone made the *hajj* and, upon his return, sought to bring the village in line with 'what he saw in

Mecca': this, he claimed, would transform it into a 'developed', 'European' village. These reformist visions of 'Alhaji Airplane', as he came to be known, strengthened Muslim factions in chiefdom politics and confirmed certain changes these factions had already introduced into the rituals of the Sande, the women's cult association. Sande initiation in this and many other villages was not eliminated, but became 'Muslim Sande' through the introduction of Islamic elements and the abolition of the Sande spirit mask: in other words, through a syncretic process of 'mixing'. One Sande leader, however, viewed the 'real' initiation as unchanged despite her apparent compliance with Alhaji Airplane and other men. For her, Ferme points out, 'Muslim Sande' meant only surface changes, not real religious synthesis.

REGIONALIZED DISCOURSES

Different positions in the social field thus generate cross-cutting sensibilities in the presence of pervasive religious traditions which are at once 'global' and 'local'. In addition to dominant religious structures and discourses, studies of syncretism are also coloured by local traditions of ethnographic research. As Fardon observes in his volume on regional ethnographic discourses:

> Regional factors influence the entry (in the broadest sense) of the ethnographer to a field that is necessarily pre-imagined, the circumstances under which fieldwork will be carried out, the issues which have been preconceived as appropriate and pressing, and, in writing up, the canons of adequate reporting and the audience to whom, in part at least, the work will be addressed and whose opinions will be the most telling.

(1990: 24)

In studies of syncretism, regional ethnography traditions intersect with the disciplinary histories and religious discourses we have outlined above. Thus syncretism in Africa, for instance, came to be defined primarily through studies of independent churches by missiologists; syncretism in Melanesia through studies of 'cargo cults' by anthropologists and sociologists; syncretism in the New World through studies of African-derived cults such as Vodun, Candomble and Santeria by American anthropologists; syncretism in Asia through studies of 'syncretistic religions' by Orientalist scholars; and syncretism in Europe through studies of 'survivals' by folklorists (see Stewart, this volume).

Some of the consequences of these intersections of religious, disciplinary and regional discourses for studies of syncretism can be seen through the example of prevailing patterns of scholarship on syncretism in Africa. Here such scholarship crystallized in studies of independent churches, especially in southern (and particularly South) Africa, most of which have been carried out by missiologists. In this literature, the vocabulary of syncretism adopted is one of pathology, hazard, decline and loss: ominous references to 'the problem' or 'the dangers of syncretism', to 'syncretistic tendencies' and to 'forfeiting the essence of Christianity' recur. One prominent scholar even characterized independent churches as forms of 'post-Christianity' which 'form easy bridges back to nativism' (Oosthuizen 1968: xi). The *locus classicus* of this 'bridgehead' idea is Sundkler's adoption of syncretism as an explanatory concept to account for such degeneration:

> the deepest cause of the emergence of Independent churches is a nativistic-syncretistic interpretation of the Christian religion . . . *The syncretistic sect becomes the bridge over which Africans are brought back to heathenism* – a viewpoint which stresses the seriousness of the whole situation.
>
> (Sundkler 1961: 297; original emphasis)

This is a discourse about syncretism which corresponds to a period of missionization before the post-1960s era of inculturation. The pejorative characterization of syncretism in these studies may be seen as a powerful example of a means 'used by religious elites to oppose unauthorized religious production' (Droogers 1989: 16). Kiernan (this volume) describes how, in South Africa, such derogatory labelling has generated an anti-syncretic backlash in which members of Ethiopian independent churches have explicitly denied and disowned the very term 'syncretism'.

A backlash can also be seen in academic studies. Peel (1968), for example, criticizes and reinterprets studies of 'syncretistic churches'. The Yoruba *Aladura* churches he worked in explicitly oppose the incorporation of African ritual elements and, Peel argues, their forms of prayer-healing and possession are not in fact syncretic as they have Western Christian rather than Yoruba origins (1968: 133–34). Instead, he prefers to reserve the term 'syncretic' for individuals and movements which explicitly unite Christian and 'pagan' Yoruba ideas and practices into an integrative scheme.

More recently, further critiques of syncretism have been developed by African scholars within theology and religious studies in South

Africa. Pato, for example, takes particular issue with the way in which syncretism has been used as a form of explanation for independent churches, thus enabling important questions of European domination and of the hegemony of mission Christianity to be downplayed:

> the new society into which the African converts were integrated relegated them to the background through a strategy of hegemonic domination that denied the power of their symbols . . . The hypothesis of syncretism as an explanatory tool of the AIC [African Independent Churches] promotes this strategy . . . [T]his approach [also] does not take seriously the context in which African conversions have taken place . . . Yet forms of expression of the Christian faith are always determined or influenced by the social context out of which they emerge.
>
> (1990: 26)

Those contexts of domination to which Pato refers are precisely the focus of Comaroff's analysis of Tshidi Zionist churches (1985), which thereby departs from previous studies of syncretism in independent South African churches. It is interesting, however, that the discourse of bricolage predominates over that of syncretism in her analysis, suggesting an implicit distancing from the latter term.

Such distancing from prevailing regional discourses of syncretism is explicit in Kiernan's chapter in the present volume. Kiernan situates the development of Zulu Zionist churches in the history of Zulu defeat and subordination and in their circumstances of violence and impoverishment in contemporary South Africa. He emphasizes, however, that church members (like members of Yoruba *Aladura* churches) reject the integration of African ritual elements into the liturgy; he also affirms (like Peel) that Zulu Zionism is not syncretic, but a thoroughly Christian variant. He argues that the healing component of Zionist church services – often cited as a paradigmatic example of the syncretic incorporation of African understandings of divination, healing and sorcery into Christianity – is in fact a synthesis of 'incontrovertibly Christian' elements even while 'it permits the conditions on which it operates to be interpreted within an African worldview.'

Studies of religious synthesis in independent African churches, then, have been indelibly marked by the 'pre-inculturation' missiological corpus discussed above, giving rise to a kind of 'negative regional tradition' around the issue of syncretism. As a consequence, many scholars in anthropology, sociology and religious studies –

especially those educated outside the optimistic glow cast over syncretism in American anthropology by Herskovits and others – have located their own studies of African churches in the context of, and in opposition to, this tradition. Kiernan and Peel thus question and take apart the easy – and politically charged – assumption that all independent African churches are syncretic. We disagree with their arguments because we are sceptical about any neat separation of 'Christian' ritual practices from the 'African' cosmologies to which they are applied (see, for example, Horton 1975; Ray 1993; Meyer 1992 and this volume). Our disagreement arises at least partially, however, from our location in different regional traditions (or sub-traditions) within and/or against which we are writing. Such issues illuminate in our own praxis precisely what is interesting about syncretism; they bring us back to the politics governing discourses and processes of religious synthesis.

AGENCY, CONSCIOUSNESS AND UNINTENDED CONSEQUENCES

In the literature on religious synthesis and conversion, agency is sometimes ascribed to religious traditions instead of religious partici-pants. Religions are frequently treated as analogous to 'rivers of tradition' which flow free of human agency, or as akin to impersonal actors (see Waldman's critique in Waldman, Yai and Sanneh 1992) with their own dispositions towards or against synthesis: Christianity, for example, may be characterized as 'radically pluralist' (Sanneh 1991), and Islam as moving inexorably toward an anti-syncretic telos (Fisher 1973; see Horton's 1975 critique and Fisher's 1985 counter-response). Views of religion such as these often lead to explanations of syncre-tism or conversion by reference to equivalences between different religious or ritual forms which are presumed to favour synchroniza-tion and interpenetration. An active search for correspondences may indeed be a common strategy among agents of different religions in interaction or competition (for example, Martin 1983; Peel 1990). But just as religions are not 'given' entities, equivalences are not simply 'there' as channels through which meanings from different religions flow automatically. In order to serve as conduits for integration, they must be perceived as equivalences and given significance as such. Not only are equivalences in the eye of the beholder, but even when they are *perceived* they do not always facilitate synthesis. Among the Diola of Senegal, for instance, a catechism school was closed amid protests that Christian teachings about the virgin birth and the resurrection revealed to uninitiated children ritual knowledge which belonged to the men's and women's cult associations (Baum 1990: 381–2).

To extend the 'flowing rivers' metaphor further: our interest is in the practical conditions and human agencies behind the building (or demolition) of embankments and weirs, not to mention the politics of water control which come into play around larger state-sponsored interventions such as the Aswan Dam. The most straightforward instances of such construction are the religious syntheses of such innovators as Alhaji Airplane (Ferme, this volume), Nishimura Shigeki (Koepping, this volume), the EPC Moderator N.K. Dzobo (Meyer, this volume) and Swami Vivekananda (Bryson 1992). Contrary to a common criticism of 'syncretism' as a term always applied to 'others' (for example, Droogers 1989: 16), one such innovator who founded a Yoruba church, Gbadebo Dosumu, acknowledged the syncretism of his church and advocated this on the grounds that most instances of 'world religions' involve the syncretizing of the universal and the local. In Dosumu's writings, 'the Teutonic festival of Easter and the English days of the week named after pagan gods are cited to support the thesis that Africans should do so too' (Peel 1968: 136).

More recently, in 1991 Chung Hyun-Kyung, a feminist theologian from Korea, astounded delegates at the conference of the World Council of Churches in Canberra by opening the meeting with an invocation which synthesized prayers and dances from Christianity, Buddhism, Korean shamanism and Australian Aboriginal ritual. After the conference, conservative theologians pronounced her guilty of 'syncretism'. But instead of denying this charge or revising her position, Chung embraced the accusation and is currently developing a theology which celebrates syncretism as part of an Asian feminist Christianity (1993).

Contrasts are sometimes made between such figures and ordinary people who enact and reproduce 'popular' syntheses passively and unreflectingly (for example, Rudolph 1979, cited in Droogers 1989). But subsections of a given population often do innovate syncretic strategies, especially if these further group interests. An example of this would be the incorporation of Muslim practices by young, enterprising Giriama farmers in coastal Kenya reported by Parkin (1970). Here, claims to be mixing Muslim and 'traditional' practices because of affliction by 'Quranic' spirits constituted 'a form of self-professed cultural diversity' (1970: 218) enabling these entrepreneurs to avoid the cultural restraints usually imposed upon the individual accumulation of wealth. And again in Ferme's chapter in this volume a conversation with two women from the Sande cult who disagreed

over whether or not the Sande had really become 'Muslim', underscores that we cannot assume 'popular' syncretism to be discursively
unavailable. Wherever religious syntheses are explicitly contested or
defended – as they were by the Giriama and the Mende – they are
unlikely to be 'unconscious'.[4]

Of course, such debates and disputes may subside. Syntheses or
erasures may become uncontested, reproduced without discursively
available intentionality (see Comaroff and Comaroff 1992: 28–9). But
if syncretic practices are no longer *consciously* syncretic, should
they still be described as such? Ferme points out that even when
religious syntheses become part of the taken-for-granted habitus,
their composite origins erased from conscious memory, they nevertheless contain the sedimentation of historical experience. As such
they may be available for retrieval and rehabilitation at the right
historical moment, such as an Islamic reform or a revival of 'tradition'.

A dramatic example is that of the Lemba or Varemba communities
dispersed over southern Africa, which appear to be distant descen-
dants of a mixed (Africans, Arabs and others) population on the
Sofala coast. By the sixteenth century they were practising a
combination of Islam (and perhaps other Abrahamic traditions) with
local ritual practices. The Lemba did not retain the 'Islamic' identity
of their ancestors, but their distinctive, syncretic forms of circumcision, burial and ritual slaughter perpetuated a sense of 'difference'
from surrounding populations. During the nineteenth century, in a
colonial context, the Lemba converted this sense of difference into
a claim to be 'the Lost Tribe of Israel' (Parfitt 1993). Still later, in
this century, certain Lemba communities in Zimbabwe, after contact
with Islamic organizations in Zimbabwe, identified elements of their
tradition as Islamic and then embarked on a phase of 're-Islamization'
(Mandivenga 1989). Because of this historical sedimentation, past
religious syntheses are always potentially available for future recon-
stitution. Past religious syntheses do not, as many have argued, cease
to exist if they are not part of conscious representations.

Other intersections of agency with religious synthesis may be seen
in distinctions in participation and expression linked to contrasts in
class, race, gender and age. Kiernan (this volume) examines how
different aspects of the 'healing synthesis' of Zulu Zionism are drawn
upon by men and women, according to gendered (and age-related)
contrasts in agency. For Zionist men, for instance, the power of the
Holy Spirit underscores their capacity to dominate as church leaders
and healers; for women, the strict Zionist moral code gives them an
authorized discourse with which to check any womanizing, drinking

and gambling on the part of their husbands. Such contrasts thus serve as a diagnostic of distinctions in power and agency.

Religious syntheses do not always, of course, arise from intentional innovations. Attempts to create meanings do not, in any case, always succeed; in fact, they may have unintended consequences. Meyer's chapter in this volume explores the phenomenon, widespread throughout the global dispersal of Christianity, of unintended syncretism through translation. Missionaries working among Ewe communities in Ghana attempted to assimilate local meanings in their translation of the Bible, selecting the deity Mawu as 'God' but collectively identifying the other Ewe deities with 'the Devil'. Having thus diabolized most of the former religion, they were taken aback by the importance the Devil was ascribed in their congregation's ideas and practices which, Meyer argues, can be seen as grassroots Africanization, a process of 'syncretism from below' (see also Meyer 1992; Waldman *et al.* 1992; Hastings 1989: 138–55; James 1988: 207–41; Lienhardt 1982).

In her contribution to this volume, Yalçın-Heckmann makes the point that anti-syncretic forms may also proceed from misinterpretations. Turkish migrants in Germany hesitate to allow their children to set off fireworks on New Year's Eve (called 'Silvester' after Saint Silvester) because they construe this as a religious festival linked closely to Christmas. The fireworks are believed to comprise part of the ritual and some parents fear that if they allow their children to participate they will be conniving in their betrayal of Islam. This is a point of debate within the Muslim community because while Silvester is, in literal terms, a saint's festival, in practical terms very few Germans perceive it in a way which could be called 'religious'. Turkish migrants are thus at odds as to whether to classify fireworks as religious or simply cultural. Here a desire to maintain religious boundaries couples with a partial understanding of the culture of the surrounding majority to create a situation of anti-syncretism as cultural resistance. Of course, as Yalçın-Heckmann points out, Germans also misinterpret Turkish Islamic customs, and such issues as the wearing of headscarves and the ban on pork have served as tropes of 'otherness' during the recent racial violence against immigrants.

SYNCRETISM, POWER AND RESISTANCE

Syncretism has presumably always been part of the negotiation of identities and hegemonies in situations such as conquest, trade, migration, religious dissemination and intermarriage. The growth of a Western-dominated world economic system, however, was accompanied by the growth of a Western-dominated world cultural system (Hannerz 1987, 1992), in which processes of capitalism and cultural hegemony transformed not only relations of power and production but also experiences of personhood, of the body, gender, time, space and religion. The appropriation of totalizing and globally spread processes such as capitalism, commodity consumption and 'rationalist' models of development is often inseparable from the appropriation of totalizing and globally spread religions. All of the contributors to the present volume situate their studies in precisely these processes. To select just a few examples, Alhaji Airplane dreams of a 'Westernized' Mende village as the outcome of his Islamic reforms (Ferme); Yawing male initiation locates a European city at the hidden core of its ritual (Kempf); the leader of a new religious movement in Japan subsumes the Bible and other foreign texts within the Japanese 'soul of language' (Koepping); unemployed Mestizo labour migrants construct the indigenous 'Indianness' of the Caicara Monkey festival in opposition to the economically devastating 'strangerhood' of Standard Oil of New Jersey (Guss); and Turkish immigrants in Germany are involved in struggles over the meaning of fireworks, Christmas decorations and women's head-scarves, which are inseparable from their struggles against racial attacks and murder (Yalçın-Heckmann). The syncretic and anti-syncretic forms which these and the remaining contributors discuss demonstrate that the processes of appropriation which we call 'globalization' and 'localization' are far from unitary.

It is significant that many recent studies of resistance through ritual have focused upon religious synthesis in contexts of colonialism and other forms of alien domination or exploitation, although they have not been explicitly 'about syncretism' (for example, Fernandez 1970, 1982; Taussig 1980, 1984; Comaroff 1985; Ong 1987; Boddy 1989). Syncretism may be (or perhaps only looks like) a form of resistance, because hegemonic practices are never simply absorbed wholesale through passive 'acculturation'; at the very least, their incorporation involves some kind of transformation, some kind of deconstruction and reconstruction which converts them to people's own meanings and projects. In colonial contexts, syncretism on the part of colonial subjects could have particularly subversive consequences, since although colonial governments created hybrid institutions such as 'native courts' all over the world, they were usually highly contemptuous and suspicious of their subjects' use of Western cultural elements in syncretic appropriations (such as 'cargo cults') whose meanings escape colonial control (see Kempf, this volume).

In many such contexts, the penetration of Western forms of capitalism and cultural hegemony has been – paradoxically – both subverted and promoted through syncretism. In Kempf's chapter in this volume, for example, colonial and missionary discourses in New Guinea informed the introduction of circumcision into Yawing male initiation, where it had not previously existed. Circumcision is now identified with Christ's crucifixion and, by getting rid of 'black' blood, is said to produce an inner state of 'whiteness' which explicitly links initiates both to the European world of powerful materiality and to the world of their own ancestors. Through this ritual synthesis, Yawing thus resist colonial ascriptions of 'darkness' and 'dirt' by asserting a hidden reality of powerful 'whiteness' within themselves. Yet in so doing they have internalized colonial and missionary definitions of 'whiteness'. Their resistance, Kempf concludes, 'possesses no "authentic niche" beyond the reach of colonial power'.

Kempf shows us that attempts to resist subordination with syncretized elements of the dominant language may be caught up in contradictions in which the contested hegemonies may be reasserted in another form (see Abu-Lughod 1990). The appropriation of dominance and the subversion of that dominance may be enacted at the same time, in the same syncretic act. Subversion may even be an *unintended* consequence of a syncretic process in which actors intend to appropriate rather than subvert cultural dominance. These conundrums of agency and intentionality make syncretism very slippery, but it is precisely its capacity to contain paradox, contradiction and polyphony which makes syncretism such a powerful symbolic process in the contexts that the contributors to this volume describe. Nor are anti-syncretic forms exempt from such contradiction. Kiernan explains, for example, that the ascetic Puritan individualism which allows Zulu Zionist members to counteract subjection to others in the workplace also cuts them off from collective political action against such subjection.

That syncretism is not exclusively at hand to subvert the dominant order is also clear when we contrast what Meyer calls syncretism 'from above' and syncretism 'from below', each representing different poles in a field of power. At one pole we have the development of religious synthesis by those who create meanings for their own use out of contexts of cultural or political domination, such as Yawing circumcision and Protestant Ewe discourses about the Devil. At the other pole we have the imposition of religious synthesis upon others by those who claim the capacity to define cultural meanings: the authorization of 'Muslim Sande' by Alhaji Airplane and other Muslim Mende men (Ferme); Christian missionaries Africanizing their churches by 'baptizing' selected deities and practices (Meyer); and Hindu nationalists claiming that Hinduism subsumes Islam (van der Veer). Syncretism 'from above' and 'from below' should not be understood as reified 'types' of syncretism, however, and of course not all religious syntheses can be neatly assigned a position at the top or bottom of a hierarchy of power. The syncretic appropriations in Japan described in Koepping's chapter, for example, may be seen both as responses to external domination *and* as discourses of reciprocal domination – and therefore as inimical to the opposition between 'global' and 'local' itself. Similarly, Matory (1994) charac-terizes the mutually englobing syntheses of Yoruba *orisa* cults and Islam as the totalizing claims of 'rival empires' rather than as a conflict between a 'local' and a 'world' religion. Here we may discern syncretism as more than just an etic category wholly invented by Western scholasticism. The instances just cited show how under-standings of religious synthesis organize indigenous theories of culture in contexts of domination (or attempted domination). They show, furthermore how such theories alternate between two opposed rhetorics: syncretism as tolerance and syncretism as hierarchical encompassment. These theories of culture can be either pro-syncretic or anti-syncretic but they are rarely free from essentialism; indeed, it appears that essentialist theories of culture require some comment on historical composition, and thus they necessarily encounter 'syncretism'.

SYNCRETISM AS ANTHROPOLOGY

Anthropology itself is both a syncretizing and creolizing discourse (as the translation and/or invention of culture) and a discourse about syncretism. Anthropologists resemble body artists who conduct syncretic experiments upon themselves. We live another culture's traditions while maintaining our own, and then we write about this experience from intimate personal knowledge. Moreover, we have recently acquired an englobing appetite for the irony of apparently incongruous cultural syntheses, which have in many ways become icons of postmodernism – 'Trobriand Cricket'; the Igbo 'White Man' masquerade on the cover of *The Predicament of Culture* (Clifford 1988). One reason we find these so attractive, we suppose, is because we can perceive them as already broken into parts, as deconstructed in advance. 'Invention of culture' writings have demonstrated the strong political significance of syncretism and hybridization in their emphasis on the challenge that such reconstruction poses to essentialized colonial representations and to Western modernist forms of consciousness in general. But they also suit our current taste for the ironic and, far from posing a challenge to us, confirm our totalizing postmodern paradigms. And just as colonial power entailed the categorizing of people into essentialized 'tribal' entities with fixed boundaries ('you are the Igbo'), anthropological hegemony now entails taking apart practices and identities which are phenomenological realities for those who use them ('your tradition is invented'). In our enthusiasm for deconstructing syncretic traditions we may have invented another kind of intellectual imperialism.

NOTES

1 We are grateful to Ken George for his permission to quote from his paper for our 1992 American Anthropological Association panel.
2 See Werbner 1989 on the location imagery used to express the estrangement of Southern African labour migrants.
3 Such an approach to missionization has faded in and out of Christian missionizing policy since the earliest times. Compare, for example, Clement of Alexandria's (second-century AD) remark as he proselytized the Greek community of Egypt : 'I will give you understanding of the mysteries of the Logos [the Word] by means of images with which you are familiar' (Protrepticus XII, 119.1).
4 Such conscious intentionality does not imply 'insincerity'. As the argument between the two Sande women illustrates, interests, strategies and 'political' contestations are very much part of the internal *constitution* of ritual or religious experience.

REFERENCES

Abu-Lughod, L. (1990) 'The romance of resistance: tracing transformations of power through Bedouin women', *American Ethnologist* 17: 41–55.

Barnes, R.H. (1992) 'A Catholic mission and the purification of culture: experiences in an Indonesian community', *Journal of the Anthropological Society of Oxford* 23, 2: 169–80.

Baum, R.M. (1990) 'The emergence of a Diola Christianity', *Africa* 60: 370–98.

Bernal, V. (1994) 'Gender, culture and capitalism: women and the renewal of Islamic "traditions" in a Sudanese village', *Comparative Studies in Society and History* 36, 1.

Boddy, J. (1989) *Wombs and Alien Spirits: Women, Men and the Zar Cult in Northern Sudan*, Madison: University of Wisconsin Press.

Bryson, T. (1992) 'The hermeneutics of religious syncretism: Swami Vivekananda's "Practical Vedanta"', unpublished PhD thesis, University of Chicago.

Burke, J.F. (1992) 'Research in a post-missionary situation: among Zairean sisters of Notre Dame de Namur', *Journal of the Anthropological Society of Oxford* 23, 2: 157–68.

Chung, H. (1993) 'The wisdom of mothers knows no boundaries: gospel and culture in Asian women's theology', unpublished paper presented in the Spring Lecture Series of the Harvard Women's Studies in Religion Program, 7 April.

Clifford, J. (1988) *The Predicament of Culture: Twentieth Century Ethnography, Literature and Art*, Cambridge, MA: Harvard University Press.

Comaroff, J. (1985) *Body of Power, Spirit of Resistance: The Culture and History of a South African People*, Chicago: University of Chicago Press.

Comaroff, J. and Comaroff, J. (1992) *Ethnography and the Historical Imagination*, Boulder and Oxford: Westview Press.

Droogers, A. (1989) 'Syncretism: the problem of definition, the definition of the problem', in J. Gort, H. Vroom, R. Fernhout and A. Wessels (eds), *Dialogue and Syncretism: An Interdisciplinary Approach*, Grand Rapids, MI: Wm B. Eerdmans Publishing Co.

Eickelman, D. and Piscatori, J. (1990) *Muslim Travellers: Pilgrimage, Migration and the Religious Imagination*, Berkeley: University of California Press.

Fabian, J. (1983) *Time and the Other: How Anthropology makes its Object*, New York: Columbia University Press.

Fardon, R. (ed.) (1990) 'General Introduction' to *Localizing Strategies: Regional Traditions of Ethnographic Writing*, Edinburgh: Scottish Academic Press, and Washington, DC: Smithsonian Institution Press.

Fernandez, J.W. (1970) 'The affirmation of things past: Alar Ayong and Bwiti as movements of protest in central and northern Gabon', in R.I. Rotberg and A.A. Mazrui (eds), *Protest and Power in Black Africa*, London: Oxford University Press.

—— (1982) *Bwiti: An Ethnography of the Religious Imagination in Africa*, Princeton, NJ: Princeton University Press.

Fisher, H.J. (1973) 'Conversion reconsidered: some historical aspects of religious conversion in black Africa', *Africa* 43: 27–40.

—— (1985) 'The juggernaut's apologia: conversion to Islam in black Africa', *Africa* 55: 153–73.

George, K. (1992) 'Origins, power and paint: etymological discourse and contemporary Indonesian Muslim art', unpublished paper presented in the panel on 'Syncretism and Agency' at the Annual Meetings of the American Anthropological Association, San Francisco.

Handler, R. and Linnekin, J. (1984) 'Tradition, genuine or spurious', *Journal of American Folklore* 97: 273–90.

Hannerz, U. (1987) 'The world in creolisation', *Africa* 57: 546–59.

—— (1992) *Cultural Complexity: Studies in the Social Organization of Meaning*, New York: Columbia University Press.

Hastings, A. (1989) *African Catholicism: Essays in Discovery*, London: SCM Press.

Herskovits, M.J. (1941) *The Myth of the Negro Past*, Boston, MA: Beacon Press.

Hobsbawm, E. and Ranger, T. (1983) *The Invention of Tradition*, Cambridge: Cambridge University Press.

Horton, R. (1975) 'On the rationality of conversion', *Africa* 45/3: 219–35 and 45/4: 85–108.

Howe, J. (1992) 'Protestants, Catholics and "gentiles": the articulation of missionary and indigenous culture on the San Blas coast of Panama', *Journal of the Anthropological Society of Oxford* 23/2: 139–55.

James, W. (1988) *The Listening Ebony: Moral Knowledge, Religion and Power among the Uduk of Sudan*, Oxford: Clarendon Press.

Lienhardt, G. (1982) 'The Dinka and Catholicism', in J. Davis (ed.), *Religious Organization and Religious Experience*, London: Academic Press.

Luzbetak, L. (1988) *The Church and Cultures: New Perspectives in Missiological Anthropology*, Maryknoll, NY: Orbis.

Mandivenga, E. (1989) 'The History and "re-conversion" of the Varemba of Zimbabwe', *Journal of Religion in Africa* 19: 98–124.

Marcus, G. and Fisher, M. (1986) *Anthropology as Cultural Critique: An Experimental Moment in the Human Sciences*, Chicago: University of Chicago Press.

Martin, L. (1983) 'Why Cecropian Minerva? – Hellenistic religious syncretism as system', *Numen* 30: 131–45.

Matory, J.L. (1994) 'Rival empires: Islam and the religions of spirit possession among the Oyo-Yoruba', *American Ethnologist* 21.

Meyer, B. (1992) '"If you are a Devil, you are a Witch and, if you are a Witch, you are a Devil": the integration of "pagan" ideas into the conceptual universe of Ewe Christians in Southeastern Ghana', *Journal of Religion in Africa* 22: 98–132.

Moffat, J. (1922) 'Syncretism', in J. Hastings (ed.), *The Encyclopaedia of Religion and Ethics*, Vol. 12, New York: Charles Scribners' Sons.

Ong, A. (1987) *Spirits of Resistance and Capitalist Discipline: Factory Women in Malaysia*, Albany, NY: SUNY Press.

Oosthuizen, G.C. (1968) *Post-Christianity in Africa: A Theological and Anthropological Study*, London: C. Hurst and Co.

Palmié, S. (n.d.) 'Against syncretism: Africanizing and Cubanizing discourses in North American *orisa* worship', in R. Fardon (ed.), *Counterwork: Managing Diverse Knowledge*, London: Routledge.

Parfitt, T. (1993) *Journey to the Vanished City: The Search for a Lost Tribe of Israel*, New York: St Martin's Press.

Parkin, D. (1970) 'Politics of ritual syncretism: Islam among the non-Muslim Giriama of Kenya', *Africa* 40: 217–33.

Pato, L. (1990) 'The independent African churches: a socio-cultural approach', *Journal of Theology for Southern Africa* 72: 24–35.

Peel, J.D.Y. (1968) 'Syncretism and religious change', *Comparative Studies in Society and History* 10: 121–41.

—— (1990) 'The pastor and the *Babalawo*: the interaction of religions in nineteenth-century Yorubaland', *Africa* 60: 338–69.

Pickering, W.S.F. (1992) 'Introduction: old positions and new concerns', *Journal of the Anthropological Society of Oxford* 23/2: 99–110.

Ray, B. (1993) 'Aladura Christianity: a Yoruba religion', *Journal of Religion in Africa* 23/3: 266–91.

Sanneh, L. (1991) *Translating the Message: The Missionary Impact on Culture*, Maryknoll, NY: Orbis.

Schreiter, R. (1985) *Constructing Local Theologies*, London: SCM Press.

Screech, M.A. (1980) *Erasmus: Ecstasy and the Praise of Folly*, London: Penguin.

Shorter, A. (1988) *Toward a Theology of Inculturation*, London: Chapman.

Spencer, J. (1990) 'Writing within: anthropology, nationalism and culture in Sri Lanka', *Current Anthropology* 31: 283–300.

Stirrat, R.L. (1992) *Power and Religiosity in a Post-Colonial Setting: Sinhala Catholics in Contemporary Sri Lanka*, Cambridge: Cambridge University Press.

Sundkler, B.G.M. (1961 [1948]) *Bantu Prophets in South Africa*, London: Oxford University Press.

Taussig, M.T. (1980) *The Devil and Commodity Fetishism in South America*, Chapel Hill: University of North Carolina Press.

—— (1984) 'History as sorcery', *Representations* 7: 87–109.

Van der Leeuw, G. (1938) *Religion in Essence and Manifestation*, trans. J.E. Turner, New York: Macmillan.

Wagner, R. (1980) *The Invention of Culture*, Chicago: University of Chicago Press.

Waldman, M., Yai, O. and Sanneh, L. (1992) 'Translatability: a discussion', *Journal of Religion in Africa* 22: 159–72.

Werbner, R.P. (1989) 'Churches of the Spirit: the argument of images from Zion to the wilderness', in R.P. Werbner (ed.), *Ritual Passage, Sacred Journey: The Process and Organization of Religious Movement*, Manchester and Washington, DC: Manchester University Press, and Smithsonian Institution Press.

1 What 'Alhaji Airplane' saw in Mecca, and what happened when he came home

Ritual transformation in a Mende community (Sierra Leone)

Mariane Ferme

'Alhaji Airplane' (*Alhaji balui*) often sat down to talk at the centre of his compound after a day on the farm. His torn work clothes still on, he kept his hands busy making one of the mats for which he was well known, while telling stories about 'what he had seen' on his pilgrimage to Mecca. His words – the words of a rural Mende *imam* who until the *hajj* had never been to the capital city, let alone abroad – were accompanied by verbal and facial expressions of wonder. First there was the airplane: he actually had *his own* seat on it, a seat which no one else could take. He was tied into it by a belt with a metallic clasp, probably because the white people who owned the airplane knew that he might try to leave it in fear. Anyhow, this was a far cry from the shoving and pushing and squeezing that characterized travel to market in the lorries driving by the junction four miles from Kpuawala.

Then there were all these white women (*puu bla, ye nyahanga*) serving him. 'Can you imagine', he would tell me in amazement, 'white women just like you, serving an old black man like me, with such dark skin (*nu lɛlei sia lee nya, nya luwui lɛingɔ mɔɔ mɔɔ*)?' He would run a finger up and down his forearm to emphasize this point. '*Allahu akbar*, God is the greatest! To think that we used to serve them as our masters, when "Mammy Queen" governed us.'[1]

> Oh my ears did hurt, up there in the airplane, and we looked out of windows . . . *a min, tai!*[3] And the land went away so fast, everything was so small. Ah, God is awesome (*ngewɔ masubangɔ*). I could not see land, up in the clouds. And when we got off the plane, in Jeddah, there was so much sand (*ŋanyɛi*), not a tree around. No bush (*ndɔgbɔ*), the sun really burns there, and it *never* rains. Imagine, people have to buy water, even water!

Ah, poor people . . . but they are rich (*gbatɛbla mia*)! And there were so many white people, and Arabs there (*Arabubla*). I used to think that Muslims were mostly black people (*nu lɛlei*), but in Mecca I saw that there are more white Muslims than black ones in the world.

The pilgrimage to Mecca transformed Alhaji's identity, becoming a key element in his new social persona. He became 'Alhaji Airplane'. This new consciousness lead him to envision a different social order.

At times Alhaji would call the whole village together early in the morning to recount a dream from the previous night, and to interpret its meaning. On one occasion, he told us he had dreamt that white people had offered to exchange the village's mud houses for a modern town of cement buildings, paved roads and water wells. For several years, the community had been trying to get a proper well dug, as well as road improvements through the area's development scheme. These efforts were recalled by people on the margins of the meeting, while Alhaji told of his dream. He concluded by asking the gathered community to bring 'small sacrifices' of food (*fangani jaa*) to ensure the auspicious outcome. He also exhorted them to pray to God like 'good' Muslims (*Mɔlibla ye yekpeisia*), instead of being jealous of their neighbours and fighting all the time.

Alhaji's vision for Kpuawala – the community of some 260 people in which he lived – was compelling to those around him. This was due in part to the cosmopolitan authority lent to his stories and projects by the narration of what he 'had seen in Mecca'. After returning from the pilgrimage, he had worked to make religious and ritual practices in Kpuawala conform to his ideal of 'good' Muslim behaviour in the larger Islamic world, and particularly in what he saw as its conceptual and spatial centre – 'Mecca.' Alhaji's efforts to bring about spiritual and material improvements were also bolstered by links between the chiefdom's political leadership and high-ranking Muslims in the region.

These high-ranking Muslims had been educated in important centres of religious learning in the Arab-speaking world, for example Cairo's al-Azhar University. There they joined organizations such as the Muslim World League, which provided Arabic texts, and financial backing for building schools and mosques, and which sponsored occasional trips to conferences that helped keep Sierra Leoneans connected with the wider Community of Faith. Thus Alhaji's dream of modernization going hand in hand with religious piety was shaped by his own spiritual and physical pilgrimage, but was also consistent with the rest of the community's perception that material wealth and 'advancement' were aspects of the integration in a more cosmopolitan Muslim community.[3]

Alhaji's modernist link between religious practices, the integration in an international Islamic community, and local development contrasted with a common perception among non-Muslim, urban Sierra Leoneans in this region, for whom Islam was equated with 'tradition'. For example, take what the DO (District Officer) for the area told me when I informed him of where I intended to carry out my research. 'Ah', he had said, 'good choice, they are very traditional Mende down there, good Muslims, you know. Very little schooling, development, or diamond mining. They just farm and are peaceful.' The DO contrasted English schooling with rural illiteracy, and socio-economic change (mining) with subsistence farming. He also made a connection between Islamic beliefs and practices, and 'traditional' Mende identity. His assessment of these connections was grounded in the historical legacy of British commercial and colonial presence in southern Sierra Leone, as well as of Christian missionary activities.

An English education in Sierra Leone was historically also a Christian education, given that missionary schools outnumbered government ones, which often had different policies regarding religious instruction and affiliation.[4] Thus opportunities for urban and government employment, and even for modern farming technologies, were generally linked with the cultural baggage brought to Sierra Leone by British commercial and colonial expansion. The cultural, economic and administrative expansion took place initially from the Atlantic coast, moving inland along navigable rivers. This south–north movement along waterways was supplemented by an eastward one on land, with the newly built railway line from Freetown, the capital city. Both phases affected territories occupied primarily by Mende, one of the two largest ethnic groups in Sierra Leone. By contrast, historically the country's northern peoples had stronger religious, cultural and economic ties with Islamic agents and centres in the savannah belt to the North (Lewis 1966; Massing 1985; Rodney 1970; Skinner 1978; Trimingham 1962: 165–70, 189–92, 224–7).

But the DO's perception that Muslim practices were an integral aspect of 'traditional' Mende identity was also consistent with an earlier, emergent historical heritage in Mendeland, in spite of the region's relative marginality to west African Islamic centres. This earlier Muslim heritage was linked to cultural and economic exchanges with traders and clerics from further north (Matthews 1788), and accounted – as we shall see – for a number of 'syncretic' beliefs and practices embedded in people's common-sense world, which were no longer marked as religious. This raises the issue of consciousness, and of its role in any discussion of syncretic agency. Alhaji was consciously trying to change ritual and religious practices to bring them in line with what he thought acceptable 'in Mecca', in the larger Muslim world. However, his project articulated with other kinds of Islamic practices and identities, and with syncretic processes at different levels, which worked against Alhaji's reforms. The outcome of this juxtaposition of syncretic processes at different levels was shaped in part by local strategies and interests. But it also articulated with elements of Mende history sedimented over time in bodily and spatial practices, in the unexamined domain of *habitus* outside the realm of conscious intentions (Bourdieu 1977; Mauss 1950).

People like Alhaji Airplane have increasingly appeared in studies of religious reform and conversion in Africa, their visions, prophesies, political alliances and timing shaping their roles as catalysts for change (see Ottenberg 1971; Peel 1968; Simmons 1979). Indeed, different perspectives on the 'catalytic' role of Islamic and Christian reformers (and belief systems) were central to important debates on processes of religious change in Africa (Fisher 1973: 28–30; Horton 1971: 104–07, 1975). Studies of religious and ritual change in particular settings suggest that the outcomes of such processes are highly variable over time, as specific configurations of power articulate with shifting communities of reference from the local to the 'universal' (see Comaroff 1985; Geertz 1968). Thus ritual transformations advocated by charismatic individuals like Alhaji, situated locally but oriented towards an encompassing, cosmopolitan, modern Islamic community, do not always 'succeed', as we shall see, and either lapse or are resisted in a variety of ways (Launay 1992: 132–48; Lienhardt 1966).

I now turn to the larger Mende context that articulated with the ideas and actions 'brought back from Mecca' by a transformed Alhaji Airplane. Debates in Kpuawala over changes introduced in Mende initiation rituals to accommodate practices and beliefs marked as 'Islamic' suggested that, in spite of the DO's views, the relationship between Muslim and 'traditional' Mende identities was far from unproblematic. Furthermore, these debates were often situated within a discourse of authenticity, in which reformed rituals were evaluated in relation to their efficacy. This pointed to the fact that often analytical and critical views of syncretism might be found in the very contexts in which it unfolded as a process. In the Mende case at hand, this debate revealed both the limitations and possibilities of a more articulated, historicized and contextual understanding of the notion of syncretism.

THE 1985 SANDE INITIATION IN KPUAWALA

In April 1985, the village chapter of the women's Sande society held its initiation. As events unfolded over the following weeks, it became apparent that initiation rituals were undergoing or had already undergone a number of changes. These transformations were pointed out by bystanders or participants, whose opinions about the resulting rituals diverged widely. Sande women seemed to agree that things had changed since Alhaji's trip to Mecca.

Sande initiation has historically marked the transformation of young girls into adult, marriageable and fertile women among a number of related ethnic groups in Sierra Leone, Guinea and Liberia. In the same region, men have undergone parallel rites of passage to enter their own society, the Poro, which emphasized training for warfare and politics (D'Azevedo 1962; Little 1965, 1966). Sande and Poro have been characterized as 'secret' societies – internally stratified societies in which leading members controlled bodies of esoteric knowledge, which could not be shared with lower-ranking initiates or outsiders (that is, children and members of the opposite sex).[5]

In the last twenty years, anthropological studies of gender have linked women's unusual access to political office in Mendeland to the gender solidarity established within the Sande society (MacCormack 1975). In particular, the analysis of the rise to power of particular female chiefs suggested that high-ranking Sande women could acquire political clout by shaping advantageous marriage alliances between the young women they initiated and men from powerful lineages (Hoffer 1974). Yet others have pointed out that the internal stratification of *both* Poro and Sande involved similar forms of control by senior members over the labour and resources of junior ones. Consequently, rather than taking at face value the model of vertical 'solidarity', this perspective stressed horizontal links between Sande and Poro leaders across gender lines, which involved the sharing of supposedly secret knowledge as well (Bledsoe 1984). Both solidarity and stratification models of the organization of Sande and Poro lacked analyses of their particular manifestations in local chapters embedded in wider communities, of their rituals, and of the historical forces with which they articulated.

In those early April days, Kpuawala's leading women were busy negotiating the timing and conditions for initiating a new cohort of Sande members. The chiefdom authorities had been alerted, and the necessary licences obtained from them. Young men were enlisted to build the *kpanguima*, the enclosure on the edge of town which was to be the centre of Sande activities for the duration of the initiation.

Families of the seven girls who were to join Sande were visited assiduously by potential husbands, who negotiated their share of payments and gifts. Sande elders, female relatives, and women in the prospective husband's lineage took an active role in these negotiations. Once an agreement was reached, the future husband was put to work by Sande elders, and had to bring his own share of firewood, water, food and gifts.

Activities in Kpuawala came to a feverish pitch on the day preceding the initiation. Female friends and relatives came to visit from near and far for the duration of the festivities. The initiates' hair was braided in elaborate patterns, and their bodies were washed and rubbed with perfumed oil. Meantime, bands of women criss-crossed the village singing, making jokes and generally having fun – often at the expense of male bystanders who were shamed into giving them money, food and other gifts.

Among these women was Kaynge, who paraded around town dressed like a man, in a long gown and cap, her face adorned with huge spectacles and a fake cigar. She conspicuously consulted her enormous wristwatch – her mocking gestures and songs eliciting bursts of laughter from female audiences and guarded smiles from men. But Kaynge was not just mocking ordinary men: she was making fun of 'big' men, particularly those flaunting their wealth and cosmopolitan modernity through the conspicuous display of foreign commodities. She did so by juxtaposing in her attire the markers of 'traditional' male authority (long gown and cap) with those of literacy, office employment and access to cash (spectacles, wristwatch and cigarettes).

But the Sande initiation performed a similar mediation between 'traditional' and modern worlds for women, a transition marked sartorially in the two most important public rituals during Kpuawala's 1985 proceedings. For the *Gani* – the first public appearance after joining Sande – initiates were barefoot, and wore 'traditional' Mende markers of feminine attire, such as headties and long *lappas* (lengths of cloth, or 'wrappers' tied around their bodies). By contrast, several weeks later they appeared for the final 'coming out' ceremony (*Sande gbuale*) wearing stylish imported sandals, knee-length tailored dresses, straightened and uncovered hair, make-up, and a variety of 'foreign' accessories such as sunglasses, watches and costume jewellery.

Thus Kaynge was in a sense mocking the men who would be desirable husbands for these young Sande women in the making, men who – like their future wives – might bridge the gap between the rural, local setting and the urban, cosmopolitan world beyond. But she also signified at another level women's appropriation of male powers in the context of Sande initiation – a process marked in other contexts as well, where Sande elders referred to themselves as warriors and chiefs, and brandished 'weapons'.[6] This appropriation was marked by the ability to laugh at men who would normally be the object of female deference.

The night was spent eating, dancing and singing. As rested women joined in, exhausted ones dropped out of singing and dancing groups making the rounds. During these night festivities, Sande elders went around to collect the girls to be initiated, and took them to the Sande 'bush' (*ndɔgbɔ*). The celebrations suddenly stopped in the early morning, and all the women disappeared from town. Those of us left could hear alternately the sounds of singing and hand-clapping coming from among the trees beyond the village edge.

Then even those sounds stopped abruptly, leaving the community silent and still. It was an extraordinary experience, all the more impressive after the sounds and motion of the previous twenty-four hours. Then a solemn procession of women led by Sande elders came to town, and went round the whole community. Leading them was a lone singer, accompanied by her gourd rattle (*sɛgbule*). 'Silence', she sang, 'silence, all you Sande women. Do not talk. I alone will speak, I and my *sɛgbule*' (*A Londo, Sande nyahagbi' baa yɛpɛ, kɛ lee nya yakpe, nya kɛ sɛgbulɛ*). The Sande voice had spoken through the feminine musical instrument *par excellence*, and everyone seemed to be listening.[7]

After this procession, dancing resumed as before. I was stunned by the dramatic contrast between the solemn procession, and the singing and dancing that both preceded and followed it. 'Oh, but you really would have been in awe', said my elderly neighbour, turning to me, 'if the Sande "head" (*ngu*) had been leading the procession, as in the past.'

Sande 'heads' are blackened helmet masks worn over layers of dark raffia, which cover the entire human body except for arms and lower legs – also concealed by fabric. These 'heads' display stylized female features admired by men and women alike, and elaborate, lobed hairdos over a ringed neck. The mask's mouth is carved with sealed lips, and it always appears in public with an 'interpreter' through which it speaks – or sings accompanied by the *sɛgbule*. But the masquerade does move and dance in public, and one of its names is *ndoli jowei*, 'dancing *sowei*'.[8] In 1985, the Sande mask did not 'come out' (*iigbua*) in Kpuawala.

In the following days, normal life and working patterns resumed in Kpuawala – though farming activities revolved around raising food and money for the ongoing initiation, and the entertainment of visitors who crowded the town for the occasion. Sande events and celebrations periodically changed the pace of everyday life. Initiates were now in seclusion in the Sande bush, having disappeared during the first night of celebrations.

Then Hawa arrived in town to be initiated. She had been in school in the city of Kenema, and had only been able to get away during holidays. Her father lived in Kpuawala but had long before separated from her mother, who had moved away. There was some discussion over where Hawa should be initiated, since she had been living elsewhere. The local Sande elders lobbied hard to keep her in Kpuawala, but her father complained that he could not afford the fees, gifts and food required for the initiation. The Sande women had their way. Hawa was initiated, albeit about ten days after her peers.

But Hawa was also to be initiated differently from the others. She was joining (I was told) the Muslim Sande (*Mɔli Jandei*).[9] She had been raised in the household of an important Muslim man, and of a leading woman in a Muslim Sande chapter. The latter told a community gathering that she would have initiated Hawa where they now lived, had there been enough other girls ready to join this year. However, Hawa was the only 'mature' girl in her peer group (*kpelangɔ*: mature, near), the only one with breasts, so her guardian had decided to make her join Sande in her paternal village.

The songs accompanying Hawa's initiation festivities were different from those of a few days earlier. These included prayers, Qur'anic references and names, and some Arabic, as opposed to the Mende songs that had characterized the earlier celebrations. The proceedings were less elaborate – although this may have been due to the delay, and Sande elders' desire to get Hawa in with her peers as quickly as possible. Dancing was rather circumscribed, focusing on the central meeting place and the nearby mosque. The women who had arrived with Hawa sang and danced, while those already in Kpuawala seemed to have lost the enthusiasm of a few days earlier. Male bystanders intervened to encourage more women to sing, but the latter did not seem interested (by contrast, see Monts 1984 for a discussion of how Muslim songs were seen as enriching and expanding the Sande repertoire among the neighbouring Vai). Alhaji Airplane was clearly pleased with Muslim Sande, and took advantage of the opportunity to preach at length on the benefits of attending Friday mosque.

From this time onwards, the new initiate joined the others in every activity. The Sande initiation exhibited features common to rites of passage elsewhere in Africa and beyond (see Turner 1967; van Gennep 1960). Following the initial seclusion, initiates appeared in public for the *Gani* ceremony. This occasion marked the beginning of a phase in which rules of seclusion were relaxed, and initiates could farm and move around the village by day wearing distinctive white headties and clay on their bodies. They returned to sleep in the *kpanguima* overnight.

The *Gani* was named after a special rice meal prepared for the occasion by Sande women, and shared with initiates in the *kpanguima*. Before eating this meal, initiates sat outside the Sande enclosure on a mat, lined up in a row, with legs stretched out in front of them. Their bodies were smeared with white kaolin clay, a sort of shell marking aesthetically their isolation from the social activities and relationships surrounding them. While the initiates sat in stony silence with downcast eyes, apparently deaf to the calls and praise surrounding them, their relatives made a show of not being able to find the daughter or sister they had 'given' to Sande elders.

For the *Gani*, initiates were decorated with multi-stranded yellow or red beaded necklaces criss-crossing their chests. Also tied across their chests and around their arms were Muslim amulets encased in leather or cotton wrappings. They were helped to walk and eat, a further mark of the process of learning and socialization they were undergoing. The whole community came to see the initiates thus displayed, offering praise and gifts of money to them and to the Sande elders solemnly sitting nearby.

Several weeks later, Sande elders gathered with the community authorities and the initiates' families to set a day for 'coming out' of Sande (*Sande gbuale*). Sande leaders requested the following for each initiate: two imperial gallons of palm oil, half a bag of cleaned rice, one large headtie, and eight Leones in cash (a little over three dollars at the time). The families suggested that these requests were excessive in the light of all the food and gifts they had already contributed throughout the initiation. But the Sande elders and their spokeswoman remained firm and defiant. They threatened to leave initiates in the Sande 'bush' if their demands were not met. Finally the community elders and families gave in, and after they brought all their contributions the concluding ceremonies began.

Upon finally being returned to the community as full-fledged, marriageable women, these newest of Sande members were a far cry from the awkward and uniformly dressed persons who had sat on the *Gani* mat, encased in their white clay shells. Now they were brought into town on the backs of older members – like 'new chiefs' (*maha nina*) whose feet could not touch the ground. Like chiefs, they were sheltered from the sun with umbrellas. As new women, their attires were individualized renditions of 'style,' (their term) – of current westernized urban fashion trends. Their skin was rubbed with oil, their nails were painted, their faces were made up, and they displayed a confident, cool demeanour as they sat in Kpuawala's central meeting place listening to music on borrowed portable tape decks.

DECEMBER 1986: SANDE REVISITED

There were no other Sande initiations in Kpuawala during my first stay, although I went along with other village women to several such occasions in neighbouring communities. Some of those Sande initiations included masked performances, others did not. As I was about to leave Kpuawala at the end of 1986, two high-ranking Sande women came to see me, and began a series of conversations to 'explain' the Sande initiation I had witnessed almost two years earlier. They discussed changes in the local Sande initiation, and compared current practices with what they had done in the past. They also compared their own Sande with other chapters.

Aminata:	Once, we used to initiate Mende Sande here . . .
Kadiatu (interrupting):	Say 'Muslim Sande' . . .
Aminata:	That's what I was about to say. We used to have Mende Sande here once. But our relatives, Alhaji's people . . . when Alhaji went to Mecca and came back, they said: 'This *sowei* we bring out, and the *sowei* headdress, let's leave them out of Sande.' They told us to stop doing those things when we women initiate Sande. Why? They said they did not see these things in Mecca. So now when we initiate Sande,

they say . . . we say, 'This is Muslim Sande.'

At that time, we Sande women agreed to men's faces, we said we'd initiate Muslim Sande. But in fact *we did not agree*. We do a mixture. Even now, Mende Sande is what we *mean* to do. We no longer bring out the mask that dances in the open: we left that because they told us not to do it. But we still do the Mende things that we used to do, *all* of them. Because the *real* Muslim Sande initiation only lasts one week. They [the initiates] spend seven nights in the enclosure, cook rice, and then circle the mosque . . . and it's over. But we still hold the 'underwater *sowei*.'

Kadiatu (interrupting): She's talking about *my* kind of Sande.

Aminata (interrupting): No, it is not your Sande! Now it's because of the chiefs that we do these things in the bush. If we brought these things to town, they would not like it. The chiefs say they do not like it.

In this exchange, Aminata and Kadiatu discussed how local Sande initiations were transformed 'when Alhaji went to Mecca and came back,' and tried to define the status of resulting 'mixed' rituals. The first thing to go was the *sowei* mask, for Alhaji and his people 'did not see it in Mecca'. Aminata later listed a number of other practices that had been dropped for the same reason, including the *kendui* procession in which Sande sacred objects were carried through town concealed under a white cloth. In response to the requests of 'Alhaji's people', Sande elders had also discontinued the practice of elaborately decorating initiates' bodies with multicoloured dots and a helmet-like hairdo – the Sande 'hat' (*Sande bɔlɛ*) – for certain rituals (see Jedrej 1980).

Kadiatu's suggestion that the local Sande chapter had been transformed into a Muslim one was rejected by Aminata on the grounds that Alhaji's reformist zeal had not affected the important rituals that still took place in secrecy. Crucial among them was the 'holding' of the 'underwater *sowei*' (*Sande hou njabu*) – the extraction of Sande ritual objects from waterways and rivers inhabited by female ancestral spirits, who were the powerful agencies at work in this society. Aminata also contrasted the longer duration of Kpuawala's Sande initiation, and its location in the segregated *kpanguima*, with the shortened 'Muslim' versions centring around the mosque.

But the case of Hawa – the latecomer in Kpuawala's initiation – suggested that this shortened, 'Muslim' version could also accommodate more easily academic demands and calendars, by lasting the length of a school holiday. Indeed, Hawa's emergence at the end of that initiation as 'Kema', as leader of her cohort of initiates, suggested that education could translate into important social capital within Sande, even in its sometimes less valued, 'Muslim' or 'mixed' form.

Aminata's main concern in her conversation with Kadiatu was to counter Kadiatu's assertions that the local Sande chapter had become 'Muslim'. Instead, Aminata claimed that local Sande rituals were 'mixed', combining Muslim and Mende elements. The women contrasted 'Muslim' and 'Mende' practices in Sande initiations, although in fact such elements were 'mixed' freely by everyone in most ritual and everyday circumstances. For example, later on in the same conversation both Kadiatu and Aminata agreed that one of the first steps taken by a woman who wanted to initiate her daughter was to consult 'Muslim people' (*Moli bla*) – diviners and ritual specialists who used the Qur'an and Muslim magic texts to determine auspicious times for holding initiations, and who suggested appropriate sacrifices in cases where the outcome seemed doubtful.

Like most people in the community, initiates wore especially made Muslim amulets, and Qur'anic inscriptions and charms were incorporated in Sande and other masquerades wherever these continued to appear (see Boone 1986; Bravmann 1983). More generally, the daily lives of Kpuawala's people were punctuated by Arabic blessings, greetings, and other loan words incorporated into their language through centuries of proximity with neighbouring Muslim people, by Friday days of rest, by the ritual repetition of even ordinary ablutions, by the eastern orientation of burials and sacred places, and by Islamic calendrical holidays. Some of these features were linked with the rather 'diffuse' Muslim identity that almost everyone in Kpuawala claimed under ordinary circumstances, but others were simply part of 'Mende customs' (*Mende hinda*).

These elements pointed to the historical articulation of Mende and different kinds of Muslim identities in this region. They were 'mixed' in everyday lives in ways not consciously identified under ordinary circumstances, but remained emergent, potentially available for encoding new or revitalized religious meanings at different times. The events and exegesis of Kpuawala's 1985 Sande initiation pointed to different levels of 'mixture', with variable meanings and values associated with them. Alhaji saw the results of his efforts as a positive, 'Muslim' ritual, now rid of masks and other elements inconsistent with 'what he had seen in Mecca'. Kadiatu seemed to share his assessment in so far as the 'Islamicization' of local Sande went, but clearly displayed her dislike for this form compared to her own 'underwater' Sande. By contrast, Aminata insisted on a third kind of Sande, a 'mixed' Sande where Islamic elements were incorporated in their superficial, visible manifestations, while remaining 'Mende' in secret, and underwater.

But Aminata's denial that the local Sande had instituted change in more than just a superficial way – to appear to comply 'to men's faces' – her assertion that 'in fact we did not agree' also suggested a denial of syncretism. The 'mixture' she was talking about was one in which Muslim and 'underwater' Sande elements existed in parallel domains without intermingling: some rituals were public, others concealed, some were for 'men's faces', others for the society's women. Though Aminata seemed to value this particular 'mixture', the way in which she defined it precluded its glossing as 'syncretism' in any simple way.

Aminata's and Kadiatu's mutual interruptions and corrections in the course of the conversation underscored their disagreements over the status of the 'mixed' Sande rituals currently performed in the community. Their disagreements also had to do with their identities and aspirations at different levels. Aminata was a member of the household that 'owned' the local Sande chapter. During the 1985 Kpuawala initiation, she had moved up to a higher rank within the local Sande chapter. Her father's ageing sister headed this chapter, as well as being a leading Muslim in Kpuawala – both women frequented the mosque, observed religious feasts, and fasted during Ramadan. Aminata made no secret of the fact that she was preparing to replace her father's sister in her role as the head of the local Sande in the future. She and her prominent aunt were also related to Alhaji Airplane.

By contrast, Kadiatu was an outsider who had married into the community, and was a famous singer and dancer. She travelled throughout Mendeland to perform in Sande initiations that continued to display the *sowei* mask, and had acquired fame and wealth in the process. She was better educated and wealthier than Aminata, and in dress and behaviour appeared to be more cosmopolitan. Though raised as a Christian in her home town further east, in the community she joined in with Muslim prayers and occasionally fasted for Ramadan. But Kadiatu's well-known fondness for palm wine made those practices appear at best as window-dressing, especially in the eyes of older Kpuawala women.

Thus Aminata's statement that local Sande initiations were still 'Mende' at the core in spite of their 'Islamic' surface characters must be seen in the context of her close kin ties with Alhaji, of her own religious identity, and of her status within a prominent Muslim and Sande family. By contrast, Kadiatu's emphasis on the similarities between the rituals described by Aminata and 'her' own ones related in part to her efforts as a non-Muslim, Mende outsider to establish her own status and authority vis-à-vis the community's Sande leadership.

The disagreement between Aminata and Kadiatu over the status of changing Sande rituals pointed to the limits of 'gender solidarity' in this conjuncture, even though gender *was* marked in Aminata's discussion. Sande rituals were changed to satisfy 'the men', particularly religious ones ('Alhaji's people'), and 'the [male] chiefs' did not 'like' initiations as they had been. But later in the conversation, disagreements between Aminata and Kadiatu over the impact of change on the efficacy of Sande rituals became so pronounced that they refused to talk any longer in each other's presence. Each woman began to question the truthfulness of the other's claim to possessing Sande esoteric knowledge, and suggested that her own ritual practices and 'medicine' (*halei*) were more effective than the other's.

Kadiatu and other leading women who had opposed the changes in their initiation rituals saw a sharp contrast between Mende and Muslim Sande. The latter was perceived as foreign, as opposed to 'Mende', in part because its rituals were shaped by what Alhaji 'saw in Mecca' – because his authority and ideals in instituting changes came from abroad. Kadiatu was determined to continue having 'Mende' – that is, 'underwater' – Sande initiations, without compromising with the male religious authorities and village elders. In practice, she did so by travelling elsewhere and taking on prominent ritual roles in *openly* 'Mende' Sande initiations. Other Sande elders in the community had also left the local chapter, to participate in 'real' initiations in different communities. While in Kpuawala, Kadiatu and these other dissenting Sande women kept a relatively low profile in the local 'mixed' proceedings.

Kadiatu's travels to perform in Sande initiations elsewhere suggested a kind of resistance to ritual change that contradicted straightforward readings of local 'mixed' practices as examples of syncretism. Even Aminata's claim that Sande leaders had not really agreed, that their rituals were only 'mixed' in so far as they *appeared* 'to men's faces' to be Muslim while remaining the same in secret, suggests that at best the resulting compromise was a peculiar and limited form of 'syncretism' as far as women were concerned. The limits of this episode of syncretism when one takes into account the agency of all parties involved became evident during a recent return trip to Kpuawala.

EPILOGUE, 1993

I first returned to Kpuawala three years after the conversation discussed above, and by then both Kadiatu and Aminata had left. Kadiatu had left her Kpuawala husband and had returned to her native town, where she later died. Aminata had gone to get started in trade and business in the diamond fields to the north of Mendeland. Sande initiations went on as they had during my earlier visits, and as before some of the local women invited me to join them in neighbouring communities where they went because they 'enjoyed' such events more when they included the 'dancing *sowei*' and other 'non-Muslim' features.

I recently returned to Kpuawala after having first drafted this chapter, and found women planning a Sande initiation for December 1993. The big news – I was told – was that the Sande 'head' (mask) had returned to Kpuawala during the preceding year's initiation, and that it had caused a big furor among the chiefdom's political and religious leadership. 'The men' – *imams*, town chiefs, section chiefs, and representatives of chiefdom authorities – had gathered, filling Kpuawala's central meeting place beyond capacity (*ndavengɔ kpaŋ*!), to persuade Sande women to retire the 'dancing *sowei*'. But at the height of the argument, the *sowei* itself appeared in the middle of the gathering, and sat down in silence, refusing to budge. The 'dancing *sowei*' had her way, and the initiation proceeded – to Alhaji's dismay.

In hindsight, my women friends believed that the political and religious authorities had given in because they thought this might remain an isolated event. But Aminata's aunt – who had been the ranking Sande elder aligned with the Muslim reformists – was now senile and unable to take an active role in the proceedings. Her own niece had returned to Kpuawala for the preceding year's initiation, and had sided with those clamouring for the masquerade's return. Kpuawala's Sande women seemed determined to dispel any notion that this had been an isolated episode, and were preparing to bring out the masquerade again.

After performing for years 'mixed' Sande initiations as a result of reformist pressures by 'Muslim' elements, Kpuawala women seemed well on their way to re-establishing ritual forms to which some among them had continued to remain partial. These were, of course, syncretic phenomena encompassing Islamic blessings, scriptures and objects. How, then, do we analyse particular agencies and interests at play in syncretic processes, given the highly selective and variable nature of the 'mixing' analysed above? We might begin by particularizing and historicizing our studies of syncretic processes, contextualizing them within specific configurations of power, where religious discourse articulates with different kinds and levels of authority.

NOTES

I am grateful for the constructive criticism of earlier versions of this paper offered by Rosalind Shaw, Charles Stewart, Richard Werbner and an anonymous reviewer. Luca D'Isanto helped throughout with stimulating discussions and research assistance, and Stefania Pandolfo provided that crucial final editorial reading. Of course I take full responsibility for the final form of this essay. Financial support for research in Sierra Leone is gratefully acknowledged from the United States Department of Education (for a Fulbright-Hays doctoral dissertation research fellowship in 1984–6), as well as the Harvard Academy for International and Area Studies (1993 trip).

1 This is a reference to Queen Elizabeth II and to the British administration of Sierra Leone, which ended in 1961.
2 Mende exclamation used when talking of sudden events, like the escape of an entrapped animal.
3 Personal accounts of the *hajj* abound in the literature. For historical narratives see, for example, Burton 1964; El Moudden 1990; Metcalf 1990; and Norris 1977.
4 For example, Qur'anic instruction was part of the required curriculum for students in the oldest and most prestigious government school in the interior of Sierra Leone, the Bo School (Fyfe 1962).
5 See Ferme 1992, especially Ch. 1, for a critical approach to the study of secrecy and secret societies in this region.
6 A discussion of childbirth and of other contexts in which this occurs can be found in Ferme 1992: 418ff. In that text, I also go further into the issue of cross-dressing and gender ambiguity raised by Kaynge and by certain offices and rituals within both Sande and Poro societies.
7 Space limitations prevent me from analysing the meaning of particular Sande initiation rituals. My concern here is rather to discuss how these rituals articulate with Islamic syncretic beliefs and practices.
8 *Sowei* is the title of the Sande society's highest-ranking members. For a discussion of structural aspects of Sande society and a summary outline of major rituals, see Jedrej 1980. The iconography and aesthetics of this society's masks and rituals are discussed in Boone 1986; Phillips 1979, 1980.
9 This form of Sande is also called 'Sunna' by Mende Muslims.

REFERENCES

Bledsoe, C.H. (1984) 'The political use of Sande ideology and symbolism', *American Ethnologist* 11: 455–72.

Boone, S. (1986) *Radiance from the Waters: Ideals of Feminine Beauty in Mende Art*, New Haven: Yale University Press.

Bourdieu, P. (1977) *Outline of a Theory of Practice*, trans. R. Nice, Cambridge: Cambridge University Press.

Bravmann, R.A. (1983) *African Islam*, Washington, DC: Smithsonian Institution Press.

Burton, R.F. (1964 [1893]) *Personal Narrative of a Pilgrimage to Al-Madinah and Meccah*, 2 vols, New York: Dover.

Comaroff, J. (1985) *Body of Power, Spirit of Resistance: The Culture and History of a South African People*, Chicago: University of Chicago Press.

D'Azevedo, W.L. (1962) 'Some historical problems in the delineation of a central west Atlantic region', *Annals of the New York Academy of Sciences* 96, 2: 512–38.

El Moudden, A. (1990) 'The ambivalence of *rihla*: community integration and self-definition in Moroccan travel accounts, 1300–1800', in D.F. Eickelman and J. Piscatori (eds), *Muslim Travellers: Pilgrimage, Migration, and the Religious Imagination*, Berkeley: University of California Press.

Ferme, M.C. (1992) '"Hammocks belong to men, stools to women": constructing and contesting gender domains in a Mende village (Sierra Leone, West Africa)', unpublished PhD thesis, University of Chicago.

Fischer, H.J. (1973) 'Conversion reconsidered: some historical aspects of religious conversion in black Africa', *Africa* 43, 1: 27–40.

Fyfe, C. (1962) *A History of Sierra Leone*, London: Oxford University Press.

Geertz, C. (1968) *Islam Observed: Religious Development in Morocco and Indonesia*, Chicago: University of Chicago Press.

Hoffer, C.P. (1974) 'Madam Yoko: ruler of the Kpa Mende confederacy', in M.Z. Rosaldo and L. Lamphere *Woman, Culture, and Society*, Stanford: Stanford University Press.

Horton, R. (1971) 'African conversion', *Africa* 41, 2: 85–108.

—— (1975) 'On the rationality of conversion', Part I, *Africa* 45, 3: 219–35; Part II, *Africa* 45, 4: 373–99.

Jedrej, M.C. (1980) 'Structural aspects of a West African secret society', *Ethnologische Zeitschrift* 1: 133–42.

Launay, R. (1990) 'Pedigrees and paradigms: scholarly credentials among the Dyula of the northern Ivory Coast', in D.E. Eickelman and J. Piscatori (eds), *Muslim Travellers: Pilgrimage, Migration, and the Religious Imagination*, Berkeley: University of California Press.

—— (1992) *Beyond the Stream: Islam and Society in a West African Town*, Berkeley: University of California Press.

Lewis, I.M. (1966) 'Introduction', in I.M. Lewis (ed.), *Islam in Tropical Africa*, London: International African Institute.

Lienhardt, P. (1966) 'A controversy over Islamic custom in Kilwa Kivinje, Tanzania' in I.M. Lewis (ed.), *Islam in Tropical Africa*, London: International African Institute

Little, K. (1965) 'The political function of the Poro', Part I, *Africa* 35, 4: 349–65.

—— (1966) 'The political function of the Poro', Part II, *Africa* 36, 1: 62–71.

MacCormack, C.P. (1975) 'Sande women and political power in Sierra Leone', *The West African Journal of Sociology and Political Science* 1, 1: 42–50.

Massing, A.W. (1985) 'The Mane, the decline of Mali, and Mandinka expansion towards the South Windward Coast', *Cahiers d'Etudes Africaines* 97, 1: 21–55.

Matthews, J. (1788) *A Voyage to the River Sierra Leone, on the Coast of Africa, Containing an Account of the Trade and Productions of the Country, and of the Civil and Religious Customs and Manners of the People; in a Series of Letters to a Friend in England*, London: B. White and Son; 1966 reprint, London: Frank Cass.

Mauss, M. (1950) 'Les techniques du corps', in Mauss, *Sociologie et Anthropologie*, Paris: Presses Universitaires de France.

Metcalf, B. D. (1990) 'The pilgrimage remembered: South Asian accounts of the *hajj*', in D.E. Eickelman and J. Piscatori (eds), *Muslim Travellers: Pilgrimage, Migration, and the Religious Imagination*, Berkeley: University of California Press.

Monts, L. P. (1984) 'Conflict, accommodation, and transformation: the effect of Islam on music of the Vai secret societies', *Cahiers d'Etudes Africaines*, 95, 24: 321–42.

Norris, H.T. (1977) *The Pilgrimage of Ahmad*, ed. and trans. H.T. Norris, London: Aris and Phillips.

Ottenberg, S. (1971) 'A Moslem Igbo village', *Cahiers d'Etudes Africaines* 11, 42: 231–60.

Peel, J.D.Y. (1968) *Aladura: A Religious Movement among the Yoruba*, London: Oxford University Press.

Phillips, R.B. (1979) 'The Sande society masks of the Mende of Sierra Leone', unpublished PhD thesis, University of London.

—— (1980) 'The iconography of the Mende *Sowei* mask', *Ethnologische Zeitschrift* 1: 113–32.

Rodney, W. (1970) *A History of the Upper Guinea Coast, 1545 to 1800*, Oxford: Clarendon Press.

Simmons, W.S. (1979) 'Islamic conversion and social change in a Senegalese village', *Ethnology* 18, 4: 303–23.

Skinner, D.E. (1978) 'Mande settlement and the development of Islamic institutions in Sierra Leone', *The International Journal of African Historical Studies* 11, 1: 32–62.

Trimingham, J.S. (1962) *A History of Islam in West Africa*, London: Oxford University Press.

Turner, V. (1967) *The Forest of Symbols*, Ithaca, NY: Cornell University Press.

van Gennep, A. (1960) *The Rites of Passage*, trans. M.B. Vizedom and G.L. Caffee, Chicago: University of Chicago Press.

2 Beyond syncretism
Translation and diabolization in the appropriation of Protestantism in Africa

Birgit Meyer

In the discourse on Christianity in Africa, the term 'syncretism' is usually either avoided, or employed in a neutral or even pejorative way to designate the mixture of Christianity and indigenous religion. 'Syncretism' has mainly been used in theories of 'acculturation' or 'culture contact' which aim to classify religious expressions along a continuum whose poles are 'traditional' and 'Western'. Used in this way, the term thus describes local versions of Christianity by reference to the origins of their elements. However, this 'mechanical assignation of cultural traits' (Peel 1968: 140) is of no aid in understanding how the mixture termed syncretism actually comes about and is conceived by African Christians themselves. Though this critique is shared by a growing number of Africanists, there are still very few studies which describe how local interpretations of Christianity evolve. It is the objective of this chapter to provide insight into this process. I will explore how this world religion is practically appropriated by people with hitherto indigenous beliefs. In my usage here, 'appropriation' means the process of making Christianity one's own – a process which can even result in the subversion of missionary ideas. I prefer this term to others like 'adoption' or 'adaptation' because it signals the necessity of going beyond the conceptualization of African Christianity in terms of acculturation and culture contact theories, and of understanding African Christians as active agents in a historical process. Another problem with 'syncretism' is that in the discourse on African Christianity it has virtually been confined to local interpretations that are formulated in independent churches, whereas mission churches are generally considered to represent missionary Christianity. Critical African intellectuals often see members of mission churches as victims of Western missionary dominance, who are unable to synthesize traditional religion and Christianity, and who need to be freed from their divided consciousness, which makes them 'slide back' into the former when the latter fails to help them solve existential problems. This is to be brought about by *Africanization*, a theologically devised synthesis of traditional and Christian elements. The terms 'syncretistic' and 'divided consciousness' both deny grassroots members of independent as well as mission churches, a developed and appropriate understanding of Christianity. By making use of these terms theologians thus contest local interpretations; they do not merely describe them (Droogers 1989: 20). At the same time the two terms suggest a difference between the ideas of the members of the two types of churches. However, since up to now missionary Christianity at the grassroots has hardly been investigated, one may have serious doubts as to whether this difference exists.

In this chapter I want to look beyond notions like 'syncretism' and 'divided consciousness' and instead focus on the historical encounter between the adherents of the religions involved, and the features resulting from it. I will deal with the appropriation of Christianity by members of the Evangelical Presbyterian Church (EPC), a historical mission church that originated from the activities of the Norddeutsche Missions Gesellschaft (NMG – North German Mission-Society) among the Ewe. In doing so, I want to discover how the amalgam called syncretism comes about.[1]

THE MISSIONARY AND THE PRIEST

Let us listen to a three-way conversation between the missionary Lorenz Wolf, an Ewe 'fetish priest' and the *fiagā* (king) in Peki, the cradle of the Ewe mission. This exchange gets us to the heart of the matter.

A fetish priest, a well-built man more than 7 feet tall, with fetish signs hanging everywhere on his body, visited me together with his entourage, posted himself boastfully in front of me and started bragging: 'God and I are one; he tells me everything.' I [Wolf] asked him what that should mean, and how he knew something about God. 'I go to God in heaven', he said. I: 'By what way?' He: 'I know it.' I: 'Show it to me.' He: 'No, God and I are one.' I: 'I am afraid you are a liar and you just talk like this to deceive the people, because if you had been to God or if you had really heard about him you would know that God hates the fetishes you claim to have received from him. God is angry with the idols.' Then the King said that all the fetishes came from God. – 'No, I said, they are from the devil.' The fetish-priest stood there silently. Then I said pointing to my Bible: 'Here is God's word, here God talks to us through his dear son, Jesus Christ, and that is why I have come so that you will hear the word of God.' – 'Yes', the fetish priest said, 'that is true. You know about God.' I: 'Do you believe that?' He: 'Yes'. – 'Well', I said, 'then give me the fetishes you wear on your chest, then I will believe that you believe my word.' He, however, refused and I said: 'Look how you are a deceiver and a liar.'

(*Mittheilungen der Norddeutschen Mission* 1848: 64, my translation)

This conversation contains some characteristic features of the interaction between missionaries and Africans. First, since mission implies communication, it makes sense to approach the interaction of the missionaries and the Ewe, which eventually led to the latter's appropriation of the former's ideas, from a language perspective. The aim of this approach, which conceptualizes religion as discourse, is 'to understand the creation of meaning, or of a meaningful praxis through events of speech and communication' (Fabian 1985: 147). Secondly, mission depends on translation. In order to be comprehensible, the missionaries had to make use of existing terms which evoked concepts they possibly wanted to replace. It is therefore reasonable to assume that through the vernacularization of the Christian message transformations of meaning occurred, and that this can shed light on the issue of 'syncretism'. A third point is the issue of diabolization. The missionary's claim that the 'fetishes' came from the Devil amounts to more than a mere insult to the Ewe religion (Meyer 1992); it demonizes the existing pantheon. Further on I will explain that the Devil can play an essential role in 'syncretic' processes.

One last issue relevant to the theme of this chapter concerns power. Although in this phase the missionary and the priest met practically as equals, only the former was able to write about their encounter, and so it is his perspective that is communicated to us. This unequal access to writing remained for long a feature of mission work. Whereas the missionaries and some of their native assistants wrote, the ordinary converts were written about. Since the historical documents thus give a limited, one-sided view of what actually was thought and happened, one may wonder whether the mission's claim of the ongoing success of the work of evangelization has to be taken at face value.

I shall advocate the thesis that the focus on vernacularization and diabolization can help to reveal the ideas of the silent majority, and that these two issues seriously limited the missionaries' power to control the Ewe Christians' ideas and actions. I hasten to say that it is, of course, not my intention to excuse the missionaries from contributing to the colonization of the Ewe; but the point I want to make is that Christianity at the grassroots cannot be reduced to the intentions and actions of the missionaries. Rather than merely reproducing the opposition of agents and victims, I am interested in discovering how these 'victims' escaped and resisted domination and thereby transcended the opposition they seem to be trapped in.

In order to pursue the lines set out here, I will turn to the translation of the main agents of Christianity – the three persons of God and the Devil into Ewe discourse. But before doing so it is important to get a broad idea about the people who use the Christian vocabulary discussed here.

THE EP CHURCH AND THE INDEPENDENT CHURCHES

The NMG missionaries began their evangelistic work in Peki Blengo, then the capital of the kingdom of Krepi, in 1847. After some decades of rather limited success, from the 1880s onwards their efforts led to the formation of congregations in many Ewe towns, including Peki Blengo. The church continued to grow in spite of the fact that, due to the First World War, the German missionaries were forced to leave.

In 1922 the mission church became officially independent. For quite some time it held the monopoly on Christianity – or at least Protestantism – in Ewe land, but around 1930 independent movements arose, to which the mission church would lose an increasing number of its members. Later members also tried to profess an alternative Christian praxis within the EPC, but since the latter would not accept any reforms a church split was imminent. For example, in 1960, as a result of a conflict over prayer healing, a secession occurred in the EPC of Blengo, which resulted in the formation of an independent pentecostal church.

Whereas in the 1960s the EPC leaders still vehemently opposed the introduction of pentecostal practices and thereby risked losing many members to such churches, by the end of the seventies the church started to Africanize its liturgy. Moreover, in 1978 a pentecostally oriented prayer group (the Bible Study and Prayer Fellowship) that had already been active for several years was formally accepted within the church. At the same time, in order to extend the project of Africanization to the doctrine, church theologians, above all the philosopher and then Moderator N.K. Dzobo (1981–92), started to develop the so-called *Meleagbe* ('I am alive') theology which conceptualized elements of the traditional religion in a positive way. This view contrasted strongly with the conviction, professed so far, that the old religion was the domain of the Devil.

Whereas most local pastors neglected this new theology, the pentecostal prayer group stood up against it. Since its members strongly believed that Satan was operating through the old gods and ghosts, they could not accept a more positive valuation of traditional religion. The group's opposition against the Moderator became vehement when in 1988 he was re-elected for a third four-year term, which, according to the prayer group, was against the church constitution. The conflict was thus cast in juridical, not theological terms. The majority of the church members – though in general not in favour of the new theology – supported the prolongation of the term, because this had been decided by the highest church authority, the synod. For them it was sufficient that the Moderator agreed to stop propagating his ideas as a new church theology. But for the prayer group this was not enough. In the course of time the conflict led to the split of the church.

Since 1991 there have been two EPCs which both claim to be the rightful successor of the missionary heritage. Whereas the old EPC remained organized as it had been before, the new EPC adopted pentecostal practices. The split occurred on both the national and the local level. During my fieldwork in 1992, the relations between the members of the two churches, who often belonged to the same families, were tense, and both sides insisted that they were right. Whereas the members of the old EPC maintained that synod decisions had to be accepted, the members of the new EPC insisted that the decision to prolong the Moderator's term for another four years was unlawful and that it was unchristian to follow a church leader with a theology that neglected the Devil. On the local level the conflict was more over constitutional issues than over problems of diabology. But it would have been difficult for the two factions to disagree on the issue of the existence of the Devil and evil spirits, since, as we shall see later on, their members shared the same cosmology.

The spiritual and pentecostal churches,[2] the new EPC included, are frequented mainly by middle-aged women and, to a lesser extent, young men with health, fertility and wealth problems. They seek relief and protection through a more spiritual Christian praxis focusing on the Holy Spirit as a power able to drive away evil spirits. The question that arises is how the emergence of spiritual and pentecostal churches can be explained and whether a person's conversion to such a church implies a complete change of ideas. Since it is impossible in the context of this chapter to deal adequately with this complex issue, I will confine myself to a brief statement. It seems that the popularity of spiritual and pentecostal churches relates to people's need to cope with the problem of evil in a practical way, that is, by naming it first and subsequently fighting it. Whereas the traditional religion provided for this need, the missionaries and mission church leaders would not accept any rituals to deal with evil forces. In earlier decades this lack did not entice church members to find effective ways to cope with evil in the framework of the mission church, because then, due to the skills learned in the mission schools, the situation of Christians in general was good enough. But if Christians had problems which they conceptualized, for example, in terms of witchcraft, they had to seek relief from a traditional priest. The spiritual and pentecostal churches which, by contrast with the mission church doctrine, did not deny the existence of witchcraft and other personified evil forces, provided an alternative to the consultation of traditional priests by offering ways and means to name and fight evil.

Though there are people with problems at any time, it is not surprising that the spiritual and pentecostal churches gained momentum in Ghana in times of economic crisis, because then the number of people facing medical, financial and social problems grew rapidly. Since the fifties, due to the continuous fall of world market prices for cocoa (Ghana's main export product), and to the devastation of many old cocoa-growing areas through disease and governmental mismanagement of resources, there is overall economic decline and people's lives are shaped by poverty (Frimpong-Ansah 1992). The total failure of the harvest and the resulting starvation experienced in 1983 worsened the situation further. Most people do not have enough money to feed themselves, to provide clothes and education for their children, and to pay for necessary medical treatment. Whereas the IMF (International Monetary Fund) structural adjustment programme is praised for having stabilized the Ghanaian economy in general, the situation of the people has not improved.

In this situation, there seems to be more need than in better times to blame evil forces for mishaps preventing progress in life, as well as a need for protection against these forces. The spiritual and pentecostal churches, which became very popular from the fifties on, and especially after 1983, provide for these needs. As we shall see, they do so by mobilizing hitherto dormant or latent dimensions of meaning – hence their popularity.

THE THREE PERSONS OF GOD AND THE DEVIL

The missionaries – at least those among them with the talent to learn languages – together with a handful of Ewe assistants, carefully studied the Ewe language in order to find adequate words and expressions to convey the Christian message. This resulted in a Christian vocabulary whose key terms, as we shall see, were not as determinate as the translators might have thought. In order to reveal the ambiguity or polysemy of Christian key terms, I will try to reconstruct the initial meanings Ewe terms probably had at the time the Christian discourse was constituted, and then proceed to contemporary Ewe Christians' understanding of these terms. The fact that the first written documents about the Ewe religion were produced by those intending to replace and even to destroy it certainly constitutes a handicap for the reconstruction of the initial meanings of terms (Peel 1990). Nevertheless, it still seems possible to infer, albeit tentatively, meanings from missionary ethnographies (Spieth 1906, 1911) which contain transcriptions of non-Christians' statements, and from Westermann's Ewe–German dictionary (1905a).

The three persons of God

The terms constituting the Trinity – *Mawu* (God), *Yesu Kristo* (Jesus Christ), and *Gbɔgbɔ Kɔkɔe* (Holy Spirit) – are from three of the four linguistic frames of reference the Ewe Christian vocabulary originates from. *Mawu* belongs to the terms taken from the pre-Christian religious vocabulary, *Yesu Kristo* is a loanword from the Bible, and the two words making up the phrase *Gbɔgbɔ kɔkɔe* originate from secular Ewe language. The last expression, like so many others, is a new linguistic creation that did not exist in pre-mission times. The Devil *Abosam*, to whom we shall turn below, is referred to by a word from the Akan (the language of the western neighbours from whom in pre-Christian times the Ewe borrowed many terms and customs) and thus represents the fourth linguistic frame of reference.

Mawu originally is not a generic term for 'God', but the personal name of a God known already in pre-Christian times. However, in those days there was no set of unified ideas about him shared by the various Ewe groups. It can be assumed that the discussions between Ewe evangelists and people who where were not (yet) Christians do not reflect the non-Christians' original ideas in a straightforward way – after all, normally they would not compare Christianity and their own religion. But in order to defend that religion against Christianity they had to compare it with, and describe it in terms of, Christianity. Nevertheless these sources reveal the Ewe's difficulty in understanding *Mawu* as a positive, caring power. One might say that listening to the Christian message triggered reflection about the old religion on a new, comparative level, and that statements on this level provide valuable insights into both the nature of the old religion and the way new influences were dealt with. The following argumentation from a non-Christian reacting to an evangelist's sermon (most probably William Lemgo), which the latter reported to the mission in 1893,[3] forms a case in point:

> One day I [William Lemgo] went into a town called Taviefe, and they had heard the good news of Jesus Christ before, but it did not please them. And one of them stood up and said that *Mawu*'s first creation were the *trōwo* [gods], and the second were the human beings, and *Mawu* appointed the *trōwo* to be the head of the human beings to look after them. And *Mawu* would divide the spirit [*gbɔgbɔ*, literally 'breath'] which is in a person into two, and he would keep half with himself and he would give half into the hands of the *trōwo* to be used in looking after people. And half of everybody's spirit is in the hands of *Mawu* himself and half is in the hands of the *trōwo*. And when a person's spirit which is in the hands of the *trōwo* is finished, then the *trō* [god] goes to *Mawu* to receive the person's spirit again, the second share which is in *Mawu*'s hand. And *Mawu* refuses and does not want a person again to receive the second part of the spirit. Then the person dies. Therefore in their eyes the *trōwo* have become more merciful than Mawu, but since he is the one who made everything and yet he does not want them to lead a long life, he is guilty . . . And there are some who say that *Mawu* did not send the *trōwo*. He sent Jesus so that they would worship Jesus. Their, the Tafi people's, Jesus is an *ameklu* [probably a guardian *trō*]; he, the great *Mawu* who made the human beings, sent a guardian to them, the Tafi people, to look after them. For that reason they would not know any Jesus.

This thoughtful rejoinder is in line with the statements of non-Christian members of different Ewe groups interviewed by Spieth (1906: 419). They considered *Mawu* to be the maker of human beings. He sent them into the world but was not concerned with their wellbeing in life. Some, like the evangelist's opponent, even accused *Mawu* of being merciless (ibid.: 789–90, 836–7). Most informants did not have much to say about *Mawu* at all, and instead talked about the female, caring earth God *Mawu Sodza*,[4] the male, aggressive thunder God *Mawu Sogble*,[5] and the money-providing God *Mawu Sowlui*. No general equally shared image of *Mawu* can be discerned from the statements of Spieth's informants. It seems that *Mawu* was considered to be far away, and if people wanted to achieve something, they addressed the various *trōwo*, gods with specific domains and responsibilities, through their priests and brought them sacrifices if requested. At least some people, including the evangelist's opponent quoted, thought that these *trōwo* acted as intermediaries between *Mawu* and human beings. For health, fertility, protection and success in life one approached the *trōwo*. This opponent took up the structural similarity of the *trōwo* and *Yesu Kristo*, but in contrast to the Christian message he used it to defend the superiority of these intermediaries to the Christian one.

I think that his emphasis on *Mawu* cannot be taken as an indication of the high God's centrality in the pre-Christian religion. His argumentation is already influenced by the Christian religion, which concentrated so much more on *Mawu* than people would have done otherwise. The missionaries were keen to emphasize the supposed monotheistic orientation of the Ewe, since this formed a valuable starting point for conversion. It is difficult to find out how far this bias really corresponded to the pre-Christian religion. Be that as it may, there is no doubt that the pre-Christian Ewe religion was practically oriented towards the *trōwo*, who had a materiality and concreteness *Mawu* lacked. Practically, *Mawu* was of no great importance in religious life, since he was thought to be too far away.

For contemporary EPC members the pre-Christian *Mawu* and the Christian God have blended, as the following fragment of my conversation with two Ewe candidate catechists in 1989 shows:

Birgit: But God as you knew him, is he the same as the one the Christians brought you?

Manfred: Yes, he is the same as *Mawu*. We call him *Mawu* and even we call him *Mawugã*, the chief

	God, or the higher God, or the all-powerful God.
Birgit:	And that is the same as the God that was brought by the missionaries?
Manfred and Isaac:	Yes.
Birgit:	So you kept the same God, but the worship changed completely?
Manfred:	Yes. The missionaries came to tell us: No, we don't have to worship God through the *trōwo* because they are evil spirits. That we have somebody who has died in our place known as Jesus Christ. Yes. And we had to worship God, too. And the missionaries came to tell us or to show us only the new way to worship God. That's the new way, and that's the acceptable way.

Mawu and the Christian God were thus connected not only by the act of translation, but also by an explanation relating the pre-Christian Ewe religion and Christianity. Through the identification of *Mawu* and God and the emphasis on the supposed original monotheism, the non-Christian ancestors turned into worshippers of the Christian God, even though unconscious of the fact. Below, we will see that this identification is not unproblematic.

But did the conversion to Christianity imply that Ewe Christians took up the new meaning the missionaries endowed '*Mawu*' with at the expense of the old? The term *Mawu*-God stood and still stands for a spiritual being that is both reachable and at a distance. The term is thus ambivalent. Whereas it should denote closeness to and love for people, it also connotes the very contrary: distance and even unconcern. I found in my fieldwork that the second dimension of meaning is always latently present. It becomes manifest when church-going and prayers do not yield the desired results. This can then prompt church members to consult the *trō* priests secretly, in the dark of the night.

Let us now turn to *Yesu Kristo*. Since, unlike *Mawu*, this name is a loan-word from a language unknown to the Ewe, it initially carried no meanings to be replaced by Christian ones. When introduced, it formed a relatively empty semantic field. But subsequently, *Yesu Kristo* became especially meaningful as an antithesis to the *trōwo*. The structural similarity between *Yesu Kristo* and the *trōwo* has already been touched on. The replacement of the *trōwo* as brokers between human beings and *Mawu* by *Yesu Kristo* did not make Ewe Christians discard them. Through the acknowledgement of structural similarity, they considered the *trõwo* to be as really existent as *Yesu Kristo*. At the same time they opposed the former and the latter in terms of evil and good. This confrontation is important for Ewe Christians' understanding of *Mawu*'s son. As a consequence of diabolization – we turn to this process below – the *trõwo* were and, as the candidate catechists' statement above reveals, still are conceived to continue their existence as real evil spirits. And it is *Yesu Kristo's* main task to fight them, since, as the catechist of the EPC that split off in Blengo assured me: 'his main aim of coming into the world is to defeat and destroy the works of the devil.' Therefore his name, which is believed to contain power, is called upon in deliverance prayers when evil spirits are driven out of people. For many people, *Yesu Kristo* is an exorcist. The fact that God's son was introduced to the Ewe by describing him as being at once similar and antithetical to the *trõwo* illustrates once more that Christianity was presented to the Ewe in terms of their existing cosmology, which had a decisive influence on their understanding of Christian key terms.

I turn now to a consideration of the Holy Spirit, *Gbɔgbɔ kɔkɔe*, a compound composed from the Ewe words for 'breath' and 'clean/pure'. The Holy Spirit in Ewe is thus a new phrase consisting of two terms which did not previously belong to religious discourse. In contrast to *Gbɔgbɔ kɔkɔe*, evil spirits were termed *gbɔgbɔ makɔmakɔwo* (*ma* negates *kɔ*, thus 'unclean breaths') or *gbɔgbɔvõwo* (*võ* 'evil', thus 'evil breaths'). These terms, too, are new creations to designate the *trõwo* and other powers now conceptualized as evil. In Spieth's ethnography of pre-Christian society the word *gbɔgbɔvõ* does not appear; his informants referred to specific spiritual agents as either *võ* or *nyuie* (good), but they did not conceptualize a large class of 'evil spirits'. The NMG missionary and linguist D. Westermann wrote that the Christian term *gbɔgbɔ* only reshapes or increases the original sense 'breathing', 'breeze' (1905b: 8).

Gbɔgbɔ also became a term designating a person's spirit. It came to replace the pre-Christian *aklama*. This is an invisible being, existing in or next to a person and deciding his or her fate. It comes into the world with the person on his or her birthday (that is, the weekday a person is born) and takes leave at the moment of death. In the pre-Christian context, *aklama* was symbolized by a statue that was placed in the house and given sacrifices as a sign of gratefulness for its protection. For this reason, the missionaries, who systematically avoided making use of terms which originally implied a ritual praxis, discarded this term. For Ewe Christians, *gbɔgbɔ*, instead of *aklama*, became responsible for a person's fate. Like *aklama*, *gbɔgbɔ* is considered to have a decisive influence on a person's life. But unlike *aklama*, a person's *gbɔgbɔ* is not conceived as a separate, independent entity, but rather as an open space in the mind which can be filled either by *Mawu*'s spirit or by an evil one. According to Christian understanding people are thus connected with a higher spiritual entity, either good or bad, that governs their lives through the possession of their personal *gbɔgbɔ*.

Christian baptism ensures that a person's *gbɔgbɔ* is to be possessed by the *Gbɔgbɔ kɔkɔe*. However, according to pentecostal Christians this connection is not permanent but has to be realized again and again through prayer. If people do not make sure that the Holy Spirit enters them, they can easily be possessed by evil spirits which will cause bodily sickness and material ruin. These evil spirits are considered to be the agents of the Devil, who is the head of all the *trɔwo* and other non-Christian ghosts (above all, the witch). Much of this is expressed in the following quotations from interviews with church members:

A woman, old EPC:	Those who are bad Christians are dominated by evil spirits. They are bad. Without the spirit of God you are bad. You are baptized with the Holy Ghost, but it must get within you.
The catechist of the new EPC:	The evil spirits are the fallen angels, they manifest themselves through human beings. Evil spirits are destructive, they take control of the mind and disrupt God's good prospects. . . . The evil spirits have to obey the command of God, if really you are prepared [to perform exorcisms] the satanic spirit will stumble and fall.

In the use of *gbɔgbɔ* we confront a very interesting phenomenon: Through translation, a hitherto secular word is vested with a new meaning which expresses an idea that did not exist in that form before. At the same time the importance of the term in its new meaning is supported by its original meaning. 'Spirit', by implying 'breath', becomes a matter of vital importance. Through the introduction of the term *gbɔgbɔ* in a suprasensory sense, the linguistic base was laid for a theory of spirit possession which integrated both the non-Christian spiritual beings and the ghost of the Christian *Mawu* as comparable, though conflicting, entities, thereby opposing them on a single, spiritual battlefield. And from possession by either good or evil spirits, it is just one logical step to the praxis of exorcism, although this has never been an official policy in the old EPC, and is instituted only in the pentecostally oriented EPC that has split off. The Christian understanding of *gbɔgbɔ* in fact called for the praxis of prayer healing and driving away of evil spirits, as realized in the spiritual or pentecostal churches. In this sense, spiritualization or pentecostalization is a logical outcome of taking the term *gbɔgbɔ* seriously, though the missionaries themselves might not have intended this by their translation. This should be taken into account in the analysis of the spread of pentecostalism in Africa, which is often attributed to American fundamentalist missionaries imposing their religion on African people. By contrast, the Ewe understanding of *gbɔgbɔ* suggests the existence of a pentecostalism or spiritualism 'from below', independent of initial missionary impacts, which provides people with remedies against the evil powers to whom they attribute their troubles.

The Devil

The term *Abosam* has been derived from the Akan language. Why the missionaries chose this term as a translation for 'Devil' is not, to my knowledge, documented.[6] As I have shown elsewhere (1992: 104–5), *Abosam* can refer to three concepts in the Akan language, which all contribute to its present meaning. First of all, it is possible to trace back *Abosam* to *(ɔ)bonsam*, which designates a male witch, wizard or sorcerer in traditional Akan discourse,[7] and the Devil in the Christian vocabulary (Christaller 1933: 38). Secondly, the term *Abosam* evokes the image of the bush-monster *Sasabonsam* which was also known and feared by the western Ewe groups who were in contact with the Asante (in Ewe: *Sasabosam*). According to Christaller this monster was 'inimical to man, especially to the priests, . . . but the friend and chief of the sorcerers and witches' (1933: 429). Rattray (1927: 28) also noted that *Sasabonsam* was in league with both the female and the male witch (*obayifo* and *bonsam*). The first and second connotation of *Abosam* thus both imply witchcraft.

Indeed, there is a strong connection between witchcraft and the

Devil. This clearly holds true for the way Ewe Christians use the term. Westermann (1905a) noted in his Ewe–German dictionary under *Abosam*: '(. . . initially sorcerer, witch, syn. *adze*), devil, Satan. To the Ewe, however, the word *abosam*, as well as the term devil, is initially foreign.' When the missionaries introduced *Abosam* to the Ewe, the latter associated him with the most feared evil power they knew, witchcraft. This was how they originally understood the term *Abosam*. Even today the witch is considered to be the foremost manifestation of *Abosam*, as my informants assured me. Almost all members in the old and in the new EPC, including many pastors, do believe in the existence of witches and conceive them as agents of the Devil. The argumentation, as formulated by an old female member in 1989, runs as follows:

> If you are a good Christian, you must believe in the existence of Satan. And if you believe in Satan, you must believe in witchcraft. And when a person behaves abnormally, he is an agent of Satan, a witch.

During my fieldwork I found that a huge majority of people participating in prayer meetings in spiritual or pentecostal churches did so because they felt troubled by witchcraft attacks. However, the EPC order disapproved of the belief in witches and other 'unimportant things' and did not institutionalize deliverance services. If people suffered from witchcraft, they could not seek deliverance within the church. This changed for about a decade through the pentecostal prayer group in the EPC, which provided the means to free people from witchcraft attacks. The prayer group thus offered a practical way to fight evil that was in consonance with the ideas of the majority of the church members. Since the pentecostalist segment broke away to form its own, new EPC, there is again no room for deliverance in the old EPC, but many of its remaining members still believe that witches are agents of *Abosam*. I am certain that if, in future, these people face problems they attribute to witchcraft, they will seek help in the deliverance meetings of other churches or from traditional priests, as has always been the case.

This widely held belief in the continued existence of witches and evil spirits is an unintended and undesired result of vernacularization. The missionaries and contemporary church leaders alike have never appreciated the existence of this belief, which they consider(ed) to be a superstitious, 'heathen' survival. But it is not surprising that this belief gained momentum, since the missionaries themselves preached that the pre-Christian Ewe gods and ghosts were agents of the Devil.

They did, however, diabolize the former religion in general terms and were, in consonance with Protestant doctrine, not prepared to provide Christian rituals to deal with specific, demonized former gods and ghosts, such as witches.

With the issue of diabolization we have come to the third possible reference of the term *Abosam*, which is *ɔbosom* (pl. *abosom*), the traditional Akan deity (Christaller 1933: 43). The missionaries' use of *Abosam* to refer to the non-Christian religion in general was eagerly taken up by the first Christians and remained a characteristic feature of Ewe Protestantism. We have already seen from various quotations that Christians consider the traditional Ewe deities to be agents of *Abosam*. The priests and other people worshipping the *trōwo* are often called *Abosamtɔ*, those belonging to the Devil, and according to the Christians they are going to end up in hell. The missionaries, in their attempt to evangelize, also told people that through the worship of the *trōwo* they were serving the Devil. This, however, contradicts the statement that the ancestors, by approaching *Mawu* through the *trōwo*, were already trying to serve the Christian God. Due to this contradiction, it is possible to judge the pre-Christian religion in opposite ways. Whereas by emphasizing *Mawu* it can be appreciated as the wrong way to the right aim, it appears to be altogether bad when *Abosam* is accentuated.

These two contradicting approaches lie at the basis of two conflicting forms of 'Africanization' present in the EPC. One is the 'Africanization' advocated by the few supporters of the more 'Africanized' *Meleagbe* theology, which, by referring to the old people's knowledge of *Mawu*, integrates 'traditional' elements into Christianity. Its supporters are mainly theologians and intellectuals who aim to restore the self-esteem Africans lost in the course of Christianization and colonization. The other is the more or less unconscious grassroots 'Africanization' or pentecostalization, which, in consonance with the diabolization of the former gods and ghosts, is based on the belief in the existence of demons. These people face existential problems which they explain in terms of evil spirits, and hope to solve by keeping them away. In contrast to the supporters of a more 'Africanized' theology, their problem is not lack of self-esteem, but the very material lack of health, wealth and fertility.

These two forms of 'Africanization' oppose each other as much as do the contradicting statements about the ancestors' godly as well as devilish orientation. Those willing to integrate traditional elements into Christianity accuse those believing in the existence of demons of being highly superstitious, whereas the latter vehemently oppose the integration of traditional elements as diabolical. The pre-Christian religion is thus approached from two perspectives. According to one, it contains something godly, whereas according to the other, it is devilish. From these two different perspectives two different forms of 'Africanization' result. There is thus not just one possible 'Africanization' of Christianity, as some African theologians seem to suggest. The existence of two contradictory perspectives on the pre-Christian religion shows that it is possible to make the past meaningful in the context of Christianity in different ways.[8]

Here, the question arises as to why the transformations of meaning brought about by translation are not interpreted by all Ewe in the same way. I would answer that polysemy, through translation, is part of the Christian key terms, but that the terms' interpretation depends on the socio-economic situation and cosmology of the people using them. In other words, polysemy is a potential which can be realized through subjective interpretation. It seems that Ewe Protestants believing in the existence of witchcraft – and this is a huge majority at the grassroots of the old EPC and the whole new EPC – are inclined to the 'Africanization' which focuses on the Devil. By contrast, the supporters of the *Meleagbe* theology do not take into account the existence of witches. Often these people have studied abroad and it seems that, through their high education and better standard of living, they have been so detached from village life that they do not (need to) hear the connotations inscribed in the key Christian terms. The adoption of one way of 'Africanization' or the other is thus closely related to the socio-economic situation people live in, the cosmology they believe in, and the problems they want to solve.

TRANSLATION

The missionaries of the NMG, of course, were aware that inter-cultural communication and translation are a *conditio sine qua non* of mission. But it seems that they did not realize that translation always alters the meaning of terms. The mission society's Bible translator Spieth made a distinction between the form of a term and its content (1907: 9). According to him, the content could be separated from its form, and then be transferred into a word-form in another language without being changed. To him, the relationship between form and content was arbitrary.[9]

This translation theory still exists today. The missionary-linguist Eugene Nida is one of its best-known representatives. Personally involved in the translation of the Bible, he published various books (1961, Nida and Tabler 1982) on how to achieve the best transmission of the Christian text into other languages. Although he is aware of the fact that the meaning might get changed through translation, his purpose is to achieve translations that mirror the original meaning as closely as possible. The transformation of meaning, for him, is a problem to be reduced to a minimum, rather than an unavoidable given to be studied. This stance is shared by other theologians and anthropologists involved in (the study of) Bible translation. The recent book on *Bible Translation and the Spread of the Church* edited by Stine (1990) is also representative of this position. These authors acknowledge the fact that the Christian message has to be expressed in a culture- and language-specific way, and hence conclude that no expression can claim to be universalistic, but nevertheless assume that all expressions derive from and refer to the same Godly source. This, of course, is a question of belief.

In the same vein, Sanneh (1991: 208) argues that '[T]here is a radical pluralism implied in vernacular translation wherein all languages and cultures are, in principle, equal in expressing the word of God.' This view, too, stems from an essentialist notion of Christianity, which assumes that the transmission of content through translation is unproblematic (see Waldman's and Yai's critical review of Sanneh's book in Waldman et al. 1992). It implies a theologically inspired perspective on language, which is unable to grasp the nature of intercultural communication. Moreover, Sanneh credits Western missionaries with having accepted the essential pluralism of Christianity and freely providing others with vernacular versions, thereby intentionally shielding them from Western dominance. By contrast, in my view indigenous interpretations of Christianity are not *given* by the mission, but *made* by converts themselves in a process of appropriation (often against the meanings missionaries intended to evoke).

In this chapter, the translations of key Christian terms are seen as products of the communication between missionaries and the Ewe. These products are different from the missionary discourse and from the pre-Christian religious discourse as well. For the missionaries, the chosen Ewe terms denoted the content they put into them; for Ewe Christians, the terms' old meanings did not totally disappear but continued to form part of them. One and the same term would thus have different meanings for the missionaries on the one hand and the Ewe Christians on the other.[10] Moreover, even though, through translation, old religious practices were excluded by avoiding terms implying ritual action, people did not accept the Protestant anti-ritualistic attitude towards religion, and endowed Christian terms with a ritual dimension. Leaving out terms in the process of translation does not guarantee that the thing they stand for is indeed excluded. Hence we can conclude that, as a result of translation, terms are transformed; they no longer mean what they meant in *either* the source *or* the target language.

This finding raises the questions of whether, given that meanings unavoidably change through translation, communication across linguistic and cultural boundaries is possible; and, on the level of translation theory, of whether this finding confirms Quine's view on the impossibility of radical translation.[11] At first sight, our finding seems to confirm his view. But more thorough reflection suggests that this is not the case. Basically, Quine's statement of the impossibility of radical translation boils down to the acknowledgement of the inadequacy of positivist translation theory. Indeed, meanings change through translation and it is impossible to find terms which objectively mirror the original one. But despite this, in practice, translations are still made. Rather than stating their *theoretical* impossibility, one should wonder what actually happens when meanings *practically* cross linguistic boundaries. Mutual intelligibility between two languages is neither a given nor an impossibility, but something to be constituted by intersubjective dialogue across cultural boundaries. Translation, then, can be understood as interpreting and transforming the original statement, and thereby creating something of a new quality (Overing 1987; Hobart 1987: 37ff; Hallen and Sodipo 1986). This is what actually happens in the process of vernacularization, although the translators themselves might not be prepared to recognize it. Through translation, key Christian terms thus acquire a new quality, which becomes an inalienable feature of those terms. This holds true despite the fact that the missionaries would not have been willing to acknowledge this and rather preferred an objectivist perspective on translation. Indeed, the recognition of translation as a creative process would have led the missionaries' efforts to control the Ewes' minds through a Christian vocabulary *ad absurdum*. However, as far as I can see, in the course of time Ewe Christians have not started hearing the terms as the missionaries heard and meant them.

The Ewe Christians' understanding of key terms eventually resulted in the establishment of spiritual and pentecostal practices upon which the missionaries would have frowned, and which the leaders of the old EPC, too, did not allow. That this practical realization of their

Christian understanding only appeared some decades after the introduction of Christianity has to be attributed to the fact that the decline of the overall economic situation started to affect a massive number of people. In more prosperous times there were fewer people confronting serious problems, which would then be dealt with by prayer or consulting a traditional priest. When, due to an overall economic decline, the life situation of a great number of Christians became increasingly difficult, church members were much more inclined to find a structural solution to their problems within Christianity. The spiritual and pentecostal churches thus made up for the lack of rituals to ward off evil effectively that distinguished mission churches from traditional religion. By providing ritual protection against evil these new churches prevented Christians from 'sliding back' into traditional religion.

The fact that Ewe Christians understood and still understand terms in a way other than that of the missionaries means that the power of the missionaries and contemporary church officials to know and control the ideas of Ewe Christians is quite limited. As a result of translation, a form of Christianity came into being which, albeit partly, evaded missionary control. This supports the finding of the anthropologist Vincente L. Rafael that '[t]he necessity of employing the native vernaculars in spreading the Word of God constrained the universalizing assumptions and totalizing impulses of a colonial-Christian order' (1988: 21; see also Fabian 1986). By studying the indigenous interpretation of the vernacularized Christian message, 'alternative native responses to the dominant and dominating interpretation' can be discerned (Rafael 1988: 21). In the case of the Ewe Christians these alternative responses manifest themselves in pentecostalization and spiritualization.

DIABOLIZATION

The missionaries, in an effort to convince the Ewe to convert, preached that the Devil was the power behind the gods and ghosts hitherto worshipped by them. The translation of the Christian message into the vernacular thus went along with the diabolization of the old pantheon. Only *Mawu* was classified as belonging to the good side. The result of the diabolization was that these spiritual beings were considered to have a real existence as demons under the auspices of the Devil. Through the Devil, the spiritual beings of the old religion became part of Ewe Protestantism. God's dark counterpart, who stands for the shadowy side of Christian belief which is open for fantasy and speculation, is the intermediary between the missionaries' variant of Protestantism and the pre-Christian Ewe religion. Through him the old could be integrated into the new, and together with the process of vernacularization this makes for the peculiarity of Ewe Protestantism (Meyer 1990, 1992).

It seems that missionaries of other denominations and nationalities in other places on the African continent followed the same device and preached that Satan was the Lord of the known gods and ghosts (for example, Kirwen 1987: 37ff.; Peel 1990: 351ff., Shorter 1973: 131). It is in no way unique or surprising that, as a result of diabolization, Christians take the demons seriously. This has been repeated over and over again in the diffusion of the Christian religion all over the world (for example, Ingham 1986: 103 ff.; Pina-Cabral 1992; Schneider 1990; Taussig 1980: 169ff.). Indeed, Psalm 96:5, which states 'The gods of the pagans are demons', became a key text for the early church fathers, who, in order to construct a coherent image of the Devil, synthesized the scattered biblical fragments. Justin Martyr (*c*. AD 100–67) was the first to argue that the pagan gods were actual demons serving the Devil. He therefore refused to sacrifice to the Roman gods, a refusal which finally cost him his life. His disciple Tatian (*c*. AD 120–80) insisted that the Devil and the demons were the fallen angels mentioned in the Old Testament, now worshipped by the Greeks and the Romans. These demons aggressively sought power over human beings, and baptism, prayer and exorcism were the only remedy against their machinations (Russell 1981: 63ff.).

From the second century AD this view, which is not stated as such in the Bible, thus became fixed in the Christian tradition, and in the course of history was applied to non-Christian religions in Europe and elsewhere, as we have seen in this chapter. Though one cannot deny that positive adaptations of non-Christian rites and gods have occurred in the spread of Christianity, to my knowledge, especially in Protestantism, diabolization has been the dominant stance towards non-Christian religion. It seems that local forms of Christianity get their peculiar, culture-specific character at least partly from the integrating capacities of the image of the Devil.

CONCLUSION

In the introductory section I stated that it is worthwhile to look beyond syncretism by exploring the field of the encounter between the adherents of two religions. Now we are able to see that the mixture called 'syncretism' can be a practical result of processes of translation and diabolization. Both make for the peculiarity of local Ewe Protestantism, and 'Africanized' it *avant la lettre*. There is no great difference between the ideas of members of mission churches with their presumed 'divided consciousness' on the one hand and independent churches with their 'syncretism' on the other. Both appropriated a version of Christianity that takes into account the existence of evil spirits, and eventually manifested in a pentecostalism 'from below' providing practical means to fight evil. Given the fact that translation and diabolization are operative in the local appropriation of Christianity, we can conclude that missionaries' control over their converts' ideas has been much more limited than critics of the mission are inclined to think. Therefore people at the grassroots do not seem to need critical theologians' 'Africanization' from above; they have already synthesized traditional religion and Christianity in their own way and according to their own interests.

NOTES

I want to thank Felix Ameka, Johannes Fabian, Gerard Roelofs, Jojada Verrips, and André Drooger's discussion group on 'Pentecostalism', as well as Charles Stewart, Rosalind Shaw and John Peel, for their valuable comments and suggestions.

1 I shall draw on material from fieldwork and historical research on the contacts between the NMG missionaries and the Ewe. During the last four years, I have conducted historical studies in the archives of the NMG (kept in the Staatsarchiv Bremen under 7,1025) and the Colonial Office archives on the Gold Coast (kept under CO 98 in the Public Record Office, London), and fieldwork in the congregations of the EPC in Peki. My research was made possible by the Amsterdam School of Social Science Research and the Netherlands Foundation for the Advancement of Tropical Research (WOTRO).
2 People in Ghana distinguish between spiritual and pentecostal churches. Both focus on the healing powers of the Holy Spirit, but whereas the pentecostals, in order to drive away evil spirits, make use of the word alone, the spirituals use holy water, candles and incense.
3 Texts written by African mission assistants are scarce. I found a compilation of the reports of Ewe evangelists in the file 'Tagebuch eines Evanglisten' in the Bremen Mission archives (file 56/8). These texts were translated by Misonu Amu and myself from Ewe into English. The quotation below can be found on p. 82ff. in the above-mentioned manuscript.
4 It is an important characteristic of the missionaries' ethnography that they tended to neglect the female dimension in indigenous notions of *Mawu*, which the Ewe express in *Sodza* as well as in the service of the *trõwo*. To them, priestesses were just 'fetish-whores'.

5 *Sogble-Sodza* are the equivalent of the Fon's notion of the dual male-female *Lesa-Mawu* (e.g. De Surgy 1988: 95).
6 It is interesting that the NMG missionaries translated 'Devil' as *Abosam* and not as *Legba*. The latter term designates a statue representing a guardian god and was used for 'Devil' in Anecho (a southeastern Ewe group in Togo) where Catholic missions were active. That the NMG chose the term *Abosam* mirrors its close connection with Western Ewe groups, who had been heavily influenced by the Akan language and culture.
7 There is another Akan term for witchcraft, *bayi*, which is used to refer to female witches that do harm in their own families. This concept is the equivalent of the Ewe term *adze*.
8 This situation is not exceptional: Droogers (1977) indicated that in African Christianity, spontaneous and theological Africanization exist side by side.
9 At the same time, however, he avoided making use of Ewe terms associated with ritual because he feared that this might confirm 'heathen' ideas and overgrow the Christian context. He thought that by avoiding those loaded terms, Christian contents could be transferred into Ewe word-forms.
10 The finding that terms change through translation is in line with the work of the catholic Ewe theologian and linguist Tossou on Bible translation (1988), who discerned transformations of meaning in the process of translation from the biblical languages into the Ewe language. However, he approached translation as a merely linguistic problem, not as a socio-linguistic process. Therefore he did not consider how the Ewe appropriated Christian terms on the basis of their own ideas.
11 Quine (1960) distinguishes in each language between the level of observation sentences and the level of standing sentences. The latter, although not stated by language explicitly, are central for the interpretation of phenomena on the observational level. Whereas foreign speakers can learn the words for visual phenomena in the native language, it is impossible to internalize the standing sentences in the same way as native speakers do. Hence the impossibility of radical translation (i.e. translation between two mutually unintelligible languages).

REFERENCES

Christaller, J.G. (1933) *Dictionary of the Asante and Fante Language Called Tshi (Twi)*, 2nd edn., revised and enlarged, Basel: Basel Evangelical Missionary Society.
Droogers, A. (1977) 'The Africanization of Christianity', *Missiology* 5, 4: 443–56.
—— (1989) 'Syncretism: the problem of definition, the definition of the problem', in J. Gort, H. Vroom, R. Fernhont and A. Wessels (eds), *Dialogue and Syncretism: An Interdisciplinary Approach*, Grand Rapids, MI: Wm B. Eerdmans Publishing Co.
Fabian, J. (1985) 'Religious pluralism: an ethnographic approach', in W. van Binsbergen and M. Schoffeleers (eds), *Theoretical Explorations in African Religion*, London: Kegan Paul International.

—— (1986) *Language and Colonial Power: The Appropriation of Swahili in the Former Belgian Kongo. 1880–1938*, Cambridge: Cambridge University Press.

Frimpong-Ansah, J.H. (1992) *The Vampire State in Africa. The Political Economy of Decline in Ghana*, Trenton: Africa World Press.

Hallen, B. and Sodipo, J.O. (1986) *Knowledge, Belief and Witchcraft. Analytic Experiments in African Philosophy*, London: Ethnographica.

Hobart, M. (1987) 'Summer's days and salad days: the coming of age of anthropology?', in L. Holy (ed.), *Comparative Anthropology*, Oxford: Blackwell.

Ingham, J.M. (1986) *Mary, Michael, and Lucifer. Folk Catholicism in Central Mexico*, Austin: University of Texas Press.

Kirwen, M.C. (1987) *The Missionary and the Diviner. Contending Theologies of Christian and African Religions*. New York: Orbis.

Meyer, B. (1990) 'Die Über-setzung des Teufels. Über die religiösen Vorstellungen von Mitgliedern einer ehemaligen Missionskirche in (Südost) Ghana', unpublished MA thesis, University of Amsterdam.

—— (1992) '"If you are a devil, you are a witch and if you are a witch, you are a devil": the integration of "pagan" ideas in the conceptual universe of Ewe Christians', *Journal of Religion in Africa* 22, 2: 98–132.

Nida, E.A. (1961) *Bible Translating. An Analysis of Principles and Procedures, with Special Reference to Aboriginal Languages*, London: United Bible Societies.

Nida, E.A. and Tabler, C.R. (1982) *The Theory and Practice of Translation*, 2nd photomechanical reprint, Leiden: E.J. Brill for the United Bible Societies.

Overing, J. (1987) 'Translation as a creative process: the power of the name', in L. Holy (ed.), *Comparative Anthropology*, Oxford: Blackwell.

Peel, J.D.Y. (1968) 'Syncretism and religious change', *Comparative Studies in Society and History* 10: 121–41.

—— (1990) 'The pastor and the *Babalawo*: the interaction of religions in nineteenth-century Yorubaland', *Africa* 60, 3: 338–69.

Pina-Cabral, J. de (1992) 'The gods of the gentiles are demons: the problem of pagan survivals in European culture', in K. Hastrup (ed.), *Other Histories*, London: Routledge.

Quine, W.V.O. (1960) *Word and Object*, Cambridge, MA.: MIT Press.

Rafael, V.L. (1988) *Contracting Colonialism. Translation and Christian Conversion in Tagalog Society under Early Spanish Rule*. Ithaca, NY: Cornell University Press.

Rattray, R.S. (1927) *Religion and Art in Ashanti*, Oxford: Clarendon Press.

Russell, J.B. (1981) *Satan. The Early Christian Tradition*, Ithaca, NY: Cornell University Press.

Sanneh, L. (1991) *Translating the Message. The Missionary Impact on Culture*, 3rd printing, Maryknoll, NY: Orbis.

Schneider, J. (1990) 'Spirits and the spirit of capitalism', in E. Badone (ed.), *Religious Orthodoxy and Popular Faith in European Society*, Princeton, NJ: Princeton University Press.

Shorter, A. (1973) *African Culture and the Christian Church*, London: G. Chapman.

Spieth, J. (1906) *Die Ewe-Stämme. Material zur Kunde des Ewe-Volkes in Deutsch-Togo*, Berlin: Dietrich Reimer.
—— (1907) *Die Übersetzung der Bibel in die Sprache eines westafrikanischen Naturvolkes*, Bremen: Norddeutsche Missions-Gesellschaft.
—— (1911) *Die Religion der Eweer in Süd-Togo*, Leipzig: Dietersche Verlagsbuchhandlung.
Stine, P.C. (ed.) (1990) *Bible Translation and the Spread of the Church. The Last 200 Years*, Leiden: E.J. Brill.
Surgy, Albert de (1988) *Le système religieux des Evhé*, Paris: Editions L'Harmattan.
Taussig, M.T. (1980) *The Devil and Commodity Fetishism in South America*, Chapel Hill: University of North Carolina Press.
Tossou, K.J. (1988) *Vom Geist der Sprache. Bewahrung und Umwandlung bei Übersetzungen. Griechisch-Ewe Metamorphosen am Beispiel der Ewe-Bibelübersetzung*, Münster: Nodus Publikationen.
Waldman, M.R., Yai, O.B. and Sanneh, L. (1992) 'Translatability: a discussion', *Journal of Religion in Africa* 22, 2: 159–72.
Westermann, D. (1905a) *Wörterbuch der Ewe-Sprache. I. Ewe-Deutsch*, Berlin: Dietrich Reimer.
—— (1905b) 'Über die Begriffe Seele, Geist, Schicksal bei dem Ewe und Tschivolk', *Archiv für Religionswissenschaft* 8: 104–13.

3 Variations on a Christian theme
The healing synthesis of Zulu Zionism

Jim Kiernan

In South Africa, apartheid has been opposed to cultural mixing and syncretism and it has attempted to seal off, spatially and politically, 'cultures' artificially identified as disparate and self-contained. Policies of racial and cultural segregation have not, however, succeeded either in eliminating interracial cooperation (see Gluckman 1956) or in suppressing cultural cross-fertilization, such as the emergence of popular culture in the townships. A long history of Christian evangelism has been a potent force in promoting cultural mingling. This merging tendency can be noted across a range of Christian denominations, particularly in the propensity of individuals to manipulate the convergence of religious traditions (Pauw 1974), but it is the independent African churches which are acknowledged to have gone furthest in synthesizing Christianity and indigenous African religion.

Africans constitute about 80 per cent of the total population, of whom 75 per cent are nominally Christians, and fully 30 per cent profess to belong to African independent churches. These independent churches encompass a wide range of diversity in their organization and worship (West 1975: 22ff.), which may be reduced to some order by appealing to Sundkler's (1961: 22, 53ff.) two dominant ideal types: the Ethiopians, who retain the structures and beliefs of the parent Christian denominations from which they split, and the Zionists, who present a novel religious orientation and a distinctive form of service, which is particularly attractive to the poor and uneducated. It would be rash to claim that the Ethiopian churches are entirely free of syncretism, but it is the Zionists who have been most readily identified as exhibiting a synthesis of different religious traditions.[1] Moreover, Zionists are numerically in the ascendant and are steadily on the increase. For these reasons, this chapter will concentrate on understanding the Zionist facility for borrowing and combining religious ideas.

SYNCRETISM

I begin by considering the discourse *about* syncretism (see Shaw and Stewart, this volume) in the African independent churches. This is a discourse with political overtones in which the labels 'sect' and 'syncretist' are applied pejoratively by white Protestant missionaries and theologians (see Pauw forthcoming) and are aggressively rejected particularly by the Ethiopian churches. The most influential voice in this discourse has been that of Sundkler who, in one powerful sentence (italicized for good measure), asserted that 'the syncretistic sect becomes the bridge over which Africans are brought back to heathenism' (1961: 397), and he concluded that there was an inevitable descent from mission church to Ethiopian to Zionist to primitive animism.[2] Not only did he identify sect with syncretism, and syncretism with barbarism, but he placed both Zionists and Ethiopians squarely in these equations. Ethiopians had long been saddled with the 'sectarian' label and it carried the implication that sect was inferior to church and denomination, a second-hand caricature of mission Christianity, a kind of bargain basement to the genuine article. Insult was added to injury when sect was made equivalent to a syncretic return to 'primitive heathenism'. In disowning these terms, Ethiopians had discerned in them a thinly disguised racial put-down and reacted by claiming to be the authentic voice of African Christianity and by excluding whites from any profession to understand African independent churches (Makhubu 1988). Being generally unlettered and certainly unacquainted with Sundkler's aspersion, Zionists are scarcely aware of this debate. Nevertheless, Zionists well aware of their origins would undoubtedly reject the application of sect and syncretist to themselves, since they regard their synthesis, with good reason, as a thoroughly Christian one.

In today's discourse, syncretism carries implications of impurity, backsliding, undisciplined sloth and indulgence, the incapacity to keep up, giving in to old ways; it implies weakness rather than strength. What is being imputed (and rejected) is a lack of agency and of power. The Zulu Zionist synthesis, it will be seen, arose on the contrary from multiple instances of agency and power.

EARLY ZULU ZIONISM

The contention that Zionism is thoroughly Christian and that it is lacking neither in agency or empowerment can be examined, first, in the context of Zionist origins around 1900 in the border village of

Wakkerstroom, situated in the south-east corner of the Transvaal close to the adjoining frontiers of British Natal and Zululand (see Figure 1). Originally occupied by the Boers in the middle of the nineteenth century, this area finally merged with three similar polities to form the Transvaal in 1860, although it was only in 1884 that the threatening opposition of the Zulu monarch to the occupation was

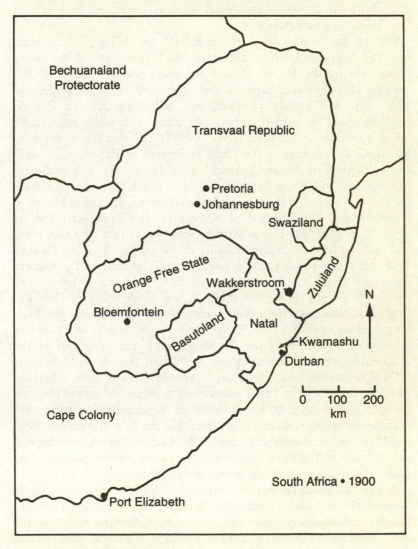

Figure 1   South Africa 1900

finally withdrawn. A short period of secure tenure was followed by
the outbreak of the Anglo-Boer war in 1902. Wakkerstroom was not
a major arena of conflict and escaped the worst of Kitchener's
'scorched earth' policy (Odendaal 1984: 36). After the war, a five-
year period of British administration under Milner culminated in an
electoral victory for Afrikaner farmers and a reassertion of their
political control in the Transvaal (Bundy 1979: 212). Shortly thereafter, both the Transvaal and Natal became constituent provinces of
the Union of South Africa.

One of the reasons cited by the British for military intervention
was 'the disgraceful, brutal and uncivilised' treatment of the native
population by the Boers, though the main concern was with the
negative effect of this on capitalist and imperialist expansion (Odendaal
1984: 30). A Transvaal constitutional ordinance decreed that no
equality could be admitted between black and white inhabitants
'neither in Church nor State' (Nixon 1972: 23), and the Boers were
notorious for continuing the Cape precedent of slavery as 'a well-
known method of obtaining cheap labour' (ibid.: 47). The treatment
of labourers and tenants was scarcely less harsh than that of slaves;
the farmers accorded them no rights whatsoever. It caused Milner to
comment that 'the position of Natives (in the Transvaal) was far
worse than anywhere else in British Southern Africa' and that there
was nothing to restrain the brutality of the ruling oligarchy (Marais
1961: 183). No ameliorating influence could be exerted by missionaries, nor could mission stations function as places of refuge and
relief. They were simply not there. It was Boer policy to clear out
English missionaries from their territory because of their proclivity
for preaching egalitarianism. In fact there was no history of missionary
activity of any kind in the Transvaal until the very end of the
nineteenth century. The condition of African tenants and labourers
in Wakkerstroom was, therefore, extremely bleak and, when we
consider that the late 1890s introduced a period of locust plagues,
drought and rinderpest, which depleted African economic reserves
in cattle especially, one can appreciate that the grip of their landlord-
employers was considerably tightened. And, in the wake of repressive labour and severe economic depression, there followed the
political uncertainties of the war and its aftermath.

It was in this environment that Zulu Zionism took root. Quite
fortuitously, the Dutch Reformed Church of the Afrikaners decided
to adopt a missionary policy and Le Roux, its first missionary to the
Zulu, took up residence in Wakkerstroom in 1893. The result of this
innovation could not possibly have been foreseen. The locus of the

missionary's work was to be the segregated settlement, at some distance from Wakkerstroom, of African labourers and labour-tenants who, upon conversion to Christianity, had to worship with the missionary apart from their white fellow-Christians, who in turn had their own dominee, a personage of higher status than the lowly missionary. Thus, the policy of segregation drove Le Roux and his wife into closer association with their Zulu converts than with their white co-residents. Secondly, Le Roux was somewhat eccentric. Of less than robust health and inclined to hypochondria, during his seminary years he had acquired an abiding interest in miraculous healing (Sundkler 1976: 19). In his personal search for wellbeing, he fell under the influence of Buchler (Johannesburg), who, in turn, was influenced by the Christian Catholic Apostolic Church in Zion (CCACZ), founded in Chicago in 1896 by J.A. Dowie, who preached a gospel of pragmatic relief to the poor through divine healing (Comaroff 1985: 177ff.). Captivated by this belief, Le Roux sought to have it accepted within Dutch Reformed Calvinism and, against mounting opposition, resigned from the Church and switched his loyalty to Zionism (Dowie) in 1903.

The Zionist teaching that healing in the spirit could be accomplished by prayer alone, without the intervention of doctors (diviners) or medicine, was already spreading among Zulu Christians by 1898 (Sundkler 1976: 22) and, in fact, it was African insistence on the efficacy of this pentecostal power that finally persuaded Le Roux to part company with the Dutch Reformed Church (DRC). He continued to preach the message of healing during the war, despite Boer attempts to silence him, with the result that, when he eventually cut his ties with the DRC, he had the support of a substantial local Zulu congregation, estimated at 800 people (Sundkler 1976: 38, 44). In 1908, Le Roux was asked to care for a congregation of European Zionists in white Johannesburg, and he and Buchler later broke away from Dowie to form the Apostolic Faith Mission, which his Zulu Zionists refused to join. They had by then begun to diverge from Le Roux's model of Zionism and to introduce innovations during his absence of which he strongly disapproved. Foremost among these was the development of prophecy; the ability to see and interpret visions for the healing of individuals and for the edification of the church. From such visions came the wearing of white robes, one of the first issues to split the congregation, and at a later stage the use of coloured apparel in the course of healing activities (Kiernan 1991). The carrying of staves was introduced, at first to ward off lightning and then to function as instruments of healing (Kiernan 1979). Le

Roux was aghast at this growing concern for ritual symbols and for the general ritualization of healing, which he attributed to 'intolerable Roman Catholic influence' (Sundkler 1976: 51).

These are the historical facts that are available to us. What do they convey about the emerging Zionist synthesis? The Zulu preoccupation with the ritual management of health was a given feature of the cultural outlook of these farm workers. It may well have been subdued, but certainly not suppressed, by conversion to Calvinist Protestantism, a literate and Bible-centred tradition with which Zulus coped by memorizing texts and selected passages. The arrangement of separate services, and the conducting of worship by officiants of unequal status, entrenched the disparity of power in the relationship of dependence between Boer master and Zulu servant. The first blow to this religious and social hegemony was struck by the arrival of a maverick missionary and his subsequent secession, along with the majority of Zulu congregants. To the biblical fundamentalism which they took with them was added a layer of divine or spirit healing, which in different ways satisfied the needs of white missionary and African converts. This 'pentecostal' strain introduced the explosive and potentially anarchic principle of an alternative channel of divine inspiration and revelation in which 'Jack is as good as his master.' At the same time, faith healing rejected all therapeutic instruments except prayer and water and thus effectively severed these Zionists from the surrounding Zulu culture, in which healing was achieved by the influence of ancestors, the intervention of diviners and a reliance on herbal medicines. The synthesis therefore emanated from a missionary innovation, clearly at odds with the prevailing religious ethos of established or mission Christianity, yet the emphasis on divine healing remained firmly within the broad parameters of Christian tradition. Ritualization was gradually added by the accretion of elements borrowed from both biblical and African culture. As time went on, these and further refinements gave rise to internal divisions and diversification; some groups remained faithful to the original model while others departed further along the path of incorporating features of African religion.

Clearly, Zulu Zionism began as a ready-made Christian import. Le Roux had his own agenda and power struggle with church authority in an early attempt to synthesise Zionist divine healing with Dutch Reformed Calvinism. Thwarted in this, but having lit the torch of Zulu Zionism, he passed on to another field of endeavour, though his wife, curiously enough, was to continue to support it in the role of 'evangelist'. In the meantime, his Zulu converts had appropriated this Christian variant and were following their own agenda of directing divine healing to African healing requirements and techniques. Had they then swopped one form of Christianity for another, for one that was more suited to their needs, or had they forged something novel from the combination of Christian instruments and African practice?

THE HEALING SYNTHESIS TODAY

One of the innovations, we have seen, has been the emergence and employment of prophets in Zionist healing. Sundkler simply equates prophets with Zulu diviners (Sundkler 1961: 24) and thus, at a stroke, rejects any claims that Zionists can be viewed either as Christians or as innovators. In his study of mainly Zionist churches in Soweto, Johannesburg, West is more circumspect. While he found that prophets are indubitably agents of the Holy Spirit, unlike the ancestral mediums (diviners), he detected some similarity in their experience and training and a measure of overlap in their functions (1975: 184, 186). He also found evidence of joint control of prophetic powers, the ancestors acting in a subsidiary capacity to the Holy Spirit (ibid.: 97). Ultimately, West perceived the synthesis to be one of form and content, the imposition of Christian meaning on historic African activities (ibid.: 188), a conclusion that closely parallels Sundkler's assertion that what has changed is that 'the *amadlozi* (ancestors) have been baptized' (Sundkler 1961: 260). Based on my own research in KwaMashu, Durban, I have argued elsewhere (Kiernan 1992) that prophets are not simply diviners in masquerade but are Christian replacements. This reflects the adamant claims of my informants that they have nothing in common with diviners, whom they consider to be the enemies of Christianity. It is significant that these Zionists all carefully preserve pedigrees of their descent from Wakkerstroom and that they consciously label themselves 'Christian Zionists' in opposition to Zionists of a different provenance.[3] It is in relation to these modern Zionists that the discussion will now be broadened, away from Sundkler's artificially narrow focus on prophets and diviners, to consider more fully the conceptual edifice that bears on their healing activities.

At the heart of every Zionist meeting, a prayer and Bible service is followed by a healing rite (Kiernan 1976a). The first of these is clearly Christian, while the second corresponds to rituals of affliction which have been part of the fabric of indigenous society. Now the mere fact that these two strains coexist side by side constitutes in itself not a synthesis but a simple contiguity of differences only. It would enable individuals to maintain a dual religious outlook whose parts could be serviced independently of one another but without attempting any meaningful combination or integration of the two. There is evidence to show that this is precisely what happens in established Christian denominations (and, no doubt, in Ethiopian churches as well). In times of misfortune, the majority of confirmed Christians can have recourse to African ancestors as an additional, that is, separate, source of help (Pauw 1974: 100ff) and, while experiencing some tension, they see no contradiction in appealing to distinct sets of religious meaning under the common label of 'spirit', albeit in different phases of worship (Schutte 1974: 116ff). However, in these instances, no concerted effort is made to Christianize ancestor spirits or to indigenize Christian beliefs.

What allows Zionists to fuse Bible and healing into a single, coherent system of meaning is not any perceived direct equivalence between the two. Even if there is sometimes a clear correspondence between biblical texts and healing, the synthesis rests not on any simple identification, presumed or otherwise, but on the presence of two coagulants or blending agents which link Bible and healing together. These are a spiritual power, namely the Holy Spirit, and a rigorous code of conduct. The Holy Spirit constitutes a conduit in that it is invoked and nourished by an extravagant mode of preaching on a biblical text, and by praying in tongues, which together build a wave of communal enthusiasm as the social manifestation of its spiritual power. The greater the euphoria, the greater the power. On the other hand, this tide of spiritual fervour is released by directing and applying it to the alleviation of individual suffering in healing. In this, the Holy Spirit usurps the traditional role of ancestral spirits as the guardians of wellbeing. Thus, the spirit provides the connection between biblical text and healing action; it feeds on the Bible in a social context and expends itself on the afflictions of individuals. Each Zionist meeting renews this cycle and reinvigorates the connection, that is, the connection does not exist in the mind only but is enacted and re-enacted. Zionists consider it unthinkable to engage in healing without first holding a Bible service, however contracted (Kiernan 1976b: 357).

There is a second connecting corridor between Bible and healing, although this persists on the level of belief only, despite being concerned with behaviour. Morally good living is enjoined by a body of unwritten behavioural rules which have their basis in biblical prohibitions but which more closely correspond to the Puritan ethic.

Proscribed are pork, alcohol (preparation, distribution and consumption), extra-marital sexual relations, gambling, politics, herbal medicines, and tobacco. There is general disapproval of idleness, that is, of time not invested in church and family. Faithful observance of biblical injunctions and of Puritan norms ensures, as far as is humanly possible, health and good fortune. Failure to observe them places one's health in jeopardy by leaving oneself open to sorcery, a belief that has its parallel in indigenous African societies, where breaches of kinship obligations may be punished by ancestors and can expose one to the malevolence of sorcerers. Again, an explicit commitment to this behavioural code is a precondition for healing, and it is all the more binding on those providing therapy, who act as channels of the Holy Spirit; any behavioural lapse is believed to deprive them of their healing capacity. The importance of conforming to this normative code, and particularly to its biblical component, is emphasized by the fact that at most meetings the Decalogue is chanted in unison by all present. In numerous ways, therefore, the Puritan and biblical prescriptions governing Zionist behaviour also serve to knit together the biblical and therapeutic, so that the resources of Christianity are harnessed to satisfy African concerns with health and wellbeing.

Clearly, this synthesis is not seamless. It is not enough, therefore, to attend to the cosmological features that are being conjoined, on the supposition that they are sucked into one another by a kind of cultural osmosis. More pertinent to an understanding of synthesis is that consideration be given to the seams, to the cross-stitching that binds the primary elements together. In the case under consideration, it is the eruption of the spirit and the regulating of social behaviour that make possible the blending of Bible service and healing rite, and these, therefore, form the key pivots of the synthesis. What social significance can be attached to these fields of fusion? Beyond their purely synthetic function, what effect(s) do they have on the lives of Zionist actors? The injection of the spirit into Zionist gatherings not only gives to healing the impress of a power superior to, independent of and of wider social span than that attributed to ancestors, but it promotes freedom of expression under the guise of visions and speaking in tongues. Every Zionist has some access to the Holy Spirit and nobody can be held to account for what is said or done when under the inspiration of the spirit; this encourages the free expression of social and personal concerns. In this respect, the activation of the Holy Spirit promotes the unbridling of normative constraints. At first glance, the Puritan code of conduct seems to represent a contrary tendency towards behavioural conformity. However, at a more fundamental level, it inculcates a quality of self-discipline and self-control, amounting to asceticism, which serves to counteract subjection to others, a common feature of everyday experience for most Africans, but accentuated among the poor where Zionists have their base. Zionists have carried this self-reliance into the workplace and it has had the effect of cutting them off both from mainstream Christians and from adherents to African tradition. In short, it has enabled them to assert a measure of social and economic independence. These merging principles of spirit and asceticism created for Zionists an area of freedom and independence, and a sense of control and empowerment, which they did not normally enjoy in everyday life.

This analysis from within Zionist discourse and practice in a modern setting is based on knowledge of what Zionists say and do in their predominantly urban congregations of the present. Its purpose was to lay bare the 'anatomy' of the Zionist synthesis and to consider in general terms the advantages it imparts to Zionists in confronting the problems of modern urban life. But does it empower all Zionists in exactly the same way? How does it meet the needs of different categories of person within a typical Zionist community; what differential usage is made of it by men or women, by young or old?

THE AGENCY OF GENDER

It can be readily observed, and is in any case openly acknowledged, that women, though outnumbering men by as many as three to one in many congregations, are subordinate to men and play secondary roles in religious services. Men are seated on the outer perimeter of the meeting room; women occupy the border with inner domestic space. Men enter by the front door; women by the back through the kitchen. Men monopolize office holding, which gives them undisputed control of the preaching function and command of the Bible as a source of knowledge and inspiration. Their control of oratory, in prayer, reading and preaching, gives men a capacity to generate communal fervour and to 'arouse' the Holy Spirit, which is denied to women. Women may acquire the gift of prophecy, but always in a minor key. Male prophets are credited with being more potent and insightful, more forceful in their utterances, than female prophets, and it is a matter of observation that the former automatically assume commanding roles in healing activities. Men thus exercise control over two very powerful resources, the Bible and the Holy Spirit, in both invocation and deployment. Women, on the other hand, because they outnumber men and because in their capacity as childbearers and nursing mothers they are most prone to sickness, are most frequently the recipients of healing ministrations. While men manage the provision of healing, women are commonly the consumers of it, and as receivers they are subordinate to the givers.

However, women are not without influence. They do not form an inert audience during male preaching and they have the capacity to fine-tune it by timely intervention (Kiernan 1990: 199). Moreover, there are regular meetings of women only, consisting of prayer and preaching (but not healing), at which women can articulate their problems with a collective force not mustered by men. What makes this collective influence so effective is that the Puritan ethic places a very powerful weapon at the disposal of Zionist women in their relations with men. The prescriptions of the Puritan code place no additional burden on women but place a shackle on characteristically male pursuits. Thus Zionist men are morally confined to monogamous marriage, they are restrained from squandering their earnings on typical male activities such as drinking, gambling and the promiscuous chase, and they are enjoined to invest their income in the support of home and family. Any noticeable deviation can be brought to the attention of the women's meeting, whence pressure can be exerted on the congregation as a whole to withdraw collective recognition from the culprit, who will consequently suffer a temporary disablement, either in the exercise of office or in his healing capacity. Thus, while men dominate the inspirational flow from Bible to spirit to healing, women are compensated on the distaff side by having a firm grip on the moral dimension. (See Figure 2.)

POLITICAL DETACHMENT

Despite the much-publicized recent appearances of leading South African politicians at annual meetings of the very large Zion Christian Church (of Legkanyane), this trend is not representative of Zionists generally, who have long been noted for sedulous political disengagement. Schoffeleers (1991) has attempted to explain this political apathy in terms of the Zionist preoccupation with healing. While not rejecting a range of other influential variables, he relegates them to secondary factors and argues that the root cause of political acquiescence is healing itself, because it is of the character of all healing systems that they 'tend to individualise, and thereby depoliticise, problems which are more often than not political' (1991:

Figure 2 The Zionist synthesis and the agency of gender

12). Professional healers apart, who may well have a vested interest in treating only the individual manifestations of social problems such as poverty, it is not entirely incompatible with more altruistic healing, of the type practised by Zionists, to see beyond the serial manifestations, to diagnose a social cause and to suggest a political solution. There have been numerous examples of this in the history of medical practice. What is it that prevents Wakkerstroom–KwaMashu Zionists from reaching this political insight and acting upon it; why do they not abandon healing in favour of political protest?

More than anything else, it is their adherence to the Puritan ethic that is the answer. This also promotes individualism – the individualism of economic achievement as the counterpart of individualized privation. For Zionists, the Puritan path of individual betterment is a preferable alternative to political action, and it complements their healing emphasis. It was clear that these Zionists did not shun politics as such. In fact, they were unwilling to recognize it as a separate domain of human activity and lumped it within a more general class of 'time-wasting' actions. This is but another expression of the moral code, the implicit positive thrust of which is to concentrate the individual's work, resources, time and energy on the cultivation of family life and religious community; all other purely secular alliances and activities are to be avoided as 'useless' and 'unproductive'. It is attachment to the Puritan ethic, therefore, that induces political conservatism and complacency, particularly among the more influential achievers, that is, the adult, married, working males.

However, the recent upsurge of violent clashes between opposed political organizations on the streets of the townships have forced Zionists to recognize politics as a disparate sphere of action and meaning. And within Zionist ranks, the tension between young and old has tightened around the recharged issue of political detachment. Before they marry, young men are not candidates for office in the church and their youth and immaturity are not the stuff of which prophets are made. Denied access to the mechanisms of producing therapeutic power (that is, Bible and spirit), they are also least likely to require healing attention. Without any compensatory benefits, they simply chafe under the moral restrictions of the Puritan code, the most vexing of which is the rule of premarital sexual abstinence. Young women find the ethical demands less irksome and see merit in the more male-oriented restraints, both as a hedge against unwanted pregnancy in the present and as a guarantee of a stable marriage in the future. It is the young men, therefore, who are ultimately driven to forsake Zionism but, while they remain, they come increasingly under pressure from their peers and from the 'press-gang' tactics of armed rival factions to join in the political action.

Although they continue to abjure violence, young Zionists call attention to this mounting pressure in an effort to loosen the autocratic control of their elders and to revise the policy of political neutrality. How this will work out remains to be seen, but senior control of the conceptual apparatus is too entrenched to yield much in the way of concession. In the meantime, an impending election presages a fresh source of strain for Zionism. Conscious of the size of the Zionist vote, political parties are beginning to woo Zionist leaders on the assumption that they can deliver *en bloc* the vote of their churches and congregations. Zionist leaders, on the other hand, express the fear that party political loyalties will split the fragile unity of their congregations.

CONCLUSION

It can be concluded, first of all, that the synthesis of elements elaborated in these pages provides Zionists in common with a dual empowerment: they are imbued with the mystical power of the Holy Spirit to counter the social deprivation which is inscribed as affliction on the human body, and they are empowered to act upon the world with the cutting edge of ascetic self-discipline. Secondly, the components of the synthesis are so related as to allow differential access to the exercise of agency and power within Zionism. Although recent political developments have given youngsters a leverage that they could not previously exert, the synthesis itself has not been breached by political interests as against those of entrepreneurial advancement, and instruments of agency and power are firmly in the hands of the dominant seniors. There are, however, discernible complementary sides to the synthesis; male and female preserves, which allow men to dominate in some respects and women in others. Thirdly, and perhaps most significantly, the synthesis is in essence no more than a Christian variant. The components were already present in the imported American model and have remained unchanged, although the understanding of how they are intertwined has been subject to modification or accentuation – for example, a failure to meet moral requirements can affect one's health and diminish one's powers. Otherwise, what Zulu Zionism has done to the model is to embroider it outwardly in some respects, such as white robes and staves, and to apply it to African purposes, most notably to opposing sorcery (Kiernan 1984). It is significant, however, that it is the synthesis that imbues the additions with meaning, not the other way round, and that Zionists strenuously reject sorcery as inherently evil and resist it with Christian might.

It is, perhaps, because Zionists are so preoccupied with sorcery, and because the visible weaponry of robes and staves that they array against it is so conspicuous, that it has been tempting to assume the presence of syncretism. But this semblance of syncretism is misleading; Zionists have assembled a purely Christian battery of ideas, which should not be confused either with the context in which these are applied or with the way they are applied in that context. While the healing synthesis is incontrovertibly Christian, it permits the conditions on which it operates to be interpreted within an African worldview. Only the problem is African; the answer is Christian.

Finally, although this conclusion may have validity only for these self-styled 'Christian Zionists' of Wakkerstroom descent, what is noteworthy about them is that they may constitute an exception to the general principle that all religions are syncretistic. Having initially borrowed a package of ideas from elsewhere, these Zionists have sought to preserve that heritage without substantial addition, further mixing, or significant alteration. A heightened consciousness of their historical roots and distinctiveness tends to curb any appreciable drift towards syncretism.

NOTES

1 For discussion of Zionism elsewhere in southern Africa, see, on the Tswana, Pauw, 1960; Comaroff, 1985; on the Swazi Sundkler, 1976; Fogelqvist, 1986; and on the Shona Daneel, 1970, 1974.
2 Sundkler later revised this judgement (1976: 316) and adopted a much more conciliatory approach, by stressing the 'newness' of content in the Zionist message and by more or less conceding (p. 317) that no religion is free of syncretism.
3 They are not averse to distinguishing between themselves and others (New Zionists) in terms of syncretism. New (that is, upstart) Zionists, in this discourse, are slack on Christian observance and are accepting of traditional practices.

REFERENCES

Bundy, C. (1979) *The Rise and Fall of the South African Peasantry*, London: Heinemann.
Comaroff, J. (1985) *Body of Power, Spirit of Resistance: The Culture and History of a South African People*, Chicago and London: University of Chicago Press.
Daneel, M.L. (1970) *Zionism and Faith-Healing in Rhodesia*, Mouton: The Hague.
—— (1974) *Old and New in Shona Independent Churches*, Vol. 2, Mouton: The Hague.
Fogelqvist, A. (1986) *The Red-Dressed Zionists: Symbols of Power in a Swazi Independent Church*, Uppsala Research Reports in Cultural Anthropology, 5: Uppsala.
Gluckman, M. (1956) 'The bonds in the colour bar', in M. Gluckman, *Custom and Conflict in Africa*, Oxford: Blackwell.
Kiernan, J.P. (1976a) 'The work of Zion: an analysis of a Zulu Zionist ritual', *Africa* 46, 4: 340–56.
—— (1976b) 'Prophet and preacher: an essential partnership in the work of Zion', *Man* 11, 3: 356–66.
—— (1979) 'The weapons of Zion', *Journal of Religion in Africa* 10, 1: 13–31.
—— (1984) 'A cesspool of sorcery: how Zionists visualise and respond to the city', *Urban Anthropology*, 13, 2–3: 219–36.
—— (1990) 'The canticles of Zion: song as word and action in Zulu Zionist discourse', *Journal of Religion in Africa* 20, 2: 188–204.
—— (1991) '"Wear 'n tear and repair": the colour coding of mystical mending in Zulu Zionist churches', *Africa* 61, 1: 26–39.
—— (1992) 'The herder and the rustler: deciphering the affinity between Zulu diviner and Zionist prophet', *African Studies* 51, 1: 231–42.
Makhubu, P. (1988) *Who are the Independent Churches?*, Johannesburg: Skotaville Publishers.
Marais, J.S. (1961) *The Fall of Kruger's Republic*, Oxford: Clarendon Press.
Nixon, J. (1972) *The Complete Story of the Transvaal*, Cape Town: Struik.
Odendaal, A. (1984) *Vukani Bantu: Beginning of Black Protest Politics in South Africa to 1912*, Cape Town: David Philip.

Pauw, B.A. (1960) *Religion in a Tswana Chiefdom*, Cape Town: Oxford University Press.
—— (1974) 'Ancestor beliefs and rituals among urban Africans', *African Studies* 33, 2: 99–111.
Pauw, C.M. (forthcoming) 'African independent churches as a "people's response" to the Christian message', *Journal for the Study of Religion*.
Schoffeleers, M. (1991) 'Ritual healing and political acquiescence: the case of the Zionist churches in southern Africa', *Africa* 60, 1: 1–25.
Schutte, A.G. (1974) 'Dual religious orientation in an urban African church', *African Studies* 33, 2: 113–20.
Sundkler, B.G.M. (1961) *Bantu Prophets in South Africa*, London: Oxford University Press.
—— (1976) *Zulu Zion and some Swazi Zionists*, London: Oxford University Press.
West, M.E. (1975) *Bishops and Prophets in a Black City*, Cape Town and London: Philip and Collings.

4 The politics of religious synthesis

Roman Catholicism and Hindu village society in Tamil Nadu, India

David Mosse

The encounter of non-Western societies with Christianity is often viewed as inextricably bound up with the spread of colonial power. Christian converts are perceived as living firmly within the orbit of the mission's influence, decultured and alienated from their religious and cultural roots. Symbolized by its European-style churches, Western clerical dress and liturgy, Christianity in India has also been judged as a legacy of the colonial past. Many Indian Christian thinkers today within both Roman Catholic and Protestant churches share this concern about cultural rootlessness and are anxious to free the church from its colonial heritage and missionary paternalism, and to develop a truly Indian form of Christian spirituality, worship and church organization. Such thinking also reflects wider changes in the church worldwide. The second Vatican councils, for example, held between 1962 and 1965, introduced a number of reforms into the Roman Catholic Church which recast ecclesiastical thinking on the relationship between Christian faith and local culture. These now endorse and encourage moves to indigenize or 'inculturate' theology, forms of worship, liturgy or architecture and to initiate inter-faith dialogue.[1]

The assumption that Christianity will supplant local systems of belief and ritual is part of a wider view of colonial experience as 'modernization', which portrays subject groups as progressively absorbed into dominant colonial cultures. This view is revised in several recent studies which attempt a writing of mission history from the point of view of the missionized themselves (for example, Bayly 1989; Comaroff 1985). The image of the passive proselyte is replaced with a view of converts as active creators and manipulators of symbolic and ritual systems which serve indigenous social and political ends. Rather than transforming local practice the missionary is, through complex exchanges, often unwittingly drawn into these systems. This chapter describes such a context and examines the strategies by which both missionaries and local Christians have used local ritual systems to serve often very different agendas.

Using archival and fieldwork material from a Roman Catholic community in rural Tamil Nadu, my aim, then, is to highlight a local type of Hindu[2] and Christian social and religious synthesis which counters the image of the politically passive and culturally isolated Christian community. In the first part of the chapter I will show how this synthesis is the product of an active incorporation of mission Christianity into local political and social relationships. In the Tamil Catholic context these are largely framed by the caste system.[3] Taking the celebration of village festivals of the Catholic saints as a prime example, I will show how Hindu-Christian forms of interpenetration have to be understood in terms of membership of a common caste order. Of course not all religious experience is shaped by relations of caste, but my focus here is largely on public forms of worship rather than belief and theologies.

In the second part of the chapter I will examine change and transformation in this 'fused' Hindu-Catholic ritual system in both colonial and postcolonial contexts. Again, I will focus on the example of the festival of a village Catholic saint. My concern will be to examine the role of changing relations of power in shaping ritual synthesis. There are two points here. The first is that the nature of *religious authority*, which the church has constructed for itself and wielded, has changed during precolonial, colonial and postcolonial times. The effects of this are evident, for example, in that practices viewed as acceptable expressions of Indian culture in one century have been redefined as heterodox compromises in another. Secondly, and perhaps more important, is the fact that in south India relations of power and authority (notably those of caste) are themselves often expressed in religious idioms. Here then is a culture in which religion and politics have not historically been separable domains of human action. In the Tamil countryside, religious institutions and their festivals have long been central to the exercise of dominance and control in local and regional political systems.[4] The key point is that local relations of caste and power have equally been articulated through public forms of *Catholic* worship (for example, festivals of the saints), which are in turn shaped by this social order. There is in fact a double and contradictory burden on the local Catholic ritual system – firstly to express Christian religion and secondly to legitimize (or challenge) caste relations. This has involved missionaries and villagers in conflicts over an endlessly disputed and shifting boundary between 'Christian religion' and 'local culture'.

In the final part of the chapter I will review some recent changes in the relationship between a local Roman Catholic church (its rites and the social thinking of its clergy) on the one hand, and caste society, popular religion and culture on the other. These indicate a number of paradoxical moves towards indigenization and anti-indigenization. Having a mandate for 'inculturation' and interfaith dialogue, the rural church, paradoxically, finds itself more separated from caste society and Hindu ritual systems than ever.

THE JESUIT MISSION IN RAMNAD: A TYPE OF RELIGIOUS SYNTHESIS

The setting for this discussion is a mixed Hindu-Christian village (Alapuram)[5] in the dry eastern plains of Tamil Nadu which comprise the modern district of Ramnad (Ramnathapuram). Most of the early conversions in this region were brought about in the seventeenth and eighteenth centuries by Jesuits of the Madurai Mission. The founder of this mission, the Italian Roberto de Nobili, began one of the earliest Christian missionary projects of 'cultural accommodation' (Pickering 1992: 104). In 1606 de Nobili settled in the city of Madurai, a major cultural and religious centre. Modelling himself on the Hindu teacher-renouncers (or *sannyasins*) he undertook in-depth study of Sanskrit and Tamil Hindu sacred texts. In doing so he was consciously separating himself from the colonial trading powers on the Coromandal coast and their Portuguese missionaries, who, by fusing Christian faith and European culture, had (in the minds of the Brahmin elite whom de Nobili hoped to influence) associated Christianity with inferior status, and conversion with joining the ritually impure community of *parangis* (firangi, franks, aliens or Westerners) (Neill 1984; Bayly 1989: 389–92). In de Nobili's view, religion was ultimately a matter of spiritual realities, belief and liturgy, and the mission's task was to present the distinctive soterio-logical message of the Gospel in Indian social and cultural form. Converts were not required to adopt new cultural identities or to abandon caste customs.[6] Indeed, de Nobili's missionaries themselves acceded to the rules of caste interaction by accepting a division among themselves – that is, between those who served Brahman converts (who, like de Nobili himself, were referred to as *sannyasins*), those who served non-Brahmans (*pandaraswamis*) and (for a short period) yet others who worked among the socially subordinate and impure untouchable castes (Dumont 1972: 250–1, 372).[7]

There was, of course no single Indian or even Tamil culture to which the mission sought to accommodate, and the *pandaraswamis* in seventeenth-century Ramnad in fact worked in a context very different from Madurai. Here the Jesuit *pandaraswamis* presented the Christian message to a Maravar caste warrior elite and their dependent service castes, and brought about large-scale mass conversions. They were far more successful in establishing church institutions in the region than was de Nobili working with the orthodox Brahmans of Madurai. One reason for this was that the Jesuits in Ramnad were able to build upon popular syncretic saint cults which had filtered inland from the Christian populations of the Coromandel coast following networks of trade and pilgrimage (Bayly 1989: 379–84). One example was the popular cult of St James (locally *Sandiyakappar*) at Alapuram focusing on a miraculous banyan tree, whose festival is the subject of discussion below. But perhaps more important was the patronage which these popular Christian pilgrimages and churches received from the regional Maravar chiefs and kings. One Hindu king, for example, gave over his tax share of the harvest of the village of Sarugani to the Christian Church 'for lighting, incensing and other religious worship', and by the end of the eighteenth century many other churches and their festivals were supported by grants of land and other gifts from Christian, but more often Hindu, regional and village leaders (Mosse, forthcoming).

The significance of such religious gifting derives from the central role played by Hindu temples (which Christian churches came to resemble) in the precolonial political system. Recent historical research has shown that the endowment of temples was an important means of extending political control into new areas for the south Indian kings and warrior chiefs of the Vijayanagar period (fourteenth to sixteenth centuries). As Stein points out, this involved an exchange in which rulers gave material resources to the temples and in return received not only ritualized public 'honours' but also political constituencies from religious leaders (Stein 1980: 469). In Ramnad these constituencies included sizeable Christian populations who, together with Hindus, participated in popular regional saint cults and festivals. As chief patron of the Sarugani church mentioned above, the Hindu king (or his representative) arranged the final procession of the image of the risen Christ in a huge ceremonial 'temple cart' (or *ter*) at the Easter festival, and, along with regional Maravar caste chiefs, received 'first honour' marked by prestations of cloth and betel nut from the hand of the presiding Catholic priest.

This synthesis of Christian and local traditions was initiated through de Nobili's 'accommodation' strategy. However, the form which it took was not the result of a passive 'accommodation' of Christianity to local Hindu practices, but rather the active incorporation of Christian centres into a local political system. Because they depended upon protection, the Jesuit *pandaraswamis* entered into exchanges with local leaders, receiving protection and granting ritual honours. This provided the basis for a thorough incorporation of Hindu ritual forms into Catholic festivals.

There are several aspects to this (described in detail elsewhere: Mosse 1986, forthcoming). Firstly, in the shape of the novena (a nine-day devotion), the Catholic festivals maintained the form of the Hindu festival of Dasara or *Navarattiri* (the 'nine nights'). On each of the nine nights the saints were decorated and taken in procession around the village on decorated platforms and chariots resembling those at Hindu temples. At the festival of St James at Alapuram (in common with other churches and Hindu temples) each of these processions was paid for and conducted by a leading Catholic caste or lineage group in the parish, in a system known as *mantakapati*.[8] The social distinction involved in being a festival donor was marked by the receipt of 'church honours' (*kovil mariyatai*). As at temples, these took the form of prestations of cloth and betel nut (see Appadurai and Breckenridge 1976). The St James festival also gave ritual roles and associated honours to a range of (Christian and Hindu) village officers, artisans and servants: the Hindu Maravar headman, the Vellalar caste accountant, the blacksmith and carpenter, the barber, the washerman and untouchable caste sweepers and drummers. These positions were all caste-specific and the holders of these offices represented their castes. In fact the church honours distributed at the start and end of the festival made explicit the caste-based division of labour and caste hierarchy of the village. The betel nut and cloth were distributed in rank order, and while high-caste Catholic festival donors and village officers received honours from the priest or high-caste catechist *inside* the church, the low and service castes were handed their betel honours *outside* on the church steps. Significantly, Catholic untouchable castes were excluded from the prestigious roles of festival donors until the 1960s.

Not only did the Jesuit *pandaraswamis* (like the Hindu religious leaders of the time) become important intermediaries in the expansion and legitimation of warrior control (Stein 1980: 469), but also, in pursuing their own goal of evangelism (and in granting 'honours' to converts) they established the same link 'between *recruitment* to the sect and the *rewards* for new recruits in the form of shares in some sort of temple service and temple honors' as Appadurai observes of medieval Hindu sectarian leaders (1981: 77, original emphasis).

In a sense, of course, this festival honours system and the novena were as much European as Tamil. The important issue, however, is not the cultural origin of individual elements, but the fact that the Catholic Church was constituted as a ritual system (centring on the presiding saint) which was perceived by both Hindus and Christians in precisely the same way as a Hindu temple, namely as a ceremonial context in which caste and relations of power could be symbolized and validated. Indeed, in ideological terms the services and honours of the churches, like those of local temples, actually *constituted* the local caste hierarchy, which was viewed ideally as an order of ritual service to the deity or the king (Hocart 1950: 17). Underlying this symbolism was a conception of divine power (of saints and deities) as localized, material and not clearly distinguished from the secular power of the king (Ludden 1985: 30–1; Bayly 1989: 48). It is not hard to see how the cult of the miraculous banyan tree of St James (himself portrayed as divine warrior and protector of the village territory) could provide a suitable vehicle for expressing local political dominance which fitted in with prevailing notions of divine and secular power. Not surprisingly – and as the 260-year record of this village church amply demonstrates – the St James festival also provided the principle occasion for contesting social rank and position and for public expressions of social mobility (Mosse, forthcoming). As a final point here, it can be noted that the missionary priests, because they controlled access to the ritual markers of social rank (the 'betel honours', the coveted roles of carrying the statues etc.) became themselves crucial arbiters of power and caste rank.

While in some senses still a Hindu institution therefore, the caste system is also able to take a Catholic ritual form. That which in ecclesiastical terms is Christianity 'accommodating' caste, is in social reality caste 'accommodating' Christianity; that is, the active construction and appropriation of Christian ritual contexts as part of indigenous social and ritual order. Saints' festivals are not the only occasions for this sort of public synthesis. Catholic life-cycle rituals such as puberty, marriage and death all retain Hindu ritual forms to express caste status. While incorporating distinctively Catholic elements and symbols, each rite has a structure similar to those of Hindus, employs Hindu ritual procedures and involves the same Hindu ritual specialists (Mosse 1986, n.d.).

It would be wrong, however, to consider the ritual integration of Hindus and Catholics as purely a matter of symbolizing social relationships of caste, as if shared meanings do not exist beyond caste. Clearly they do. I have already alluded to a deeper level at which Catholics share Hindu notions in conceptualizing the divine power of saints like St James, and the same is true of other contexts (for example, conceptions of the dead: Mosse 1986: 413–36, 465–76). Moreover, the popular synthesis of Catholicism and Hinduism is not restricted to caste-based ritual. I have elsewhere described ways in which, for example, the cult of saints is conceived and ordered by principles held in common with village Hinduism, and the way in which Hindu deities are incorporated into Catholic conceptions and ritual practice (Mosse 1994).

The eighteenth- and nineteenth-century Jesuits' tolerance of Indian cultural traditions, including those of caste, contrasts sharply with their strong rejection of what was understood as Hindu *religion*. Fundamental to salvation was the rejection of Hindu religious practices, and the diaries of Jesuit parish priests indicate severe sanctions imposed upon those who 'attend pagan worship and secure the things offered to the devil'.[9] Ironically, it was precisely this intolerance of Hindu 'religion' which actually encouraged the incorporation of Hindu ritual forms (and no doubt with them Hindu conceptions) into Catholic contexts. For example, it was largely to facilitate the rejection of Hindu religious worship (that is, worship directed towards Hindu divinity) among converts that Jesuits permitted or encouraged the elaboration of 'customary practices', not only in the organization of the festivals, but also in allowing 'Hindu' forms of devotion in the worship of the saints. What mattered was not the form but the object of worship; Christians should 'render to the Lord above homage which hitherto had only been rendered to the prince of darkness' (Saint-Cyr 1865). Undoubtedly, in relation to both the celebration of festivals and the cult of saints, what the Jesuit missionaries failed to appreciate was the extent to which for the actors themselves meaning lay not in the religio-cultural content (saint rather than deity; church rather than temple) but in the ritual form. The social organization of Catholic festivals and the conceptual ordering of the cult of saints both had Christian content but retained Hindu meanings. By distinguishing 'form' from 'content' or 'religion' from 'caste', missionaries conceived local ritual practice in ways which differed significantly from those of the actors themselves.

Finally, it would be quite wrong to consider Catholic ritual practice as 'culturally absorbed' (Pickering 1992: 104) – that is, wholly ordered and understood in terms of notions shared with Hindus – or to forget that the missionaries created ritual contexts and communicated values which were clearly seen as overriding the demands of caste and opposing Hinduism (Mosse 1994). None the less, as far as caste goes, in the minds of both de Nobili's followers and many villagers today, the point is that the distinctive truth and values of Christianity relativized but did not deny the obligations of caste. Moreover, this non-contradictory relationship between Christian faith and caste society could be conceived in an indigenous way – namely using the model of the Indian renouncer in relation to caste society (ibid.). The values of the renouncer are individualistic, transcendent and absolute (beyond both society and religion); those of caste are relative and concern hierarchy, purity and relations of control (both human and divine).[10]

As a 'local model' of the relationship between Catholic religion and its Hindu socio-cultural context, this in fact fails to grasp the constant interpenetration of caste and Christian worship, and the way in which the boundary between Catholic religion and caste society has itself constantly been subject to contest and redefinition. It is to these matters of conflict and change that I want to turn.

CHURCH AUTHORITY AND THE CREATION OF A CATHOLIC RELIGIOUS DOMAIN

The equation of Christian spirituality with the world of the renouncer lying beyond caste society is precisely that which informed de Nobili's practice of 'accommodation'. The Jesuit *pandaraswamis* held a very other-worldly view of religion which clearly dichotomized the spiritual and the temporal. Caste was viewed as a matter of 'worldly honour'. While the equality of all before God, manifest as the *religious* right of all castes to hear mass in the same church or to 'render honour to the saints', was stressed, there was no decisive objection to expressions of rank or social honour at festivals or even in the central rite of the mass. This view held force throughout the eighteenth and nineteenth centuries. Thus up until 1919, in Alapuram, low-caste (Pallar) Catholics received the sacrament after high castes and at a separate rail at the back of the church where they sat. Many churches had separate entrances and exits for different castes, separate burial grounds and often entirely separate churches dedicated to different saints and celebrating different festivals (although as a matter of religious principle a single mass was usually celebrated in the central parish church).

Consistent with the clear separation of spiritual from worldly matters, the Jesuit *pandaraswamis* in precolonial Ramnad provided a distinctively spiritual leadership as renouncer-teachers. They administered the sacraments and presided at Christian ceremonies, but did not claim exclusive authority over the churches and their festivals, in which local headmen, regional chiefs, and representatives of different serving caste groups held recognized rights.[11]

British colonial rule allowed for a significant change in the position of the missionary priests. Most fundamentally, colonialism brought with it a distinctly European conception of religion as a domain separate from politics over which bureaucratic control could be imposed. By the mid-nineteenth century this had already brought about a major change in local temple systems (Dirks 1987; Appadurai 1981). This bureaucratic conception of religion, together with the colonial administrative and judiciary system which implemented it, made it possible for Catholic priests to impose an exclusive authority over popular cults like St James' at Alapuram. However, they did not immediately use this power to challenge the rights held by Hindu headmen and others in 'their' churches. On the contrary, they sought to embellish and extend certain ritual privileges and caste honours in the churches and their festivals. The principle reason for this was a competition over jurisdiction of the parishes of Ramnad between two Catholic missionary agencies – the French Jesuits under the authority of Rome, and the 'Goanese' Padroado priests under the patronage of Portugal.[12] Each side claimed the legal right to patronage on the grounds of the popular support which they commanded from villagers. The two missions in turn sought to solicit this support by manipulating the existing system of church honours and by exploiting their old role as custodians of festival privileges and arbiters of caste rank. In a series of moves and counter-moves both parties therefore inaugurated new festivals and honours, elaborated old ones or transferred rights from one caste group to another as a way of rewarding their supporters (Mosse, forthcoming).

This ecclesiastical conflict over patronage between Jesuit 'intruders' and Goanese 'schismatics' intersected with a series of local conflicts over precedence and status between caste groups. (These conflicts in turn reflected wider socio-economic changes resulting from British rule: Mosse, forthcoming). While the missionaries used the honours system to win local support, caste leaders were also able to challenge the priests' authority and judgements through threats to withdraw support or to convert to other sects. In other words, caste groups manipulated missionary patronage to serve their own goals in the competitive demonstration of caste honour and position. The complex cultural synthesis at festivals like St James' at Alapuram in the 1850s was more than ever an expression of contests of power.

By 1860 the Jesuit Fr. Favreux had (through the courts) won jurisdiction of Alapuram and began to assert a new administrative control over this church and its parish. No longer a renouncer priest, he employed distinctly royal idioms and symbols of overlordship to express his new 'rule'. Like other priests he began building and endowing churches, and took over the kingly role of chief festival donor and other symbols of overlordship, such as arriving for processions on horseback under a processional umbrella. The challenge to the local caste and political leaders (who continued to claim rights in the festival system) was more than symbolic. Throughout the nineteenth and twentieth centuries, Catholic priests used the courts gradually to erode rights in the churches and their festivals claimed by Hindu kings and village headmen. In some cases old churches were demolished entirely in attempts to erase these pre-existing rights. As late as 1956, the priest of Sarugani (see above) challenged the rights of Hindu headmen of the area to conduct the large chariot procession of the risen Christ on the grounds that this 'is not a part of Christian ritual' and that the only rights existing in Catholic religious observances were those granted by canon law administered by the bishop.

In 1936 the Jesuit priest at Alapuram decided to refuse to hand 'betel honours' to the Hindu village headman inside the church 'as it is not becoming chiefly when there is the Blessed Sacrament.'[13] The headman's threat to stop the festival was thwarted by a heavy police guard at the honours distribution that year. But following this public affront the headman managed to have the distribution of church honours (*kovil mariyatai*) abolished entirely. These it will be recalled involved a hierarchy of Christian and Hindu village officers, artisans and village servants. From 1937 onwards, with the removal of the honours system, Hindus participated in the festival only as individual devotees and without socially determined rights and honours. This marked the collapse of the St James festival as a village festival which integrated Hindus and Christians into the same social and ritual system, and its transformation into a Christian religious festival. The honours and privileges which remained (the right to pay for processions, carry the statues etc.) continued to be contested among Christians of different castes but were now separate from the bundle of rights of which they had originally been a part.

In moves such as this, and supported by the colonial administration, Catholic priests helped make concrete the European conception of religion as 'a bounded domain of action separate from other domains'; and at this point the Christian *kovil* (temple or church) ceased to resemble the Hindu *kovil* (Stein 1980: 452). Churches like St James' became religious institutions under the exclusive authority of the priest, which was clearly separate from the secular authority of the Hindu village headman. Rights in the church, including the shares in the worship marked by honours, which had historically been inseparable from rights in the village (rights to office or 'shares' in the village harvest) and which had been instituted by the king of Ramnad in the eighteenth century, were now exclusively Christian.

Significantly, the priest challenged the caste rights of Hindus on the grounds that they compromised Catholic religious practice or the Catholic sacred space. Practices which earlier Jesuit (and Goanese) priests had considered as secular and separate from Catholic religion now compromised it. It is difficult to separate out questions of power and authority from those of religion here. The Alapuram Hindu headman's presence in the church as a matter of social right, for example, was clearly viewed as anomalous. This was not, however, because he participated in an institution (the honours) which was now viewed as a part of Hinduism. After all, Catholics continued to receive honours. His claim was anomalous rather because it took place in an area of Christian ritual over which the priest now held authority, and potentially compromised this. It was this domain of church authority which defined the presence of Hindus and (later) all expressions of caste rank as out of place. In effect the realm of Catholic religion had become firmly institutionalized as, and synonymous with, that of church authority. The view of Catholic religion as institution was significantly different from its earlier equation with the renouncer. As institution, Catholicism would no longer permit expressions of caste – as a ritual and social system – in the church, and these were progressively challenged.

This began with the sacrament and the physical space of the church itself. In 1919, despite considerable high-caste protest, church seating arrangements were changed so as to give low castes apparent equality in the receipt of the sacrament. In 1936 Hindu social honours had become incompatible with Christian sacred space and were denied to the village headman. In 1982, following instructions from the All India Catholic Bishops Conference, all remaining caste-based privileges were eliminated from the celebration of Catholic festivals, and in 1989 the priest refused to bless any festivals which were celebrated separately by different castes in the same village.

SOCIAL PROTEST, SOCIAL ACTION AND THE DISMANTLING OF TRADITION

The significance of these moves is not, however, restricted to the assertion of a Catholic ecclesiastical authority. As earlier, Catholic priests intervened in a changing social context in which caste honour and power were constantly being challenged and redefined. During the final procession of the Alapuram festival of Our Lady of Lourdes in 1969, for example, a group of untouchable-caste Catholics (Pallars) grabbed the statues from the hands of the high-caste festival donors and carried them back to the church. Implicitly supporting this act of social protest (but explicitly to avoid further conflicts), the priest (now Tamil rather than French) moved to grant Pallars equal rights to organize processions in the village. Although initially (in the 1920s and 1930s) the priests extended such privileges to low castes explicitly on the grounds of their religious rights as Christian individuals, the disputed honours were widely understood as the signs and symbols of low-caste social aspirations. Indeed the conflicts over untouchable access to festival 'honours', which raged throughout the twentieth century, clearly indicate that Catholic festivals had become an important context for social protest and political mobilization among untouchable castes until the 1960s (Mosse, in press).

While this particular development was unintended by the clergy, priests had in fact become progressively more active in matters of education and social welfare, and were increasingly willing to support low castes simply on the grounds of social discrimination. When in 1981 the All India Catholic Bishops' Conference decided to abolish what remained of the caste-based system of festival donors, the *mantakapati* (which continued to exclude untouchables), it was not simply a matter of the church asserting authority over its forms of worship or of upholding the religious rights of parishioners. It was also a question of social ethics, and a desire to bring the church more in line with both the anti-caste position of the modern Indian state and a post-Vatican-II emphasis on social justice. The firm dichotomy between secular and religious action which priests had inherited was largely displaced.

In 1983 all caste privileges in the festival of St James were abolished and the festival was celebrated on a single day and organized by a committee representing all castes in the parish. In the short term the move continued a trend to 'equalize' participation in terms of caste, and as such was strongly supported by low-caste villagers and opposed by a significant proportion of high-caste

Catholics, who withdrew from the festival. In the longer term, however, a more significant change had taken place. With the abolition of the *mantakapatis* all remaining shares in the worship of the church held by villagers as members of social groups were eliminated. Today, participation in the festival is not by virtue of membership of particular kin or caste groups but by an individual's relationship to the church. That is to say most of the key roles (carrying the statues etc.) are now performed by officers of the church (the priest, the catechist) or by laymen condoned by the priest.

Here then is the final stage in the transformation of the St James festival from a political institution to a Christian ceremony. Not only has the St James festival ceased to be a village festival and become a Christian festival, but it has now also ceased to be a social event and become a religious ceremony, divorced and disengaged from the local social order and exclusively controlled by the church. The festival no longer incorporates Hindu socio-ritual forms and no longer provides a context for the articulation of local caste relations.

CONCLUSIONS, IMPLICATIONS AND RECENT DEVELOPMENTS

The Catholic Church and caste society

Let me recapitulate some of the themes addressed, starting with that of the shifting relationship between the Catholic Church and caste society. De Nobili's missionaries dichotomized reality into the spiritual and the temporal. This placed the ultimate matters of Christian faith beyond caste and allowed a remarkable incorporation of Catholic ritual into the working of a local caste system. In turn this generated a Hindu-Christian cultural synthesis in forms of Catholic worship and ritual. In the nineteenth century, however, a different conception of religion informed the action of missionaries who began to impose a distinction between the institutions of Catholic religion (that is, the church, festivals – embodying the authority of the priest) and those of caste society (for example, festival honours). Village Christians, however, continued to treat church ceremony as a ritual dimension of caste entirely compatible with Christian faith. These inconsistent understandings of the demands of Catholic religion generated a long series of disputes between priests and villagers. These were generally won by the church, which, by degrees, institutionalized Catholic religion as a domain ritually separate from Hindu and caste society.

The earliest stages of this process were driven by concerns about the priests' religious authority. The more recent and final separation of the church from caste society, however, derives particularly from a critique of hierarchical social and ritual forms. Indeed this has extended to criticism of hierarchy within the church itself and led to some experimentation with consultative decision making, particularly in the form of a new structure of parish councils. While sometimes generating new institutions (youth clubs, women's groups etc.) the strong critical involvement of priests in village society has, however, in general resulted in a greater separation of church ritual from traditional village social institutions, and in particular, has dismantled the festivals as a ritual context for statements about caste status.

Changes in popular Catholicism

A second theme is the shifting relationship between Catholic and Hindu religious systems. Earlier I suggested that the strong proscription on Christian participation in Hindu religious activities encouraged the incorporation of Hindu ritual forms into the practice of Catholic religion. To some extent this generated a shared religious culture among Hindus and Christians. Most publicly this was expressed in the recognized roles for Hindus in Catholic festivals, which also gave these a central integrating role in the village. When Hindus withdrew from the St James festival, Hindu and Christian ritual systems became in social terms uncoupled and separate.[14]

To some extent this increased separation of Christian and Hindu religion is mirrored in areas of shared belief and ritual other than festivals. As far as I know there has never been widespread Catholic participation in Hindu cults. Hindu gods have been recognized, even feared, but I know of only isolated cases where they receive regular cults from Catholics (Mosse 1994). As in the case of the festival, it is around *Catholic* cults that a shared religious culture has developed. Not only are Hindus active participants at most Catholic shrines, but, as I have described elsewhere (ibid.), the conception and ordering of these cults is influenced by principles shared with popular Hinduism. This common symbolic order has always been confined to a 'pragmatically oriented' area of religion concerned with health and misfortune and involving the saints, the 'good dead', village deities and malevolent demons and ghosts. Hindu principles, and certainly Hindu participation, are absent from 'salvation-oriented' (transcendent) religious action focusing on the priest and the sacraments. Today this latter aspect of religion receives almost exclusive emphasis in the church.

There is less and less support for the cult of saints as a form of Catholic worship. Saints are de-emphasized in favour of a focus on Christ and the church as the sole mediators between God and humans. Devotions and saints' festivals are encouraged because they bring people to confession and offer opportunities to communicate social messages, but today's Catholic priests in Ramnad emphasize the saints as exemplars of the Christian life rather than as sources of supernatural power (Houtart n.d.: 299; see Stirrat 1979). At the festival of St James, for example, the implicit focus on the saint's power and protection is replaced by an explicit emphasis on social and moral education, involving slide shows, scripted dramas, or festival banners more often than not carrying anti-caste and social justice themes. In other words the part of Catholic religion where conceptions of divine power are most closely fused with Hindu ideas, and where Hindu participation is greatest, is now marginalized.

Local saint cults continue to be popular, but to nothing like the extent of nineteenth-century descriptions.[15] The exceptions are those centres, like the nationally popular shrine to Our Lady of Velankanni, where a more clearly universal Catholic religion is again emphasized. In short, whereas the church formerly embraced both 'pragmatic' and 'transcendent' (Mandlebaum 1966) elements of religion, the contemporary emphasis is almost exclusively on social and salvation-oriented aspects, from which Hindus and popular Hindu concepts are absent.

One response to the 'decoupling of village religion from institutional religion' might be a lapse from sacramental practice and an emphasis on local cults. This is how Barnes reports an Indonesian Catholic context in which the church increasingly fails to establish a 'Catholic culture' (1992: 17). But in Ramnad, Catholic withdrawal from church services and the establishment of independent saint cults are rare or short-lived. More important by far as a recent development is the rapidly growing participation in pentecostal and charismatic forms of Christianity, both within the Catholic church and outside it.[16] Not far from Alapuram, for example, is the 'Prayer Garden' of the Church of Truth and the Spirit, established by a Tamil ex-Roman Catholic priest in 1990, which reportedly now attracts between four thousand and five thousand people to prayer, worship and healing events held every Wednesday. The guiding principle – 'worship in spirit and truth' (John 4: 24) – involves a radical assertion of Christian fundamentalism and individualistic spirituality which erases all signs of Catholic or Hindu ritualism, public ceremony and all non-Christian symbols (including the marriage *tali* worn by

Catholic women). The sacraments of the Catholic Church are abandoned or recast in radical Protestant form and the 'church' remains distinctively uninstitutionalized (if at all, taking local shape as village prayer groups). Caste-based practices are certainly rejected but the strong emphasis on personal salvation and change eschews social action. Since salvation, healing and the power of the Holy Spirit orient this movement, salvation- and pragmatic-oriented religion are again combined. As Caplan says of pentecostalism in the context of healing and exorcism, charismatic Christianity 'provides a Christian context for popular modes of explaining misfortune as well as a Christian means of dealing with it' where the church is increasingly unable to do so (1983: 30). The emphasis on power and healing at the 'Prayer Garden' also attracts large numbers of Hindus, which perhaps only underscores the point that popular conceptions of power remain part of a common Hindu-Christian religious culture which is now excluded from the established church (Caplan 1987).

The remoulding of Catholicism in rural Ramnad as a world religion separated from local culture and religion is, ironically, taking place when the ecclesiastical policy of 'inculturation' emphasizes a more tolerant attitude towards Hindu religion, actively encourages dialogue, and, through forms of art, music, architecture and liturgy, attempts to bring Hindu and Christian religious symbols closer together. Thus the Catholic Bishops' Conference in India in 1969 approved '12 points of Indianisation' in the liturgy, including use of local gestures, and rites of greeting, oil lamps instead of candles etc. (Houtart *et al.*, n.d.: 300–1).[17] There is a double paradox here. As I have suggested, the manifestly European churches, Latin liturgy and foreign missionaries of the nineteenth and early twentieth centuries, together with an emphasis on conversion which consciously polarized Hindu and Christian religions, all disguised and perpetuated a deeper cultural continuity between village Christians and Hindus. Yet today's interest in inculturation and interfaith dialogue occurs at a time when the church emphasizes fundamental differences in belief and social ethics between Christianity and Hinduism, and when the religious lives of Christians and Hindus are separate to an unprecedented degree.

'Indigenous culture', counter-culture, whose culture?

The imposition of church authority and the dismantling of an indigenous form of public worship at Catholic festivals have been contested; not, however, on the grounds of lost cultural tradition, but rather because they erode specific privileges symbolic of high-caste social dominance. For exactly this reason, the erosion of tradition and its replacement by church administration have won widespread support from low castes. (An example is the recent organization of festivals according to residentially defined parish 'zones' instead of caste *mantakapatis*.)

This low-caste support for anti-indigenizing moves is in fact part of a wider discourse in which indigenous (dominant) cultural forms (and the church honours would be included here) are rejected by low castes because of the hierarchy and subordination they imply. This presents a dilemma to established Christian churches in India, which are attempting to 'inculturate' in the context of a firm commitment to social justice *and* have a membership which is overwhelmingly low-caste (or tribal). The problem is this: challenging social subordination isolates the church from local cultural traditions (as in the case of the St James festival); but indigenization accommodates hierarchy. Emerging out of this dilemma is the new tradition of 'dalit theology'[18] – the theology of 'the oppressed, the down-trodden, or broken'. Through the 'concrete subjectivity . . . of the oppressed, their particular experience and histories, and aspirations' (Chatterji 1989: 9), dalit theology aims to provide an analysis of the socio-religious roots of oppression in India (principally focusing on caste). Combining traditions of liberation theology and inculturation, it generates a critique of hegemonic Hindu religious culture and sets about constructing liberating dalit counter-cultures (Prabhakar 1989; Irudayaraj 1990). In this, dalit theology draws on the wider 'dalit movements', which are untouchable-caste or tribal (dalit) political and cultural movements asserting socio-religious identities for dalits which are separate from the dominant 'Hindu culture' (including those of the non-Hindu religions of Buddhism, Christianity and Islam: Mosse, in press). To this, dalit theologians add a critique of Indian Christianity's 'Latin and Sanskrit captivity' (Prabhakar 1989: 4), and emphasize the authenticity of Indian subaltern religious traditions (low-caste or tribal religion, often characterized as non- or pre-Hindu) as the proper basis for a dalit Christian inculturation (Ayrookuzhiel 1983). Dalit theology is strongly critical of forms of inculturation which draw on high-caste or Brahmanical traditions, and would probably characterize the Hindu-Catholic synthesis arising from de Nobili's mission as simply a Christian form of high-caste Hindu hegemony.

The present Indian context, in which religious identity is highly politicized, is sure to affect these contemporary efforts at inculturation and counter-inculturation. In rural Ramnad the politics of religion and that of caste intersect. The rise of militant Hinduism, which implicitly reasserts caste hierarchy (Omvedt 1990), is likely to encourage further alignments of caste with religion. Thus untouchable castes, who have long used conversion to non-Hindu religions as a form of social protest, have begun to do so again. At the same time high-caste Catholics find much common political ground with Hindu fundamentalists. In this connection it is significant that when the militant fundamentalist Hindu RSS (Rashtriya Swayamsevak Sangh) organized public meetings in the village to protest against the Catholic priest's erosion of customary traditions and caste honours in church festivals, they were able both to speak for high caste Catholics and to win their tacit support.

Over its 300-year history in the Ramnad countryside, Roman Catholicism has maintained a changing frontier with Tamil village society and religion, which has generated always unstable forms of religious synthesis. These have themselves been vehicles for the legitimation of political control, for asserting ecclesiastical authority and even for social protest. De Nobili's socially 'inculturated' Catholic tradition was progressively replaced during the nineteenth and twentieth centuries through assertions of Catholic religious integrity which were profoundly un-inculturated. After the Second Vatican Councils, however, wide-ranging measures of 'Indianization' have been suggested, approved and experimented with at Catholic centres, retreats (ashrams) and parishes. While the 'ordinary liturgical reforms' which, for example replaced Latin with the vernacular in the mass have been uncontroversial, the wider moves to 're-inculturate' Catholicism have won limited local support. On the one hand, one section of the clergy (a narrow majority of priests surveyed in Ramnad in 1976) reject Indianization of the liturgy and the introduction of 'Hindu' gestures, rites etc. as a threat to the distinctive religious identity of Catholics (Houtart *et al.* n.d.: 299–316). On the other hand the same inculturation measures are rejected by 'dalit' thinkers, who view them as Sanskritic or Brahmanical symbols. (Ironically, Indianization often finds its strongest support from among Western members of the churches, for whom perhaps it validates a postcolonial, intercultural Christianity.)

The concern with culture is inextricably linked to another contemporary shift in the practice of the church, namely one away from an other-worldly pietism and a stress on conversion towards social action in religiously plural communities. As a new policy this too divides the clergy in Ramnad. Those priests critical of 'Indianization' on the grounds of its threat to distinctive Catholic identity tend also to retain an emphasis on conversion, and support a distinctly sacramental and spiritual role for the church. They welcome the recent decoupling of church from local society and consider that priests should be relieved of secular responsibilities such as the management of schools, lands or development programmes (Houtart *et al.* n.d.: 277–8, 291–7). At the other end of a spectrum of opinion is an increasing number of younger priests, influenced by liberation theology and emphasizing a strongly anti-caste 'social gospel'. The rejection of a separation between the sacred and the secular, and the replacement of individualistic spirituality with direct involvement in social and political action, depart fundamentally from the very basis of de Nobili's 'accommodation' method. Here, concerns with inculturation and interfaith dialogue are subordinated to the goal of working for justice among the oppressed irrespective of religion. While some of these priests have been influenced by the caste-based analysis of dalit theology, a majority emphasize class or gender in social and political mobilization.

However, while inculturation and the social gospel dominate contemporary concerns in the established church, it is the growing popularity of charismatic and pentecostal Christianity which is the most significant recent change in popular Catholic practice. As Caplan argues for urban Protestants, this itself marks a rejection of both the 'liturgical coolness and priestly mediations' (Caplan 1991: 379) of the orthodox church, and the secularism in the 'social gospel' of its more radical sections, in favour of informality, emotion and direct access to divine power. In its fundamentalist charismatic form, Christianity in Ramnad is at once more radically separate from Hindu religion and caste society than ever, and yet in its ideas of divine power and healing, more deeply rooted in a shared popular religious culture. Yet another religious synthesis emerges.

NOTES

I should like to express thanks to Charles Stewart for comments on an earlier draft of this chapter, and to the ESRC who funded the research on which it draws. Historical material derives mostly from parish diaries held at the Jesuit Madurai Mission Archives, Sacred Heart College, Shembaganur, Kodaikanal, Tamil Nadu.

1 The term 'inculturation' has a rather specific usage in contemporary missionary discourses (e.g., Shorter 1988), and there is a long history and a vast literature on theological, cultural and social dimensions of the *Indian*ization of Christianity in both Protestant and Roman Catholic traditions (e.g., Boyd 1975; Shiri 1982). This chapter will not address the 'inculturation' concept directly, but rather look at a local social context in which these ideas come into play.

2 I use the term 'Hindu' in two senses: firstly to refer to a hereditary religious identity (and I use 'Christian' or 'Catholic' in the same sense); and secondly to refer to indigenous religious and ritual practices. The latter does not imply a clearly defined system of doctrine, belief and practice equivalent to Christianity (see Fuller 1992).

3 Conceptualizing the 'caste system' in the context of religious pluralism presents problems. On the one hand the caste system is fundamentally a (Hindu) religious institution involving ideas and ritual practices which are not clearly separable from those of Hindu religion (see Dumont 1972); but on the other hand caste is also an idiom of social and political relationships. Whole mission strategies in India have depended upon whether the distinctions of caste are viewed as constituting a civil institution (a predominantly Roman Catholic view) or, as an enquiry sponsored by the Anglican Bishop of Madras concluded in 1845, 'as unquestionably religious . . . originating in and maintained by, the operation of Hindu idolatry' (Forrester 1980: 39). Yet other missionary traditions (for example Lutherans) distinguished the Hindu 'caste spirit' from the secular 'caste distinctions', allowing a qualified acceptance of cast among converts (ibid.: 18–19). In the present context, when describing a caste order common to Hindu and Christian villagers I refer to a system which is both political and religious, and, moreover, which is expressed through both Hindu and Catholic religious institutions. This will be explained below.

4 See the recent historical research on the political role of south Indian religious institutions in Stein 1980; Appadurai 1981; Appadurai and Breckenridge 1976; Dirks 1987; Bayly 1989.

5 The pseudonym for a village in which I carried out fieldwork in 1982–4 and intermittently in 1987–91 and 1993.

6 De Nobili's experiment was a marked departure from the post-Tridentine standardization of Catholic missionary practice. Disagreements with Rome (especially over questions of caste in the Church) eventually led to the suppression of the Society of Jesus by Papal Bull in 1773, and the Jesuits were expelled from India (see Neill 1984).

7 Even in the twentieth century, and well after the disappearance of this division among missionaries, there were separate categories of catechist serving high castes (*kovilpillais*) and untouchables (*pandarams*).

8 As Reiniche argues, implicitly the term *mantakapati* refers to the expenses of organizing a ritual passage in which the deity ordinarily resident inside his temple (*kovil* or royal seat) becomes exposed outside among his devotees (literally on the hall or *mantapam* outside the sanctuary) (1979: 87, n. 7). This ritual passage denotes both the special presence of the deity (and saint) during his festival and, through the processions, his royal rule over the village.

9 Alapuram Parish Diary entry, Fr. Gnanaprakasam, 4.8.1896.

10 Dumont argues that the relationship between renunciation and 'worldly Hinduism' is replicated in that between the Hindu 'sect' (founded by the renouncer) and caste (1972: 230–7). The point here is that being a Catholic in Ramnad resembled affiliation to a Hindu theistic devotional sect – what Dumont calls a 'religion-of-choice'. A new path to salvation – the *kiristu markkam* or 'Christian path' – was superimposed on the obligations of caste, relativizing but not denying these.

11 Contrast this with Catholic Sri Lanka where priests introduced Christianity in a colonial context and asserted a strong authority as political mediators with the state as well as religious leaders. Here socially more homogenous Catholic communities developed separate socio-religious identities as client groups of the Church (Stirrat 1992: 11ff.).

12 The 'Goanese' priests had taken over the administration of the churches of Ramnad after the Society of Jesus was suppressed in 1773. Jesuits of a newly reinstituted Madurai Mission returned to India in the 1830s and staked their claim to be true administrators of the churches of Ramnad.

13 Alapuram Parish Diary entry, Fr. Sousaiyamanikam, 17.7.1936.

14 While in Ramnad Hindus have gradually been denied formal roles in church festivals (although many do still continue), in Sri Lanka post-Vatican-II indigenization takes the form of, for example, introducing Buddhist drummers into festivals (Stirrat 1992: 45–6).

15 Here again there is an interesting contrast with Sri Lanka, which has witnessed the rapid increase in popular saint cults as centres of healing and demonic exorcism, which in Stirrat's analysis also carry a message about the political position of the Roman Catholics as a minority community in modern Sri Lanka (1992). In rural Tamil Nadu, by contrast, Roman Catholics remain firmly part of a caste society shared with Hindus and certainly do not project a common political identity.

16 See Caplan (1983, 1987, 1991) for accounts of the growing pentecostal religion in a south Indian urban setting.

17 The contemporary discourse of 'inculturation' is in important ways quite different from de Nobili's 'cultural accommodation' (Pickering 1992). The shift away from a spiritual/temporal dichotomy means that in contemporary Jesuit 'formation' the model of Indian spirituality comes, for example, from the Gandhian ashram with its distinctive combination of contemplative spirituality *and* social action, rather than from the traditional Hindu ashram which has no notion of social involvement. Other departures from de Nobili would include the emphasis on regional or local religious and cultural traditions (rather than primarily on textual traditions) and therefore a positive reappraisal of popular Hinduism; also the emphasis on personal experience of these (Hindu traditions) and on life in communion with Hindus (Clementin-Ojha, forthcoming).

18 This term was first used following the first National Conference of Christian dalits in 1985, organized by the Dalit Liberation Movement (Prabhaker 1989: 35).

REFERENCES

Appadurai, A. (1981) *Worship and Conflict Under Colonial Rule: A South Indian Case*, Cambridge: Cambridge University Press.

Appadurai, A. and Breckenridge, C. (1976) 'The south Indian temple: authority, honour and redistribution', *Contributions to Indian Sociology* (n.s.) 10, 2: 187–209.

Ayrookuzhiel, A.M.A (1983) 'The religious resources of the Dalits in the context of their struggle', in S.K. Chatterji (ed.), *Essays in Celebration of the CISRS Silver Jubilee*, Madras: Christian Institute for the Study of Religion and Society.

Barnes, R.H. (1992) 'A Catholic mission and the purification of culture: experiences in an Indonesian community', *Journal of the Anthropological Society of Oxford* 23, 2: 169–80.

Bayly, S. (1989) *Saints, Goddesses and Kings: Muslims and Christians in South Indian Society, 1700–1900*, Cambridge: Cambridge University Press.

Boyd, R. (1975) *An Introduction to Indian Christian Theology*, 2nd edn, Madras: The Christian Literature Society.

Caplan, L. (1983) 'Popular Christianity in urban south India', *Religion and Society* 30: 28–44.

—— (1987) *Class and Culture in Urban India: Fundamentalism in a Christian Community*, Oxford: Clarendon Press.

—— (1991) 'Christian fundamentalism as counter-culture', in T.N. Madan (ed.), *Religion in India*, Delhi: Oxford University Press.

Chatterji, S.K. (1989) 'Why Dalit theology?', in M.E. Prabhakar (ed.), *Towards a Dalit Theology*, Delhi: Indian Society for Promoting Christian Knowledge.

Clémentin-Ojha, C. (forthcoming) 'Des Indiens en quête de leur indianité: la formation "inculturée et contextualisée" des jesuites de Patna (Bihar)', in (provisional title) *Christianisme et Islam en Milieu Hindou: Pratiques et Debates*, Paris: Centre d'Etudes de l'Inde et de l'Asie du Sud.

Comaroff, J. (1985) *Body of Power, Spirit of Resistance*, Chicago: University of Chicago Press.

Dirks, N.B. (1987) *The Hollow Crown: Ethnohistory of an Indian Kingdom*, Cambridge: Cambridge University Press.

Dumont, L. (1972) *Homo Hierarchicus: The Caste System and its Implications*, London: Granada.

Forrester, D.B. (1980) *Caste and Christianity: Attitudes and Policies on Caste of Anglo Saxon Protestant Missionaries in India*, London: Curzon Press.

Fuller, C.J. (1992) *The Camphor Flame: Popular Hinduism and Society in India*, Princeton, NJ: Princeton University Press.

Hocart, A.M. (1950) *Caste: A Comparative Study*, London: Methuen.

Houtart, F. (n.d.) *A Socio-religious Analysis of East Ramnad District*, report prepared for the Madurai Archdiocese.

Irudayaraj, X. (ed.) (1990) *Emerging Dalit Theology*, Madras and Madurai: Jesuit Theological Secretariat and Tamilnadu Theological Seminary.

Ludden, D. (1985) *Peasant History in South India*, Princeton, NJ: Princeton University Press.

Mandlebaum, D.G. (1966) 'Transcendental and pragmatic aspects of religion', *American Anthropologist* 68: 1174–91.

Mosse, D. (1986) 'Caste, Christianity and Hinduism: a study of social organisation and religion in rural Ramnad', unpublished DPhil thesis, University of Oxford.

—— (1994) 'Catholic saints and the Hindu village pantheon in rural Tamil Nadu', *Man* 28: 1–32.

—— (in press) 'Idioms of subordination and styles of protest among Christian and Hindu Harijan (untouchable) castes in Tamil Nadu', *Contributions to Indian Sociology*.

—— (forthcoming) 'Honour, caste and conflict: the ethnohistory of a Catholic festival in rural Tamil Nadu (1730–1990)', in (provisional title) *Christianisme et Islam en Milieu Hindou: Pratiques et Debates*, Paris: Centre d'Etudes de l'Inde et de l'Asie du Sud.

—— (n.d.) 'Tamil Roman Catholics, purity and impurity and the caste system', unpublished ms.

Neill, S. (1984) *A History of Christianity in India, I: The Beginnings to AD 1707*, Cambridge: Cambridge University Press.

Omvedt, G. (1990) 'Hinduism and politics', *Economic and Political Weekly*, 7 April 723–9.

Pickering, W.S.F. (1992) 'Introduction: old positions and new concerns', *Journal of the Anthropological Society of Oxford* 23, 2: 99–110.

Prabhakar, M.E. (ed.) (1989) *Towards a Dalit Theology*, Delhi: Indian Society for Promoting Christian Knowledge.

Reiniche, M.-L. (1979) *Les Dieux et les Hommes: Etude des Cultes d'un Village du Tirunelveli, Inde de Sud*, Paris: Mouton.

Saint-Cyr, L. (1865). 'Letter, 17 Sept. 1841', in J. Bertrand (ed.), *Lettres Edifiantes et Curieuses de la Nouvelles Mission de Maduré*, Tome 2, Paris – Lyon.

Shiri, G. (1982) *Christian Social Thought in India, 1962–77*, Madras: The Christian Literature Society.

Shorter, A. (1988) *Towards a Theology of Inculturation*, London: Geoffrey Chapman.

Stein, B. (1980) *Peasant State and Society in Medieval South India*, Delhi: Oxford University Press.

Stirrat, R.L. (1979) 'A Catholic shrine in its social context', *Sri Lanka Journal of Social Science*, 2: 77–108.

—— (1992) *Power and Religiosity in a Post-Colonial Setting: Sinhala Catholics in Contemporary Sri Lanka*, Cambridge: Cambridge University Press.

5 Ritual, power and colonial domination

Male initiation among the Ngaing of Papua New Guinea

Wolfgang Kempf

The Western presence had a deep-reaching effect on the male cult and secret initiation rites that were a central component of the social and cultural life of many of Papua New Guinea's societies. Systematic studies focusing specifically on changes in this male ritual sphere have rarely been undertaken. Ethnographic interest has thus far primarily been concentrated on societies with allegedly archaic ritual systems, seemingly part of the continuity of precolonial tradition (for example, Herdt 1982). Preference for an ethnography of timeless and authentic male ritual activities was linked to a specific conceptualization of change. While the creeping influence of the Western world in the ethnographic present was viewed as a process only involving the periphery of the cultural system, leaving (for the time being) certain core domains intact, further Western penetration mainly evoked visions of future decline and demise. This notion of change, which confined itself to diagnosing future cultural *tristesse*, stressed the continuity and authenticity of the investigated ritual system. 'The great narrative of entropy and loss' (Clifford 1988: 14) was constitutive for research into Papua New Guinea's male cults and initiation rites.

That missionary activities and colonization have led to the disappearance of a considerable number of such ritual complexes is beyond question. Mention need only be made, as representative of this development, of the Gahuku-Gama of the Eastern Highlands (Read 1952, 1980) or the Ilahita Arapesh of the East Sepik region (Tuzin 1980) – both of whom have, in the meantime, abandoned their male cult practices and initiation rites (Read 1986, Tuzin 1989). But even when ritual activities do disappear, this is invariably preceded by a differentiated historical process which, depending on the local specifics of colonial influence, could be sustained across variously long time periods, and result in new diversities emerging in ritual life.

However, the dissolution of male ritual is by no means an inevitable outcome. Incorporation of indigenous cultures within colonial Western structures has also given rise, on the local level, to numerous processes of invention within the fields of male ritual activity, which have proved durable enough. This chapter will attempt to point up these phenomena of change in the male cult and secret initiation arenas.

The focus of attention here will be on changes to men's ritual activities in Yawing,[1] a village belonging to the Ngaing linguistic group and located in the hinterland of the Rai Coast in the northeast of Papua New Guinea (see Figure 3). As a result of the encounter with Western hegemonic[2] structures, men's initiation rites among the Yawing underwent significant changes: circumcision was introduced and made into a central component of local initiation. The presentation of secret paraphernalia such as gourd instruments and bull-roarers, which used to be at the heart of initiation, has now declined in importance. However, ritual introduction to handling these objects

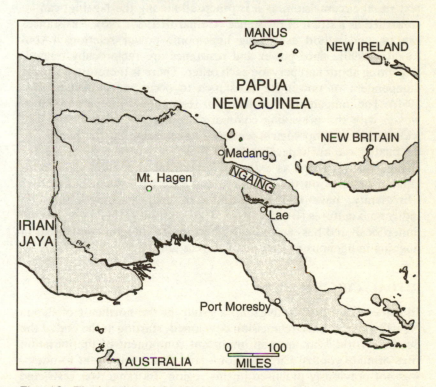

Figure 3 The location of the Ngaing, Papua New Guinea

continues to be respected as a domain of local knowledge and power. This attention to the phenomena of change in connection with men's ritual practices represents, indeed, an altered perspective, a move towards a historical approach to rituals. In this chapter, I investigate the historical processes that led, in Yawing, to the establishment of the circumcision ritual. I will be concerned to show how colonial discourses and practices have pervaded indigenous space and bodies alike, permitting a terrain of power structures to emerge that query local forms of knowledge and power. I would like to show that the Yawing, as a result of their experience with colonial contestations of local discourses and practices, were led to take over the circumcision ritual in order to reconstitute their own power domains. Here it can, I think, be cogently argued, that in the course of colonial encounters and influence, the Yawing have internalized white discourses to the point where they now draw on the very same argumentation to formulate their resistance.

In the following pages I will attempt to show that in a colonial context ritual circumcision, as it is practised among the Ngaing, can be construed as a ritual of resistance (Comaroff 1985: 196). Resistances can be understood as tracing hegemonic power relations (Abu-Lughod 1990), since power and resistance are reciprocally related; they bring about and pervade each other. There is therefore no space independent of power for resistance to occur in (Foucault 1978, 1980). The indigenous articulation of resistance is inseparably inter-woven with the prevailing colonial discourses (Kaplan 1990). The widespread anthropological tendency to celebrate the 'authentic', to be fixated on unchangeable 'traditions', is partly responsible for change being treated as external, superficial and, ultimately, marginal. I believe, on the contrary, that external influences, such as Christianity, have had a multitude of deep-reaching effects on indigenous cultures (Barker 1992). The 'external/global' pervades the 'inner/local' and has, accordingly, become an integral component in ongoing indigenous articulation (Marcus and Fischer 1986: 77).

RITUAL CIRCUMCISION

In some villages of the Ngaing, a group in the northeast of Papua New Guinea, ritual circumcision developed, starting at the end of the Second World War, into an important component of the initiation rites of male youths. Circumcision – and this is important to note – was not previously practised in this region. Its range was restricted to the Austronesian-speaking coastal populations. Most of my field research was carried out in Yawing, a village in the upper part of Ngaing territory. Here circumcision has been conducted for more than four decades. In Yawing, it is stressed that circumcision belongs to the innovations of local ritual life and is, in fact, the 'tradition' of the coastal people. The men, however, certify that they have not given up their traditional practices as a result. They are proud of their secret instruments, made from gourd components. These instruments must be washed at river sections exclusively reserved for this purpose, before they can be played in the men's house or at nighttime dance festivals.[3] Men continue to compose new melodies for the gourd instruments and are moved when they hear old ones being played. Old men tell stories of earlier initiations into this secret domain, of how they were presented with these instruments and the bullroarers for the first time, of what hardships, fears and physical torments they had to go through then. The men in Yawing still to this day consider the secret gourd instruments and bullroarers, along with the accompanying cult practices, as an integral part of their tradition and, as such, meriting their respect. Old men certify that knowledge of how to perform traditional initiation rites is in fact still at hand. At the same time, they express the conviction that Western influence has heavily transformed their local world so that the ritual practices of the ancestors alone no longer suffice. Thus circumcision has come to be considered a vital step on the way to full masculinity.

Circumcision was probably introduced in Yawing at the beginning of the fifties. The accounts given by the men involved at the time all agree that it was an indigenous medical orderly stationed in Yawing who first put them on to practising circumcision. This orderly, who had received a basic Western medical training, came from Meibu, a village of the Rawa people in the adjoining Finisterre Range. Here, it was stated, circumcision had already made inroads. The justification repeatedly tendered in connection with the introduction of circumcision was that whites also practise circumcision. Allusion, for example, is made to the practice of circumcision in local Papua New Guinean hospitals, where white doctors are said to have performed such operations as treatment for venereal diseases and to have recommended its use as a hygienic measure.

The men of Yawing attach fundamental importance to the argument that maternal blood is 'impure', 'makes sick' and is 'black'. This female blood must be removed from the body of a male adolescent. Only when nothing but 'pure', 'bright' blood predominates can he become a healthy and powerful man, a man whose skin 'shines'. An older man, who was among the first men in Yawing to undergo circumcision, put it this way:

> When our mother brings us into the world and [our umbilical cord] is cut from our belly [pointing to the navel], then a part of it remains. They cut the umbilical cord and some of our mother's blood remains in us . . . and that is why this is done . . . [Lowering his voice] We are circumcised to get this bad blood out so that only fresh, new blood is left. Then we are strong. Strong enough to fight . . . To go on the hunt, to go hunting with bow and arrow. Or women and all that.

In Yawing, circumcision is mostly undertaken when there are from three to six candidates. The circumcision that I was able to attend took place in the bush near a small hamlet. The initiates were permitted to eat their fill for a last time – this was also referred to as the 'last supper' – before having to submit to various purification procedures. The area where the circumcision was to be performed was associated with a mythical old woman said to have lived there in earlier times. Shortly before the circumcision rite, the candidates had to make a 'confession of sins' (called *konfesio* in Tok Pisin), in which each youth had to disclose to his guardian, or to the circumciser, the exact number of times he had indulged in premarital sex. Then followed a longitudinal incision on the foreskin. The 'pure' blood, which flowed out after the black maternal blood, was caught in small bamboo tubes or flasks and, later on, partly mixed with oil. The containers with this mixture of blood and oil were tied up with the bullroarers so as to form a bundle, which was then handed over to the young man for careful safekeeping. The bundle is considered to help him increase his attractiveness; with its aid, he can 'bind to him' the wife he will later take; it will also serve, from time to time, to fortify his declining male powers. In strict isolation from women, candidates then observed a three- to four-week period of seclusion. During this time, they were also instructed in traditional knowledge and practices. They had to observe taboos on food and water, submit to further ritual procedures intended to fortify themselves, and receive moral instruction. The clan elders not infrequently considered it crucial to induct initiates into the men's secret domain – seen as having been of fundamental importance in earlier times. Thus initiates were shown bullroarers (*ngumbung walinang*) which, when bound to a long cord and rotated in the air, produce sounds. Their use was considered important for assuring the success of the hunt. Frequently too, the initiates' camp resounded with the reverberations of the gourd instruments, as both novices and overseers joined in with equal alacrity. The night before the public presentation of the newly circumcised young men, their bundles were readied and preparations made for the decorations that were to follow. After watch had been kept the whole night – mainly spent playing the secret *tambaran* instruments – the decoration of the initiates took place at first light. First they were thoroughly cleansed and then an array of different mixtures was rubbed in to make the skin 'shine'. Dressed in European clothes, wearing a feather in their hair, carrying on the left shoulder a netbag (which contained their bundle), the initiates were then ceremoniously presented in public.

For many Yawing these secret practices of the men are quite compatible with the Christian faith, which they have adhered to for decades. They are convinced that the missionaries – and incidentally all whites – only present them with superficial truths while keeping the really important knowledge for themselves. The Yawing therefore think it essential to study the 'outer' representations if their 'inner' meanings are to be got at. Thus the Bible has become an important source of legitimation of their ritual activities. For instance, Jesus' baptism by John the Baptist at the River Jordan has come to be associated with displaying the traditional gourd instruments. John is considered to be Jesus' classificatory mother's brother and, as such, is held to have initiated him into the domain of the secret gourd instruments which, as it happens, are associated with water. The Yawing men know too that Jesus was circumcised. The young men particularly interpret the crucifixion of Jesus as his ritual circumcision. The Last Supper is, accordingly, compared with the last meal eaten by the Yawing candidates the evening before their circumcision. Judas is not considered as a betrayer but as Jesus' classificatory mother's brother. He led him to Pontius Pilate who, for his part, was a member of an oppositional patriclan and thus responsible for the circumcision. Pilate is believed to have questioned Jesus thoroughly on his premarital affairs but could not establish that Jesus had 'sinned'. This cross-examination is the equivalent of the confession conducted before circumcision at Yawing. Then the crucifixion took place, this being nothing but Jesus' circumcision. The three days after Jesus' death are interpreted as his three weeks of seclusion. Finally, the resurrection is identified with the public presentation of the initiates at the close of the circumcision rites.

COLONIAL DISCOURSES

Initiation in Yawing, with its new and 'traditional' elements, emerged from the encounter with Western colonial discourses and practices. The Yawing region first came under influence from the missions in the twenties. The Rhenish Mission Society had despatched a Samoan pastor to the Rai Coast, along with indigenous evangelists. These ambassadors of the Lutheran mission first focused on the coastal strip, but soon turned their attention to the immediate hinterland. Their mission work in and around Madang convinced the Rhenish Mission that the men's ritual activities, centring on secret gourd instruments and a *haus tambaran* off-limits for women, were a cardinal barrier to their conversion to Christianity:

> In New Guinea it is a secret cult, a bizarre ceremony, to which only the male world has access. Whatever has anything in the least to do with the ceremony is assiduously kept from the women and enveloped in the darkness of an awe-inspiring secret . . . It is a remarkable but demonstrable fact that the repeated murder and conspiracy designs mounted against the rule and lives of the whites were devised and brought to fruition at these Mesiab or Asa festivities [= secret cult]. This secret cult is also the mightiest bulwark of Papuan heathendom.
>
> (Rheinische Missions-Berichte 1918: 55)[4]

The Lutheran mission saw their task as bringing the 'Light of the Gospel' to the dark spaces of indigenous 'heathendom'. By discursively constituting uncontrolled spaces, which were presented as a threat to white dominance, the mission justified their claim to power and their manner of operation. The avowed aim was to shine light into secrecy, inwardness, darkness, and to reorganize and control these spheres. Between 1925 and 1930, attempts to translate the missionaries' vision of Christianized space did in fact get under way. A tabooed area (*tut*), held to be an ancestral precinct, was cleared of vegetation so that a house for the evangelists and missionaries could be erected there. Scattered hamlets were moved to a single large settlement in Yawing where a church was then erected. In preparation for baptism, secret paraphernalia (gourd instruments, bullroarers etc.) were exposed and burned in order to clear the way for a Christian life. The indigenous body was to be brought under control and cleansed; it was to be transformed from a dirty, not particularly industrious body – such as might frequently be encountered at nightly dance festivities wearing traditional ornamentation – into a clean, disciplined body attired in European apparel. For all that many Yawing were initially cooperative, there were some who resisted these Lutheran demands and carried the secret paraphernalia to safety. When an epidemic eventually broke out in the new settlement – evidently costing a large number of the local people their lives – the cause was seen as lying in the public destruction of the secret objects. Hence those voices in Yawing who were committed to preserving the traditional order soon regained the upper hand (Kempf 1992).

Support for the men's ritual activities and their retention proved forthcoming from the Australian administration, which not only viewed them as an area of local tradition worth preserving, but also perceived an interest in averting armed conflict between those favouring and opposing abolition of male cult practices. In the thirties, the administration tried to promote exploration of the region and to bring the resident populations under their control. Pacification and mapping of indigenous space were important prerequisites for regular patrolling by administration officials. The population was instructed to maintain pathways, build proper housing, install latrines, and keep the villages clean; people were made to turn out before the administration officials and be counted, registered and medically examined. Violations were punished by forced labour or imprisonment. Thus the administration created a colonized space, consecrated to hard work, order, hygiene and law-abiding habits, and geared to promoting the development of the indigenous people.

Towards the end of the forties there originated a politico-religious movement named after its figurehead, Yali, who came from a Ngaing village. Stimulated by Yali's concern with local religion, the people began to devote themselves more closely to their own traditions, the result being that the traditional *tambaran* activities were intensified (see Lawrence 1964; Hermann 1992, n.d.). Disappointed by the whites – especially the missionaries, who, in the eyes of many, refused to share their knowledge and wealth – the people started to revive their ancestral religion systematically in the hope of attaining white living standards. Missionaries and administration officials soon found themselves confronted with ritual activities aimed at acquiring Western goods – hence dubbed 'cargo cults'. The hostility to the mission shown by the movement prompted the Lutherans especially to conduct intensive enquiries, which linked the men's secret cult to the so-called 'cargo cult' practices. The very fact that the men's cult had been revived was interpreted by the missionaries as a sign that Christianity had not really been internalized, but simply 'put on like a new robe over a soiled body' (Wagner 1949: 3). Missionary discourse of uncontrolled, subversive 'inner' space – the preserve of a 'cargo' movement which not only showed anti-European tendencies, but was accused of having had the temerity to assume the administration's functions – finally made the Australian administration enter the lists too. Countermeasures seemed called for to deal with this challenge to white dominance and restore order. Here, for the first time, the administration deemed it appropriate to penalize *tambaran* activities. Years later an administration official summed up the situation as follows:

> The legal position I believe is that the Tamboran Singsing has never been gazetted as being prohibited. The actual position at present is that apparently several years ago during some disturbances the singsing was forbidden. When the trouble was over the natives were told they could dance the 'outside' part of the ceremony but the 'inside' ceremony remained forbidden because of past associations with cultism. I have maintained the status quo but from what I can find out I can see no objection to the Tamboran Singsing practised in the manner of their ancestors.
>
> (Dyer 1956/7: 5)

The prohibition was, in fact, at the people's instigation, lifted several years later when the administration considered the situation to have more or less returned to normality. Care was still taken to send out regular patrols, to keep the local situation under continuous scrutiny and extend the presence of administrative power. The administration took the view, though, that in the long run only school education and incorporating subsistence farmers into the Western cash economy could counteract indigenous ideas of ritual acquisition of Western goods. The upshot of this policy was that, initially in the fifties, growing European vegetables for sale on the local markets was encouraged in Yawing. Later this was displaced by coffee growing, which until the present remains the main source of income. The region's school education remained almost exclusively in the hands of the Lutheran and Catholic missions. The latter was able to expand its influence after initiating its activities in 1933, achieving its first successes among the Ngaing in the villages adjacent to the coastal region. From the fifties on, more and more of the Yawing people passed through the Catholic-run schools – after they had begun to open up to the Catholic mission. The main reason for this new orientation was that the Catholics had become known as more tolerant than the Lutherans towards local tradition. Today the majority of the Yawing people are Catholic, which, in my opinion, has contributed to the fact that a local combination consisting of the 'traditional' *tambaran* and the newly accreted practice of circumcision could emerge in the form it did.

For more than seventy years the men's ritual practices have been exposed to the assaults of the colonial regime. With colonial penetration, discourses and practices were launched which denounced indigenous spheres – like the *tambaran* – as 'dark', immoral, backward, intimidating and criminal, and which established and routinized the indigenous body as dirty, disease-prone and undisciplined. Thus a colonial terrain of power and knowledge was set up that perpetually controlled, occupied, relocated and reorganized indigenous space and body. For the Yawing men, this colonial experience meant a devaluation of their own spheres of power, such as their *tambaran* activities.

Introduction of circumcision represented a change in the men's ritual practices, one that allowed the Yawing to reclaim their indigenous space and bodies against the colonial power. Like the white doctors in New Guinea, the Yawing could now draw on the medical discourse of hygiene and health when ritually purifying their black male bodies. But, at the same time, the men invoked their own ritual practices and local knowledge in order to perform successful circumcision and provide the young men with powerful substances for their future lives. Like the European priests, the Yawing could now invoke the Bible too – but in connection with ritual circumcision. At the same time, the Yawing men laid claim to their own reading of circumcision as redemption and cleansing from sin, the 'confession of sins' being heard shortly before the operation and Jesus' crucifixion being interpreted as his circumcision. The indigenous association of *tambaran* practices with Jesus' baptism in the River Jordan is located in this discursive field of redemption from sin too. Associating *tambaran* and circumcision with key passages from Jesus' life permits the ritual practices to be correlated and evaluated – by virtue of their sequence – whereby circumcision emerges as the more dramatic of these events. By means of these discourses and practices, the Yawing attempt to constitute anew their secret 'inner' power spaces, their male bodies, their local knowledge of practices and meanings; they are, in so doing, opposing a colonial order premised on the ascribed inferiority of black skin and culture.

WHITENESS/BLACKNESS

Change in Melanesia, induced by the West's influence on indigenous societies, was frequently treated in anthropological studies as an external phenomenon that had no impact on core areas of tradition (Barker 1992: 149–52). For instance, Peter Lawrence and Mervyn Meggitt, in their introduction to a reader on Melanesian religions, expressed the following opinion:

> In spite of the extensive consequences of the impact of the West, Seaboard religions have proved far more durable than is generally supposed. The changes introduced impinged mainly on the super-structure of native life, the external form of the socio-cultural order.
>
> (Lawrence and Meggitt 1965: 21)[5]

This concept of change in indigenous societies assumes a stable traditional culture, capable of being authentically transmitted as a self-contained system. But precisely this fixation on 'authentic tradition' can no longer be plausibly maintained. Allan Hanson (1989) has succeeded in bringing out clearly, with reference to Derrida's philosophy of difference (1976, 1978), that change happens *en permanence*. The assumption of a tradition that remains constant implies that an original meaning has been logocentrically fixed upon, a centre from which all other meanings have been derived. Derrida has called in question this presence of a transcendental signified, which can dispense with signifiers and eludes signification (1978). Instead, he postulates an infinite alterability of meanings – a sign-substitution in an open-ended play of signification within systems of difference (Derrida 1978: 280). This approach has been usefully deployed by Hanson to permit the analysis of processes of change (see Hanson 1989: 898–9). Jettisoning the concept of traditional culture as a fixed, transmissible corpus in favour of that of an open system of ongoing cultural construction (Linnekin 1992) also opens up a new perspective on religious change. The cultural construction approach encourages a decentred view of change, construing it as a continuous motion devoid of both origin and the fixed point of 'tradition'. 'Truth' and 'tradition' are viewed now as discursive configurations, as objects of dialogic processes, of history in the making.

Historical practice, as shown in the previous section, does not occur in a power-free space. Yawing is a colonized space where the black inhabitants define themselves in relation to whites. The subtle processes of hegemonic domination have resulted in the incorporation of colonial hierarchies into body and mind. White skin, in a colonial context, came to represent purity, power, knowledge, prosperity and moral superiority. With the internalization of white discourse predicated on the fundamental inferiority of black skin and culture, white skin acquired an aura of redemption from blackness (Lattas 1992). Incorporated into the network of colonial ascriptions, the Yawing perceive themselves as black, unclean, powerless and peripheral.

A narrative that circulates among the men makes this clear. In their portrayal of Creation, the first tree was a type of palm, whose parts can be found inside the Earth, keeping the world from breaking apart. This palm tree represents ultimate power and is associated with the Holy Trinity by some. Most importantly, the wood of this palm is used to make the bullroarers, the means through which this power can be manipulated, through which the cosmos can be influenced. The Yawing men are convinced that the white interior plays a decisive role in the growth of this palm, and hold this whiteness to represent the whites who have the capability to produce tangible, sophisticated things like cars, aeroplanes, factories and the like. The black exterior enclosing the inner white part of the palm merely plays a supportive role in the eyes of the Yawing, who inter- pret this as representing the blacks themselves, who are incapable of producing anything on their own. Thus the tree as a symbol of real power now stands for the colonial hierarchy in which the blacks are doomed to lead a powerless, peripheral existence. Nevertheless, this narrative also expresses the Yawing men's significant insight that this inner (white) power constitutes the central element of their local world. In addition, this story also explains the secret of the bull- roarers, which, as 'external' objects, are able to mobilize this 'internal' power. Whiteness is construed as the inner condition of blackness and hence as manipulable, as susceptible to influence.

The ritualized purification of the male body of dark, female substances should also be seen against the colonial background. This represents an attempt by the men to counteract their social (de-) placement and marginalization. The Yawing men claim to possess the knowledge and ritual practice to constitute an altered external appearance and efficacy, this being achieved by modifying the body inside:[6] pure, bright, male blood is essential for a 'shining' skin, for a masculine body, for the ability to prevail in a colonial environment. It is apparent that gender constructions are woven together in the structures of black and white. The construction of maleness through the ritual of circumcision is developed in relation to femaleness[7] – which, depending on context, can be seen as negative/contaminating/ black or as positive/creative/white. The men point out that circumci- sion serves to remove the black, polluting maternal blood so that full masculinity can be attained. Here black/polluting is associated with femaleness. However, this negative association of black and female is not invariably found.

Femaleness can also be associated with powerful/white. Thus Yawing circumcision was performed at a place within a locality that had once belonged to a mythical old woman. The story goes that the woman had disappeared after an earthquake, only then to appear in a dream to an initiate while he was undergoing his period of seclusion. Together with the other ancestors, she was present in the circumcision area as a white woman. The latter location, the place of the construction of masculinity, was here associated with femaleness/power/white. The men resort to circumcision in order to approximate discursively to whites and thus set up a field of power where women are contained. The women's presence is essential if this power relationship is to be constructed. Given the colonial hegemony of the whites, power appears synonymous with the condition of whiteness. Circumcision constructs the gender relationship within the framework of this colonial situation.

Both ritual circumcision and the narrative of the crucifixion as circumcision – also that of the true nature of the palm tree – are local forms that subvert colonial power relationships. By placing the focus on these small, local resistances (and those treated here represent only a small fraction) I do not wish to be taken as presenting an image of romantic refuges, beyond the influence of colonial power. Rather I have attempted to come to grips with the relational character of power and resistance. Resistance cannot exist outside the constellations of power (Foucault 1978: 95–6; 1980: 142). Resistance is woven into power relationships and can therefore function as 'diagnostic of power' (Abu-Lughod 1990: 42). The ritual of circumcision and the narratives told by the Yawing men signify controversies with colonial power; they are expressions of a struggle for meaning. This creative and subversive appropriation of meaning invariably also involves contradiction and paradox (Kondo 1990: 222–5). Through the meaning they attach to the crucifixion, for example, Yawing men subversively appropriate the central Christian scenario of forgiveness and redemption from sin. But in their struggles to escape from Christian ascriptions of 'sinful', 'black' etc., they reproduce this 'Manichean' discourse and so contribute to the legitimation of Christian concepts and images. Here Christianity has clearly become an essential component of local culture. The Yawing formulate and practise their resistance, but without being able to escape the hegemony of the white culture. There is no space in their local world that lies beyond this power relationship. A narrative is told among the young men in Yawing which serves to illustrate this once again.

THE CITY OUTSIDE/INSIDE

The story is told of a young man who wants to flee from a marriage arranged by his parents. The local white missionary procures a passport for him, and so the young man arrives in a big city outside of Papua New Guinea. However, he is unable to find his bearings in the big city. The young man drifts around aimlessly until he finds a white woman who feels sorry for him. She takes him home with her. When her husband comes home from work that evening they eat together. During the conversation, the two whites finally disclose that they are his deceased grandparents. He may stay with them, but is informed that a particular room is taboo to him. When he does secretly enter the room he cannot perceive anything at all. It is dark. His grandparents observe that the taboo has been broken and send him back to his village to undergo the rite of circumcision. He returns to his village in Papua New Guinea, goes through the ritual, and sets off once again for the city. When he meets his grandparents he certifies that he has been circumcised, whereupon he is allowed to enter the forbidden room. Once he gets inside he can behold his village, his parents, the place where he was circumcised, and other things. He can even hear them talking. It is understood that he is still in the city.

The Yawing know that their dead turn into whites and that they live in places resembling those of the whites. This knowledge is revealed to them in dreams, visions and states of trance. The candidates whose initiation I could observe lived in an area of seclusion identified as a 'city' several years ago by a ritual specialist. The dreams of these candidates during their seclusion dealt with ancestors who appeared as whites in such 'city' surroundings. Explicit reference was made to the correspondence of the dreams with the trance reports of the ritual specialist.

When the Yawing perceive their dead as whites in a Western environment – or tabooed places as 'cities' populated by 'whites' – the power of whites is, by implication, transformed into the power of their own ancestors. Perceiving the local world from inside the tabooed room is tantamount to adopting the perspective of the dead, their own ancestors – and thus being in a position of power. The important point is that the act of circumcision lays the foundation for assuming this position of power; this first requires removal of the impurity that leads to 'darkness' and impedes the acquisition of knowledge. These constructions evolve from rituals such as circumcision and, for this reason, ritual plays a vital role in historical practice (Kelly 1988). The practice and experience of circumcision define the male body; the authority of the ancestors (as whites) is created through performance of the ritual (see Kelly 1988: 54). Ritual acquires this power by virtue of its restrictive nature. The participants must submit themselves to a higher authority (the whites/ancestors), and partake in the realization of this authority during the ritual act (Kelly 1988: 54; Kelly and Kaplan 1990: 139–41). The Yawing draw on ritual circumcision to deconstruct colonial definitions of black and white, outer and inner, thus revealing that outer appearance embodies a different and powerful interior. The Yawing draw on these constructions to make of the whites and their world the most powerful aspect of their own world. But when they attempt to appropriate the knowledge and power of the whites by making their own ancestors into whites – that is, by discursively creating a common origin and kinship ties – the Yawing concede the superiority of white skin and culture. Paradoxically, their subversion of colonial power relationships contributes to these being reproduced. Their resistance cannot be conceived of as a separate entity; it possesses no 'authentic niche' beyond the reach of colonial power; instead it is linked in with the hegemony of white culture. Blackness without whiteness has become no longer conceivable. Caught up in this complex situation – which frequently leads to contradictions – the Yawing organize their life in their local world.

CONCLUSION

The introduction and ongoing practice of ritual circumcision is closely associated with the colonial hegemony of Western culture. The inferiority experienced vis-à-vis the white colonizers – the diabolization, criminalization and partial suspension of ritual activities in the process of establishment of colonial domination – left behind men who perceived themselves as weak, unmanly and powerless. This experience of being deprived of power engendered resistance in the Yawing, drawing them into a continuous struggle for meaning. Through their refigurations of colonial ascriptions, they lay claim to the power to define the relationship and the true nature of inner and outer. Ritual circumcision enables knowledge to be elicited, and given currency, to the effect that 'blackness' is predicated on 'whiteness', that black bodies, indigenous culture and local environment *embody* 'whiteness'. The circumcised man with his pure, clear, male blood, the bundle consisting of containers of pure circumcision blood with the bullroarers wrapped around, the primeval palm tree in the Earth's interior endowed with a white centre and black outer covering, the tabooed room in the distant city affording a view back into the local world in New Guinea – these are various manifestations of their model of power. The Yawing men fashion themselves and their world into embodiments of external, white power. The whites have become *central* to the Yawing; possessing power is now, for them, synonymous with reference to the white presence.

Intrinsic to the new initiation ritual would seem to be the fundamental paradox that incorporation and distancing are conjoined. Adoption of circumcision was both a reaction to the colonial devaluation of indigenous ritual activities and an adaptation to a different, altered world. But by incorporating the circumcision ritual an act of distancing has also been performed, whereby the Yawing integrate their own 'traditions' that enable them to set themselves off from the Europeans (see Keesing 1989). 'Tradition' among the Yawing would no longer be conceivable without these new elements. Circumcision helps to constitute 'tradition' (for example, in the male cult domain); it specifies 'old' local traditional knowledge and practices and is therefore integrally involved in its construction. Ritual activities are not an expression of authenticity; rather they produce authenticity. The making of men should be seen as an integral component of indigenous history making within the framework of colonial power relationships. 'Authentic traditions' are products of their respective historical contexts and, as such, are cultural constructs of an indigenous past that are subjected to contemporary conditions of knowledge and power. Present-day initiation rites in Yawing indicate that men's ritual activities, irrespective of whether they are maintained or disappear, can only be adequately understood if these practices are construed as the result of the interaction of 'inside' and 'outside', as reticulations of local culture and global influences.

NOTES

Fieldwork among the Ngaing in Papua New Guinea was conducted between 1988 and 1990. I am most grateful to my Ngaing informants for sharing with me their knowledge and philosophies in the making. The project was generously supported by a postgraduate scholarship, made available under the 'Landesgraduiertenfoerderungsgesetz' of the state of Baden-Württemberg, as well as by an additional grant from the German Academic Exchange Service (DAAD). The 'Tübinger Stipendienstiftung' provided funds for attending the EASA conference in Prague, where this paper was first presented. Thanks to Bruce Allen, who has translated my manuscripts into English. For critical reading and helpful comments on preliminary versions

I wish to thank Thomas Schweizer, Rosalind Shaw, Charles Stewart and, above all, Elfriede Hermann.

1 The name is a pseudonym.
2 In anthropology, the Gramscian concept of hegemony (Gramsci 1971) has gained considerable recognition in recent years; the concept covers forms of domination in which the colonized adopt, internalize and reproduce the discourse of the colonizers (for example, Comaroff 1985: 196–7, 261; Keesing 1989: 25; Ortner 1984: 149).
3 In the Ngaing vernacular this ritual domain of the men is called *gabu*, in Tok Pisin – the lingua franca of Papua New Guinea – *tambaran*.
4 The text has been translated from German into English.
5 The editors introduced the term 'Seaboard religions', since a distinction was made, in their volume of collected essays, between the 'highland societies' of Papua New Guinea and other Melanesian societies that had settled the islands, the coasts and the coastal hinterland. The Ngaing, whose traditional religion was described in this volume by Peter Lawrence (see Lawrence 1965), were assigned to the 'Seaboard religions' group.
6 M. Strathern's insights on 'knowledge about internal capacity or enablement, and about external efficacy in interaction with others' (1988: 128) have helped me to clarify this point.
7 On the relational character of gender constructions see M. Strathern (1988). She has investigated this relationship between maleness and femaleness, though not within the framework of a black–white hierarchy.

REFERENCES

Abu-Lughod, L. (1990) 'The romance of resistance: tracing transformations of power through Bedouin women', *American Ethnologist* 17: 41–55.
Barker, J. (1992) 'Christianity in western Melanesian ethnography', in J.G. Carrier (ed.), *History and Tradition in Melanesian Anthropology*, Berkeley: University of California Press.
Clifford, J. (1988) *The Predicament of Culture: Twentieth-Century Ethnography, Literature, and Art*, Cambridge, MA: Harvard University Press.
Comaroff, J. (1985) *Body of Power, Spirit of Resistance: The Culture and History of a South African People*, Chicago: University of Chicago Press.
Derrida, J. (1976) *Of Grammatology*, Baltimore: Johns Hopkins University Press.
—— (1978) *Writing and Difference*, Chicago: University of Chicago Press.
Dyer, K.W. (1956/7) 'Patrol Report Saidor No. 4 of 1956/57, Saidor Subdistrict, Madang District', unpublished ms, National Archives of Papua New Guinea, Waigani.
Foucault, M. (1978) *The History of Sexuality. Vol. 1: An Introduction*, New York: Random House.
—— (1980) *Power/Knowledge: Selected Interviews and Other Writings, 1972–1977*, ed. C. Gordon, New York: Pantheon Books.
Gramsci, A. (1971) *Selections from the Prison Notebooks*, eds Q. Hoare and G.N. Smith, New York: International Publishers.
Hanson, A. (1989) 'The making of the Maori: culture invention and its logic', *American Anthropologist* 91: 890–902.

Herdt, G.H. (ed.) (1982) *Rituals of Manhood: Male Initiation in Papua New Guinea*, Berkeley: University of California Press.

Hermann, E. (1992) 'The Yali movement in retrospect: rewriting history, redefining "Cargo Cult"', *Oceania* 63: 55–71.

—— (n.d.) '"Kastom" Versus "Cargo Cult": emotional discourse on the Yali movement in Madang Province, Papua New Guinea', paper presented at the First European Colloquium on Pacific Studies, Nijmegen.

Kaplan, M. (1990) 'Meaning, agency and colonial history: Navosavakadua and the Tuka movement in Fiji', *American Ethnologist* 17: 1–20.

Keesing, R.M. (1989) 'Creating the past: custom and identity in the Pacific', *The Contemporary Pacific* 1–2: 16–35.

Kelly, J.D. (1988) 'From Holi to Diwali in Fiji: an essay on ritual and history', *Man* 23: 40–55.

Kelly, J.D. and Kaplan, M. (1990) 'History, structure, and ritual', *Annual Review of Anthropology* 19: 119–50.

Kempf, W. (1992) '"The second coming of the lord": early Christianization, episodic time and the cultural construction of continuity in Sibog', *Oceania* 63: 72–86.

Kondo, D.K. (1990) *Crafting Selves: Power, Gender, and Discourses of Identity in a Japanese Workplace*, Chicago: University of Chicago Press.

Lattas, A. (1992) 'Skin, personhood, and redemption: the doubled self in west New Britain cargo cults', *Oceania* 63: 27–54.

Lawrence, P. (1964) *Road Belong Cargo*, Melbourne: Melbourne University Press.

—— (1965) 'The Ngaing of the Rai Coast', in P. Lawrence and M.J. Meggitt (eds), *Gods, Ghosts and Men in Melanesia*, Melbourne: Oxford University Press.

Lawrence, P. and Meggitt, M.J. (1965) 'Introduction', in P. Lawrence and M.J. Meggitt (eds), *Gods, Ghosts and Men in Melanesia*, Melbourne: Oxford University Press.

Linnekin, J. (1992) 'On the theory and politics of cultural construction in the Pacific', *Oceania* 62: 249–63.

Marcus, G.E. and Fischer, M.M.J. (1986) *Anthropology as Cultural Critique: An Experimental Moment in the Human Sciences*, Chicago: University of Chicago Press.

Ortner, S.B. (1984) 'Theory in anthropology since the sixties', *Comparative Studies in Society and History* 26: 126–66.

Read, K.E. (1952) 'Nama cult of the Central Highlands, New Guinea', *Oceania* 23: 1–25.

—— (1980) *The High Valley*, New York: Columbia University Press (1st edn 1965).

—— (1986) *Return to the High Valley: Coming Full Circle*, Berkeley: University of California Press.

Rheinische Missions-Berichte (1918) 'Die Arbeitsgebiete der Rheinischen Mission: Deutsch Neu-Guinea (Schluß)' 75: 53–6.

Strathern, M. (1988) *The Gender of the Gift*, Berkeley: University of California Press.

Tuzin, D. (1980) *The Voice of the Tambaran: Truth and Illusion in Ilahita Arapesh Religion*, Berkeley: University of California Press.

—— (1989) 'Visions, prophecies, and the rise of Christian consciousness', in

G. Herdt and M. Stephen (eds), *The Religious Imagination in New Guinea*, New Brunswick and London: Rutgers University Press.
Wagner, H. (1949) 'Offenbarer Rueckfall in's Heidentum an der Rai-Küste', unpublished, Az 52/23, Archives of the Evang.-Luth. Missionsanstalt, Neuendettelsau.

6 Syncretism as a dimension of nationalist discourse in modern Greece

Charles Stewart

Virtually every culture or religion is synthetic; they have all changed over time, adopting and incorporating exogenous elements and ideas along the way. As Hannerz (1987) and others have suggested, creolization, hybridization, interculture, or whatever one wishes to call it, is now the rule not the exception. I would only add that it has probably been this way for a very long time, not just since colonization or the emergence of global capitalism. The notion of a pure tradition is only an ideal but, like the notion of a pure 'race', a potentially dangerous one.

Although syncretism everywhere exists, the recognition of it is far from objective and automatic and cases where syncretism is denied, or left unnoticed, require attention just as much as those cases where it is explicitly recognized. Appropriations and attributions of 'syncretism' are bound to have political motivations and consequences and we must be aware of these, for they contextualize the usual analyses of syncretism which proceed from an objectivist, etic position to describe the cultural hybridity of particular rituals, cults and cosmologies (for example, Herskovits 1937).

The following contribution does not, therefore, attempt to examine and weigh the 'real' evidence for the synthesis of Ancient Greek religion and Christianity in modern Greece. Instead I explore the discourse of syncretism, the various expressed opinions on the subject of Helleno-Christian synthesis which were entertained by Greek society beginning in the last century. At the same time I attempt to situate the political interests underwriting these various statements in the context of European and modern Greek history.

In the last century 'race' was thought to determine the culture of a people and thus there was considerable overlap between domains explicable in terms of 'race' and syncretism. Below I examine how an argument from 'race', namely that the modern Greeks were racially impure and thus not successors to the ancients, was countered by the assertion that they possessed a religion which syncretized Ancient Greek elements, thereby rescuing them as inheritors of the Ancient Hellenes.

Syncretism is a technical, social scientific term, but this does not make it a strictly academic concern, nor should it be allowed to obscure the simplicity of the ideas it introduces. Syncretism asks whether parts of a religion are borrowed and, if so, how these borrowings are used and how their presence should be interpreted. Syncretism poses historical questions about roots, cultural contacts and received influences. These are questions which ordinary people are entirely capable of formulating in their own terms to understand religions as well as other cultural phenomena; anthropological analyses are merely professionalized extensions of this popular mode of thought. At the very least the principles underlying syncretism comprise a mode of describing religion, and at the most they can amount to a theory of religion. Of course anthropology has numerous alternative theories of culture (as sign system, as structure, as process etc.), many of which are less continuous with popular theorizations.

CLASSICISM, PURITY AND THE *BILDUNG* OF EUROPE

Consider the portrayal of classical Greek civilization, as a pure, autochthonous and *sui generis* phenomenon. Not everyone has held this opinion; in fact the Ancient Greeks themselves thought that their culture had borrowed heavily from Egypt. As Bernal (1987) has shown, however, beginning in the early modern period all Near Eastern or African influences of any significance for Ancient Greek culture were steadily excluded, overlooked or otherwise dismissed from European classicists' representations of Ancient Greece. The German classicist K.O. Mueller refined the technique of excluding outside influences into a clear, if flawed, method in his *Introduction to a Science of Mythology* (1825). Here, as in the rest of his work, he assumed that the true Greeks had entered Greek territory from the north and progressively spread their civilization southwards, eventually reaching Egypt and the Near East. He assumed that, 'if similar cults, myths or names could be found in Greece and the Near East, they must be Greek . . . Furthermore, if cults or names were widespread in Greece or the Aegean, they had to be indigenous and not the result of foreign introduction' (Bernal 1987: 311). Mueller maintained these arguments even against the authority of ancient historians such as Herodotus who accepted foreign influence as a fact. These exercises in the 'science of mythology' proceeded as if the Ancient Greeks had foolishly entered into a discourse of syncretic borrowing from the Near East which could be, indeed needed to be, proved false by the methods of philology.

Classicists such as K.O. Mueller were working during a period of German nation-building stimulated, in part, by the Napoleonic invasion and occupation of Prussia in 1806. They were also working in the wake of Herder's and Fichte's formulations of the relativity of cultures and nations, each of which was seen as an essentially unique organism characterized by its own language and customs. Each such nation, it was thought, should ideally have the right to autonomy and self-regulated development (Dumont 1986: 113ff.). It is not surprising that the convictions supporting the construction of the German nation, and indeed the very qualities attributed to this nation, such as philosophical reason, love of music and athleticism, should also influence the historiography of Ancient Greece, especially since the Hellenes were cast as spiritual forebears and fellow Aryans. Purity and autochthony were two important *desiderata* of the ideal nation and they came to be asserted for both Germany and Ancient Greece. Wilhelm von Humboldt, for example, stressed that the chief virtue of the German language was its authenticity and purity, qualities which he also attributed to Ancient Greek (Bernal 1987: 288).

The manifest fact of intercultural contact and borrowing, whether in antiquity or in nineteenth-century Germany, was something of a stumbling block for Herderian cultural relativism. How could cultures be unique if they borrowed elements from one another? This quandary was solved not by denying that contact occurred, but by asserting a hierarchy of cultures in terms of perfection and achievement. The Germans were one such superior nation and as a result they exerted a civilizing influence over other peoples with whom they came into contact (Dumont 1986: 131). The Ancient Greeks were held to share this exemplary quality and Hegel presented the situation in the following terms:

> They [the Greeks] certainly received the substantial beginnings of their religion, culture . . . from Asia, Syria and Egypt; but they have so greatly obliterated the foreign nature of this origin, and it is so much changed, worked on, turned round and altogether made so different, that what they – as we – prize, know and love in it is essentially their own.

> (Cited in Bernal 1987: 295)

This view offers an early example of the rhetoric of encompassment which often features in anti-syncretic denials of borrowing and mixture even in the face of contradictory evidence and competing claims (van der Veer, this volume). Todorov (1984: 185) has broadly labelled this assimilative denial of the other's distinctiveness 'rapprochement', and he considers it one of the three modes of reaction to alterity. German culture, like Greek, was sufficiently developed and integrated to absorb foreign influence without altering its own essential nature.

If Greece had been overcome and influenced by any invaders, then the most significant of these were Dorian Greeks who came from the north, like the Germans themselves. On entering Greek territories (or what would become such) the Dorians amalgamated with other Greeks such as the Ionians, who had migrated earlier but who had been somewhat orientalized through contact with Near Eastern cultures. The Dorians thus reinfused this faltering strand of Hellenism with Greekness and generally raised its level. Elsewhere, they encountered Pelasgians, altogether pre-Hellenic inhabitants of the region, but they had no difficulty in subjugating this primitive population and assimilating them to their own standards. By the late nineteenth century the Dorians came to be seen as very close to Germans in their pure-blooded Aryan-ness. It was even thought by some that they had migrated from the region of what is now Germany into Greece (Bernal 1987: 293). These ideas influenced classical scholars in other countries such as Britain, where the historian J.B. Bury wrote in his *History of Greece* (1900):

> The Dorians . . . keeping their own Dorian stock pure from the mixture of alien blood, reduced all the inhabitants to the condition of subjects . . . The eminent quality which distinguished the Dorians . . . was that which we call 'character' and it was in Lakonia [that is, Sparta and its vicinity] that this quality was most fully displayed and developed itself, for here the Dorian seems to have remained most purely Dorian.
>
> (Cited in Bernal 1987: 293)

The Ancient Greeks were viewed as an extraordinary people and that is why the Germans stood to gain so much from the study of them; ancient history was a means of experiencing their transcendent perfection. Such thinking justified the promotion of classical studies. When asked to reorganize Germany's educational system in 1809, Wilhelm von Humboldt gave a central place to what he termed 'Humanities' and most of all to the study of classical antiquity. This was the cornerstone of the pedagogical concept of *Bildung*, a term which denotes 'formation' but can perhaps be rendered more freely as 'self-cultivation' (Dumont 1991: 108ff.). Not surprisingly this educational strategy was modelled on Ancient Greek paedagogics, in particular the concept of *paideia* which held that children were not fully formed but more like embryonic beings. It was the task of education to overcome this by establishing form (Dumont 1991: 120; Gourgouris n.d). *Bildung* rapidly came to be seen as indispensable to the education of properly cultivated Europeans. Certainly the British adopted it in designing the public school curriculum around the study of Greek and Roman civilisation. As von Humboldt wrote,

> Knowledge of the Greeks is not merely pleasant, useful or necessary to us – no, in the Greeks alone we find the ideal of that which we should like to be and produce. If every part of history enriched us with its human wisdom and human experience, then from the Greeks we take something more than earthly – almost godlike.
>
> (Cited in Bernal 1987: 287)

Against this triumphalism Dumont (1991) has forcefully argued that *Bildung* developed into the instrument of an anti-Enlightenment form of nationalism. In the Ancient Greek model, individual freedom coupled with self-cultivation ideally led to a spontaneous, voluntary embrace of citizenship and participation in political life (Mosse 1985: 8). In nineteenth-century Germany, however, the content and process of *Bildung* were increasingly influenced by nationalist assumptions, so that it came to produce German citizens rather than individuals who then chose to be Germans. Free choice was thus short-circuited; universalist human equality downplayed in favour of local cultural determinism and obedience. In the service of Herder's and Fichte's concepts of the *Volk* – a people linked together by a common spirit and sensibility – *Bildung* furthered the realization that culture determined individuals at their very core (Mosse 1985: 13, Dumont 1991: 184).

'RACE' AND MIXTURE

The reluctance to see Ancient Greece as syncretic was consolidated and formalized in the early nineteenth century, and can be seen as consistent with romanticism and the suppositions of scientific racism which took shape in the same period. According to 'race'-thinking in this period, the characteristics of populations were determined by

their physiological type, although there were almost as many classi-
fications and names for these 'types' as there were contributors to
the debate (Banton 1987). In his *Systema Naturae* (1758) Linnaeus
divided mankind into seven main varieties: *ferus, americanus, euro-
paeus, asiaticus, afer, monstrosus* and *silvestris* (orang-utan, which he
differentiated as a nocturnal variety), while roughly sixty years later
Cuvier discerned three principal subspecies – Caucasian, Mongolian,
Ethiopian – each of which was further subdivided according to
geographical, linguistic and physical criteria (Banton 1987: 4, 29).
These early anthropologists[1] faced a problem similar to that encountered by the German classicists, namely how to account for the
preservation of 'types', especially those 'types' whose biological
make-up endowed them with exceptional capacities and characteristics, in the face of manifest contact and interbreeding between
all the various types.

They overcame this problem simply by legislating that 'type' (or
'race' in some formulations) was immutable and stood apart from the
actual fact of contact and mixing between populations. Much like the
philologists with their picture of the Dorians, then, they were able
to maintain the notion of pure 'races' which perdured and whose
presence was, so it seems, detectable only by a select circle of
discerning racial theorists. As the Americans Nott and Glidden
expressed it in an 1854 work:

> Every race, at the present time, is more or less mixed . . . [but]
> there is abundant evidence to show that the principal physical
> characters of a people may be preserved throughout a long series
> of ages, in a great part of the population, despite climate, mixture
> of races, invasion of foreigners, progress of civilization, or other
> known influences; and that a *type can long outlive its language,
> history, religion, customs, and recollections*.
>
> (Cited in Banton 1987: 41, emphases in original)

The issue of racial mixture was none the less closely scrutinized,
for hybridization could lead either to degeneration or improvement
depending on the exact 'types' being mixed, and their proportions.
The interbreeding of animal species yields infertile offspring (for
example, the mule) and in some quarters it was thought that whole
populations would similarly stagnate if 'races' were to mix. The mid-
century English racial theorist Knox, for example, was anti-colonial
because he thought that the Anglo-Saxon 'race' would decline
outside the British homeland, both because of interbreeding and
because of the unsuitable climate of the tropical colonies (Stepan

1982: 42). Another representative of this line of thinking was the
Alabama physician Josiah Nott, who published an article in a medical
journal in 1844 entitled, 'The mulatto is a hybrid – probable exter-
mination of the two races if the whites and blacks are allowed to inter-
marry' (Banton 1987: 40). Innumerable observations and experiments
were conducted in this period to study the effects of interbreeding.
Such ideas were central to Gobineau's *Essay on the Inequality of
Races* (1853–5), a work in which he speculated upon the results of
every imaginable racial mixture. His initial postulate was that the
superior, white Aryans had migrated to all corners of the world.
Were it not for this no civilization could have been achieved anywhere,
since some admixture of white blood was necessary for cultural
advancement. In the European context Gobineau argued that the
Germans represented the purest Aryan strain and thus the greatest
civilizing force on the continent. Some degree of Germanization was
desirable for other European 'races' such as the Italians, for it could
help them overcome their otherwise feminized condition (Gobineau
1966: 93). Similar admiration for German culture and its high level
of achievement could be found in numerous other non-German racial
theorists, such as Knox (1862: 360) and Thomas Arnold (1842: 33).
This portrayal of German culture as dominant and assimilative vis-
à-vis other nations in mid-century racial theories was remarkably
consistent with the German philologists' depictions of the Greeks,
and this is a point to which we shall return.

CHRISTIANITY AND THE RECOGNITION OF SYNCRETISM

Classical studies in nineteenth-century Germany offer one example
of how the socio-political context of the observer can influence the
impetus to deny cultural mixing. In that case a set of observers,
northern European intellectuals and pedagogues in the process of
their own nation-building, pronounced upon the nature of Ancient
Greece, a foreign, historically distant society.

The case of European Christianity could be offered as a slightly
different example, one where *members* of a group – lay Christians
and clerics alike – insist on the authenticity and integrity of their own
religion. This is an enormous subject and I only wish to point out
that it is the common, expressed view of the educated laity and
certainly the clergy everywhere in Europe that their denomination
faithfully preserves the spirit and true form of Christianity. Each
church, for different and specific reasons, is convinced of its own
orthodoxy and orthopraxy. Obviously they cannot all be right at the

same time, and the history of European religious wars confirms the fervour with which differences have been sanctioned. The usual charge in these matters was 'heresy', which did not just castigate difference but also pointed to a betrayal; a heretic was a former member of one's own faith. The adherence to religious texts and scholastic, theological pronouncements no doubt facilitated the erection and close invigilation of religious boundaries, which, without the aid of literacy, might have remained a series of gradual, permeable transitions. It is interesting to note that the term 'syncretism' was first introduced into modern discourse in this historical context (seventeenth-century), to refer to the attempt to reconcile and harmonize the different sects of Protestantism and ultimately all Christian bodies.

At the same time, non-Christian local customs which had amalgamated with Christianity at the time of conversion and after, resulting in cults of unusual saints, water sources, mountain tops and even holy greyhounds (Schmitt 1983), received a more inconsistent treatment. Periodically the church (mainly the Catholic or the Orthodox in the earlier periods) tried to extirpate what it saw as pagan customs and influences, and many strictures against such practices were enacted at the early councils (Stewart 1991: 223) and again during the Reformation and Counter-Reformation. Ultimately, with the passage of time, many of these local practices simply became naturalized as parts of the accepted Christian tradition of a particular place, region or country; thus, for example, the preponderance of holy wells in Ireland or mountaintop shrines in Greece. Whereas once they had been discerned as remnants of paganism, such sites and the beliefs surrounding them now became part and parcel of a validated Christian tradition.

These examples suggest that the passage of time may dull the recognition of 'syncretism', especially for those who practise the religion in question – everything becomes equally traditional and inseparable. This cycle of conversion, accommodation and naturalization is then repeated in the process of missionization, with the difference that instead of church councils excoriating divergent forms of 'superstition' while legislating proper practice, we now hear charges of illegitimate 'syncretism' when the missionized do not get the missionaries' form of Christianity right.

FALLMERAYER'S GREECE

I turn now to modern Greece where the two traditions mentioned so far, Christianity and classical Hellenism, intersect. At the very moment when European classicists were convincing their countrymen that they were the cultural and spiritual heirs of the Ancient Greeks, Greece was embroiled in a war of independence against the Ottoman Empire (1821–33). The military support which the Great Powers finally furnished the Greek revolutionaries could be viewed as the political acknowledgement of the opinion that Greece was quint-essentially Hellenic. It was not at all clear, however, that the majority of ordinary Greek people truly thought of themselves as Hellenes (Herzfeld 1982: 15, 124). Throughout the middle ages they had referred to themselves as 'Christians' or as *Romii*, eastern Romans. Up to this point the adjective 'Hellenic' had meant 'pagan', as for example in church prohibitions of 'Hellenic customs' such as jumping over bonfires or divining by the form of clouds. Even into the twentieth century, oral traditions circulated in Greece about 'Hellenes' who were thought to be giants who had occupied the land in a distant past (Kakridis 1967). Now, caught up in the enthusiasm for classical culture, it was a foregone conclusion that the new country would be called Hellas, thereby implicitly claiming a cultural continuity and identity with a civilization that had disappeared almost 2000 years earlier.[2]

The problem with this idealistic Hellenism was immediately apparent to anyone who travelled to the country: the Greeks did not really seem like Europeans, but rather more like the Ottomans from whom they had liberated themselves. There were also significant non-Greek minorities in the Greek nation, notably Albanians (later the state would encompass increasing numbers of Vlach and Slavic speakers). These and other considerations moved the Austrian historian Jakob Fallmerayer to assert in 1830 that the Greeks were not really Greek at all; rather, they had been thoroughly Slavicized and Albanianized during the middle ages. In registering these contentions Fallmerayer was the first to introduce the word 'race' to the modern Greeks, who, having received only partial exposure to the Enlightenment and romanticism, had no equivalent concept.[3]

This charge of racial discontinuity also implied cultural discontinuity since it was held that 'race' determined culture and character traits.[4] Fallmerayer maintained, however, that the 'Greek genius' was not dead; it had simply moved northwards. To remove any uncertainty as to the exact destination he pointed out in a footnote that no fewer than three German cities now called themselves 'New Athens'. And for good measure he added, 'All three are, as one knows, well grounded in their claims' (1877: 480).

For the Greeks, the most irritating aspect of Fallmerayer's claims was that they threatened to subvert Greece's recently established national identity, which depended on a close link with Ancient Greece. Although many redressed his assertion that the Greeks were Slavs by re-examining the evidence of medieval migrations and settlements in the Peloponnese, few grasped the broader political context of this charge. They considered Fallmerayer a Slavophile, and when he visited Greece in the 1840s crowds of people taunted him with shouts of 'Slav! Slav!' when he walked the streets (Fallmerayer 1877: 545). Yet Fallmerayer was actually more of a Slavophobe, as numerous scholars have recently pointed out (for example, Herzfeld 1982: 77; Gourgouris n.d.). In particular he feared Russia and the threat which pan-Slavism could pose to German and Austo-Hungarian interests in central Europe. In his view the Ottoman Empire, which was progressively weakening and losing its grip on its Balkan territories in the nineteenth century, needed to be kept in place as a check against Russia. Thus he supported Turkey against Russia in the Crimean War (1853–6) and was opposed to the goals of Greek irredentism, which called for, and eventually achieved, the successive annexation of the Ottoman territories of Thessaly, Macedonia and Thrace, which lay to the north of the original Greek state of 1833.

In making the Greeks Slavs, Fallmerayer also assimilated them to the status of peoples such as the Czechs, Poles, Slovenians and Croats whom the Prussians and Austro-Hungarians were used to controlling.[5] He likened Greece to 'an extremely lost wandering star in the Sarmatian solar system, receiving light and warmth only from Kiev with its golden domes' (1877: 481). In the last century 'Sarmatia' referred roughly to Poland and Russia and it was even used as a racial category. On the evidence of the similarity of (his own?) sketches of Greek and Russian head profiles, Knox (1862: 44, 362ff.) argued for the inclusion of Greeks as Sarmatians, a people he characterized as untrustworthy (in contrast to Turks), obedient and bound to be ruled. 'Slavonians', on the other hand, were transcendentalist and abstract if 'deficient in elegance of form' (ibid.: 356). He considered their chance of independence, surrounded by the purer Germans, small.

The views of other racial theorists on the Slavs were quite diverse. In 1849 the German Carus published the view that the Slavs should be classed as Eastern twilight people (a category including Hindus, Mongolians and Turks among others). The Germans were to be seen as day people responsible for illuminating the way toward civilization for the less able twilight peoples (Banton 1987: 20). Gobineau pointed out that the Slavs were 'ignorant of the western world and its movements', but basically admired them as an Aryan people who had also benefited from additional Germanization (1966: 74ff.).

These parallels from 'race' theory help to contextualize Fallmerayer's position, but Fallmerayer himself should not be considered a full-blown follower of these theories. Although he introduced the term 'race' into the discussion, he supported his argument with volumes of linguistic and cultural-historical evidence (Veloudis 1982: 40). He did not mount a sustained argument in biological and human evolutionary terms.

Fallmerayer's position was not shared by the majority of scholars outside Greece; certainly it was disdained within Greece (Veloudis 1982), but it had the positive effect of stimulating a fluorescence of academic Greek historical and folklore studies (Skopetea 1988: 172; Herzfeld 1982). The study of folklore and linguistics were designed to show that there were still vestiges of Ancient Greek culture to be found in the everyday practice of contemporary Greeks, especially the rural peasantry. By and large the Greeks conceded that they were racially mixed, but they rejected the essentialist overtones of racial theory and maintained that culture could be learned and maintained regardless of race. Indeed the very idea of 'race' was immediately dismissed from the discussion, as by the German philhellene Wachsmuth, who wrote:

> Or might we, therefore, not be Germans anymore, just because we have absorbed a good quantity of Slavic and Wendish blood. A nation's essence and particularity lie, I think, incomparably more in its language, its thought and its sensibility, its whole style and civilization.
>
> (1864: 10, cited in Herzfeld 1982: 89)

Intellectuals asserted language to be a more important correlate of culture, and they pointed to the manifest fact that they still did speak the Greek language (even if it was grammatically simpler than the ancient language and contained numerous Turkish loan-words). Furthermore they could point to various religious beliefs and practices as continuations of Ancient Greek religion. In this they were aided by a host of romantic foreign scholars who also wrote books on this subject (Herzfeld 1982). Practices such as funeral lamentation, beliefs in demonic figures such as *neraides* and *gorgones*, which preserved the names of ancient forerunners even if their form and function were now different, reverence for various saints which could be shown to have absorbed and continued the cults of ancient gods – these were all now explored and held up as evidence that the moderns were heirs of ancient culture.

CULTURAL CONTINUITY AND THE ORTHODOX CHURCH

While statements to the effect that one could find relics of Ancient Greece in the new Greece were commonplace, it must surely have been difficult for the church to accept the view of certain romantic folklorists like the British scholar Lawson, who wrote in 1910 that: 'with all this external Christianity they [the modern Greeks] are as pagan and as polytheistic in their hearts as were ever their ancestors' (1910: 47). The nationalist folklorists recast Greek Christianity as basically syncretic, although they did not use this term. Instead they spoke in terms of 'survivals'. The doyen of modern Greek folklore studies, Nikolaos Politis, defined these as traits, 'which are in no way unseemly but preserve their original rationale and meaning, and which can be regarded as the partial but unbroken continuation of an earlier life' (cited in Herzfeld 1982: 104). In denying that they were 'unseemly' Politis was revising Tylor's use of 'survivals' – which referred to retentions from primitive phases of human evolutionary development – and refashioning it to suit the Greek situation, where the survivals were relics from highly developed ancient forebears (ibid.: 102ff.). But in insisting that they preserve their original rationale and meaning Politis was opening the way to conflict with the church, for his position implied that the modern Greeks potentially engaged in a dual form of religion. Perhaps realizing this, Politis and most other Greek folklorists focused mainly on the linguistic, ritual and material cultural evidences of continuity and refrained from comment on the issue of spiritual continuity (ibid.: 92).

In principle the church still opposed religious practices which it identified as pagan. Paradoxically, nationalist folklorists were likely to uncover just such rites and bring them to public attention in order to celebrate rather than censure them. Considering this collision course, it is surprising how few cases of significant public conflict there were between the church and the folklorists. One reason for this might be the church's principle of economy (*oikonomia*), which disposed it to a relatively accommodating attitude towards local practices, even when these conflicted with established doctrine. This flexibility differentiates the Eastern Orthodox Church from the more rigidly legalistic Catholic Church, and it allowed popular customs to continue and even exert some influence on the institution of the church (Kokosalakis 1987: 41). Another consideration is that the Greek Orthodox Church broke away from the Ecumenical Patriarchate of Constantinople and became autocephalous shortly after Greek independence. This move freed the church to take a more partisan stance on national issues and perhaps inclined it to turn a blind eye to some of the folklorists' discoveries. The Ecumenical Patriarchate would have been above such national concerns and more impartially focused upon theological, doctrinal consistency (Kitromilides 1989: 166).

This is probably why the best example of conflict between the church and survivalism in the nineteenth century issued from Constantinople. It involved a report on the firewalking customs of the Greek communities of Bulgarian Thrace, presented to the director of the Greek theological school at Constantinople and published in 1873 (see Danforth 1984: 69ff.). The author of this early ethnographic study, Anastasios Hourmouziadis, contended that this ritual, known as the Anastenaria, carried on ancient practices associated with Dionysos and thus demonstrated the continuity of Greek culture. As a religious man he decried the followers of the rite as improper Christians who danced ecstatically over hot coals while holding sacred, Christian icons. To reconcile this ambiguous situation he theoretically accommodated the survival of ancient paganism within a surrounding Christian frame. He spoke of an ancient 'nature' encased and overcome by a Christian 'form'. As Danforth puts it: 'By pointing to a syncretism that combines Christian 'form' and pre-Christian 'nature' and by stressing the 'very Christian' quality of the Anastenaria, Hourmouziadis tries to appease the Church without sacrificing his claim for Greek culture' (1984: 72).

The Bulgarian Greeks studied by Hourmouziadis were eventually forced to resettle in northern Greece in the early twentieth century, where the tensions between nationalist folklorists and the church resurfaced. When Greek folklorists learned that the Anastenaria was being continued covertly by the refugees, they encouraged them to perform it openly. After the first such public performance in 1947 the Holy Synod of the Church of Greece denounced the rite as 'an idolatrous survival of the orgiastic worship of Dionysos [that] must be abolished using all the spiritual means at the disposal of the Church' (cited in Danforth 1989: 135). In 1970 the local bishop actually confiscated the Anastenarides' icons, causing cancellation of the ritual for that year, and only returned them when a court order declared they were private property (ibid.: 137). Defences of the Anastenaria insist upon its importance as an indicator of Hellenic, Greek identity. Today the rite continues to be performed under the aegis of the local folklore society before ever-increasing audiences of pilgrims and tourists.

Like Hourmouziadis, later folklorists have also fashioned their own theories of pagan Hellenic and Orthodox Christian syncretism.

The folklorist Megas, for example, revised Hourmouziadis' terms and spoke of the Anastenaria as presenting ancient religious 'forms' and Christian 'meaning' (Danforth 1984: 84). Another theorization of the relation of Ancient Greek to Christian culture was that advanced by the nineteenth-century folklorist/intellectual Zambelios, who held that the ancient Greeks were already essentially Christian in nature and the coming of Christ simply set the seal on this without radically altering it (Herzfeld 1982: 44). Perhaps one of the most intriguing formulations is that of the Cypriot scholar Loukas, brought to light by Herzfeld (1982: 93ff.). Loukas observed that the modern Greek personification of death, Charos (from Ancient Greek Charon), alternates in popular usage with the Archangel Michael. The two figures are almost completely interchangeable. Commenting on this, he wrote, 'In general, whenever they [the Greeks] mention or invoke Charon, they also have the Angel in mind, and whenever they shout and revile the Angel, they are reviling Charon too' (cited in Herzfeld 1982: 96). Notice his use of the Ancient Greek form, Charon, implying that this figure from ancient Greek cosmology was the subject of modern Greek thought. Loukas implied that the Greek people were simultaneously faithful to two distinct religious traditions.

CONCLUSION

In the Greek case, recognizing syncretism was no simple objective matter, but an engaged nationalist stance which situated one in a domestic social field where not everyone shared the same viewpoint. Greek national interest called for an identification with Ancient Greece and this was bound to lead to a certain amount of synthetic theorizing. Yet there was no consensus of opinion in the nineteenth-century social field about the relation of Ancient to modern Greece. Writers such as Fallmerayer disputed it on racial and historical grounds, while the Orthodox Church acknowledged the connection but disputed the continuity of Ancient Greek religion. The folklorists and ideologues of nationalism, by contrast, devoted themselves unreservedly to proving the reality of Helleno-Christian synthesis. Ultimately their view has attracted the broadest assent. In recent years the military dictatorship (1968–74) breathed new life into this equation, popularizing it in the slogan 'Greece of the Helleno-Christians' which could be found scrawled on walls up and down the country. And in a speech in 1982 to a conference of Orthodox clergy in America, the then Prime Minister Karamanlis declared that, 'Orthodoxy, by enriching the shining cultural tradition of classical

antiquity constituted with it the strong spiritual and ethical foundation of Hellenism . . . For this reason the concepts of Hellenism
and Orthodoxy have been interwoven inseparably in the consciousness of the nation' (cited in Kokosalakis 1987: 45). The Greek
case thus presents us with an example of how religious amalgamation
amounting to syncretism could be seen as a valid and positive
phenomenon.

Herzfeld (1987: 111) has labelled the modern Greek balancing act
between classical Hellenism and Byzantine Christian Orthodoxy
'disemia', meaning that the Greeks have available two parallel traditions, two sets of signs, for representing themselves. The discourse
of syncretism examined above represents one particular instance of
disemic negotiation. It could be argued, however, that formulations
such as those of Loukas, Hourmouziadis and Megas transcend
disemia by fusing the Hellenic and the Orthodox into a single sign
rather than maintaining them as alternatives. In the models of the
latter two, analysis of Anastenaria practices reveals the dual presence
of pagan and Christian elements although the participants' understanding of the ritual is *solely* Christian. Loukas, on the other hand,
argues that a single sign (*either* Charos *or* the angel) gives rise to a
cosmological dualism indicative of bi-religiosity. These two types of
synthesis are certainly different, and this difference was potentially
significant to the church, which might excuse the first but would
almost surely condemn the second.[6] I think that both forms of
synthesis may none the less be considered examples of 'syncretism'
by anthropologists taking this term broadly as any synthesis of
different religious traditions.

Note also that the Greek example was unusual in the nineteenth
century, because its upholders used cultural and linguistic evidence
to argue against Fallmerayer's biological assertion that the Greek
'race' had been erased by waves of foreign invaders. They did not
attempt to deny that there had been invasions and mixture between
Greek, Slavic and Albanian populations; rather, they asserted that
such issues were irrelevant to the transmission of culture. Populations
were everywhere mixed, the Greek scholars pointed out, even in
Germany (Veloudis 1982: 33, 39). Their key argument was for the
continuity of Ancient Greek culture and the documentation of its
survival in modern Greece. The dubiousness of some of their
assertions need not concern us; for those who subscribed to these
arguments the modern Greeks really were Hellenes.

The Greek case thus does not entirely conform to Just's (1989: 77)
prediction that a biological notion of 'race' will be asserted when all

the usual criteria of ethnicity (language, culture, territory) are too inconclusive to establish the distinctive identity of a people. In Greece the reverse seems to have happened, namely a racial assertion against Hellenic identity was countered and defeated by arguments phrased in terms of culture.[7] In nineteenth-century terms, an ethnological argument triumphed over an anthropological one (see note 1). This does not, however, diminish Just's (1989) larger point that 'race' and ethnicity are just versions of each other, one involving biology, the other omitting it. Essentialism is the pinnacle – or should I say 'nadir'? – where 'race' and ethnicity arguments converge. This is a wholly abstract, almost mystical, space created neither by biology nor by cultural attributes, but rather by pure belief and assertion. How much difference is there, ultimately, between the Greek historians' claim that Hellenic culture had assimilated all medieval influences (see Veloudis 1982: 74), and Gobineau's opinion (see note 4) that the Greek 'race' had absorbed all invaders? The preservation of cultural 'character' (or 'style' or 'sensibility') and the maintenance of a racial 'type' are equally articles of faith.

Finally, I have shown that the Greek discourse on syncretism applauds the mixture of two discrete and, from the point of view of the Orthodox Church, incompatible religions. At first sight the strategy of refuting racial mixture by asserting religious mixture appears an original, possibly even progressive, means of establishing cultural authenticity; all the more so when the usual negative reaction to syncretism as indicative of inauthenticity is considered. We should not, however, lose sight of the fact that syncretism in Greece is entirely subordinate to the larger nationalist assertion of cultural continuity. Nationalism created Greek syncretism in the first place, and then demanded its positive evaluation.

NOTES

1 The difference between ethnology and anthropology in the nineteenth century was that the former viewed culture as independent of biology and understandable by reference to factors such as climate, language and history, while anthropology sought to explain culture in terms of biology, as a function of 'race' (Stocking 1971: 374ff.).

2 Bearing in mind the success of this nominalist move it is not surprising that Greeks today are unwilling to see 'Macedonia' as merely a name; they know from experience how such names claim both history and identity (Danforth 1993).

3 The word appears in his writing (for example, 1877: 488) in its English or French form 'race' (not in the German form *Rasse*) as if he had picked it up directly from Cuvier or one of the English writers on the topic, possibly

Sir Walter Scott, who popularized the word in his 1820 book *Ivanhoe* (Banton 1987: 13).

In the nineteenth century the words *genos* and *phyli*, which today mean respectively 'lineage' and 'race', were commonly applied to the Greek nation. But they apparently designated 'nation' in a corporate, culturo-political sense (Skopetea 1988: 171). By the same token, *phyletismos* meant 'nationalism' or 'ethnic chauvinism', not 'racism' as it does today. *Phyletismos* was not introduced until *c.* 1872, while the term *ethnophyletismos* (ethno-nationalism) was coined slightly more than a decade earlier. Both terms were critically applied by the Ecumenical Orthodox Church to charac-terize the Bulgarians who broke away and established their own auto-nomous church in 1870 (Koumanoudis 1980). Kitromilides (1989: 181, 191) considers the problem of translating *phyletismos* as 'racism'.

4 In 1878, more than 45 years after Fallmerayer made his initial charges of Greek racial discontinuity, Gobineau pronounced differently on the pedi-gree of the Greek 'race'. Although he considered it to be mixed, he main-tained that an Ancient Greek nucleus had absorbed external influences rather than vice versa. The result was a strong alloy, since the Greeks had integrated the best traits of the peoples with whom they came into con-tact. His final verdict was that the Greeks demonstrated all the requisite qualities to earn the accolade 'nationality' (see Vacalopoulos 1968: 104ff.).

5 It could be argued that Germans did rule the early Greek state. The first king of Greece was a Bavarian, Otto, but he did not support Fallmerayer's views; neither did the majority of German scholars.

6 The Catholic Church would probably excuse Megas' account as indicative of 'inculturation' and condemn Loukas' representation as evidence of a 'dual system' (Schreiter 1985). Only the latter would earn the pejorative label 'syncretic'.

7 A comparable progression from a racial to a cultural/ethnic conception of national identity may also be observed in the Basque case (MacClancy 1993).

REFERENCES

Arnold, T. (1842) *Introductory Lectures on Modern History*, Oxford: John Henry Parker.

Banton, M. (1987) *Racial Theories*, Cambridge: Cambridge University Press.

Bernal, M. (1987) *Black Athena: The Afroasiatic Roots of Classical Civilization*, New Brunswick: Rutgers University Press.

Danforth, L. (1984) 'The ideological context of the search for continuities in Greek culture', *Journal of Modern Greek Studies* 2: 53–85.

—— (1989) *Firewalking and Religious Healing*, Princeton, NJ: Princeton University Press.

—— (1993) 'Claims to Macedonian identity: the Macedonian question and the breakup of Yugoslavia', *Anthropology Today* 9: 3–10.

Dumont, L. (1986) *Essays on Individualism: Modern Ideology in Anthropological Perspective*, Chicago: University of Chicago Press.

—— (1991) *L'ideologie allemande: France–Allemagne et retour*, Paris: Gallimard.

Fallmerayer, J. (1877 [1845]) *Fragmente aus dem Orient*, 2nd edn, Stuttgart: J.G. Cotta.

Gobineau, A. de (1966 [1853]) *The Inequality of Races*, trans. A. Collins, Los Angeles: Noontide Press.

Gourgouris, S. (n.d.) 'The punishment of philhellenism', unpublished ms.

Hannerz, U. (1987) 'The world in creolization', *Africa* 57: 546–59.

Herskovits, M. (1937) 'African gods and Catholic saints in New World Negro belief', *American Anthropologist* 39: 635–43.

Herzfeld, M. (1982) *Ours Once More: Folklore, Ideology and the Making of Modern Greece*, Austin: University of Texas Press.

—— (1987) *Anthropology Through the Looking Glass: Critical Ethnography in the Margins of Europe*, Cambridge: Cambridge University Press.

Hourmouziadis, A. (1961 [1873]) 'Peri ton Anastenarion kai allon tinon paradoxon ethimon kai prolipseon', *Arkheion tou Thrakikou Laographikou kai Glossikou Thisavrou* 26: 144–61.

Just, R. (1989) 'Triumph of the ethnos', in E. Tonkin, M. McDonald and M. Chapman (eds), *History and Ethnicity*, London: Routledge.

Kakridis, J. (1967) *Die alten Hellenen und neugriechischen Volksglauben*, Munich: Ernst Heimeran Verlag.

Kitromilides, P. (1989) '"Imagined communities" and the origins of the national question in the Balkans', *European History Quarterly* 19: 149–94.

Knox, R. (1862 [1850]) *The Races of Men: A Philosophical Enquiry into the Influence of Race over the Destinies of Nations*, 2nd edn, London: Henry Renshaw.

Kokosalakis, N. (1987) 'The political significance of popular religion in Greece', *Archive des sciences sociales des religions* 64: 37–52.

Koumanoudis, S. (1980 [1900]) *Synagogi neon lexeon*, Athens: Ermis.

Lawson, J.C. (1990) *Modern Greek Folklore and Ancient Greek Religion*, Cambridge: Cambridge University Press.

MacClancy, J. (1993) 'Biological Basques, sociologically speaking', in M. Chapman (ed.), *Social and Biological Aspects of Ethnicity*, Oxford: Oxford University Press.

Mosse, G. (1985) *German Jews Beyond Judaism*, Indiana University Press/ Hebrew Union College Press: Bloomington and Cincinnati.

Schmitt, J.-C. (1983) *The Holy Greyhound: Guinefort, Healer of Children since the Thirteenth Century*, Cambridge: Cambridge University Press.

Schreiter, R. (1985) *Constructing Local Theologies*, London: SCM Press.

Skopetea, E. (1988) *To 'protypo vasileio' kai i megali idea*, Athens: n.p.

Stepan, N. (1982) *The Idea of Race in Science: Great Britain 1800–1960*, London: Macmillan.

Stewart, C. (1991) *Demons and the Devil: Moral Imagination in Modern Greek Culture*, Princeton, NJ: Princeton University Press.

Stocking, G. (1971) 'What's in a name? The origins of the Royal Anthropological Institute', *Man* 6: 369–90.

Todorov, T. (1984) *The Conquest of America: The Question of the Other*, New York: Harper & Row.

Vacalopoulos, A. (1968) 'Byzantinism and Hellenism: remarks on the racial origin and the intellectual continuity of the Greek nation', *Balkan Studies* 9: 101–26.

Veloudis, G. (1982) *O Jakob Fallmerayer kai i genesi tou ellinikou istorismou*, Athens: E.M.N.E.–Mnimon.

Wachsmuth, C. (1864) *Das alte Griechenland im neuen*, Bonn: Max Cohen.

7 Syncretic inventions

'Indianness' and the Day of the Monkey

David M. Guss

It has no European or African roots whatsoever. This is native. It's the only festival in Venezuela, and perhaps the world, which is celebrated on just one day only: the 28th of December. And it has no European influence nor any African. It's native to the indigenous Carib culture, and what's more, I'd say, to the region of Caicara. Descended from the Chaima, the Guarao, and the Guaiqueri.

Edgar Baquero

It is always the specificity of power relations at a given historical moment and in a particular place that triggers off a strategy of pseudo-historical explanations that camouflage the inventive act itself.

Werner Sollors 1989: xvi

While American anthropologists, taking their lead from Boas, may have viewed cultures as syncretic formations for many years, participants in these cultures have often resisted such self-ascription.[1] Notions of ethnic purity, often fuelled by nationalism or religious ideology, have militated against openly embracing the many contributors responsible for any collective identity. As will be clear from the contributions to this volume, decisions to acknowledge or deny the relative importance of any group's influence are constantly tempered by a host of political and socio-economic situations. In my own work, I have looked at festive behaviour in Venezuela to determine how these cultural performances have been used to articulate competing ethnic, religious and national interests. Like Lévi-Strauss's famous 'bricoleur,' these festivals, as a direct result of their syncretic composition, have enabled participants to recombine elements continually, forefronting some and ignoring others, depending on the particular message those in control of the festival wish to convey.

One example of the on-going reinterpretation of a festival by its participants is that of St John the Baptist or San Juan, a holiday primarily celebrated in the black coastal communities of Barlovento from 23 to 25 June. By viewing this holiday in the historical context of a 45-year period, it has been possible to identify a number of strategies used to enable participants to address various concerns within their communities. To do so, they have explored, experimented with, and manipulated many of the different elements that have combined to give San Juan its present configuration. For the last decade, this festival has been used to articulate particular issues of racial identity and oppression. The elements presently highlighted by the Afro-Venezuelan Sanjuaneros who dominate this celebration therefore are those of African history, maroonage and drums (Guss 1993). But other Venezuelan festivals, which are also derived from the union of African, European and Amerindian, have chosen to accentuate quite different elements from this grand *mescolanza* or 'mix.' And yet, while strategies may vary, intentions are often remarkably similar – the reassertion of community and the construction of a unique cultural heritage.

In Caicara, a small, uniformally mestizo farming community in the easternmost state of Monagas, a celebration known as El Día del Mono, or Day of the Monkey, has been used to assert the singular 'Indianness' of its participants' pasts. But the Day of the Monkey may not have always been an indigenous celebration and, according to some Caicareños, was very probably not even known by that name. If so, it may be an irony of this festival's current elaboration that, in seeking to establish its purity of origin, it has underscored its own syncretic invention. For the debate engulfing this discussion has exposed more clearly the many competing interests which this celebration helped to unite.

Like most of Monagas' first towns, Caicara was established by Capuchin missionaries for the express purpose of settling Indians into one location where they could be both converted and put to work. But historians and local residents are unable to agree as to when exactly this occurred. Some put the date as early as February 1728 while others claim it occurred the following year. Many, however, insist that the town was not established until 20 April 1731, for its acknowledged founder, Father Antonio de Blesa, did not even arrive in Venezuela from Puerto Rico until January of that year. When an official seal was designed for the community, the debate was resolved by displaying all three dates with equal prominence (Chitty 1982: 85–7; Ramírez 1972: 12–28).

The Indians, whom Father de Blesa was continually chasing after, were from various groups. There were Pariagotos, Coacas, Cores, Kariñas and, most numerous of all, Chaimas. Carib-speakers like the others, the Chaimas inhabited a territory spreading from the coastal Turimiquire range to the mesas overlooking the Guarapiche River, the site where the new community was to be placed. The town's official name was Santo Domingo de Guzmán de Caicara, and it was Santo Domingo, the patron saint, who was said to have saved the town soon after its founding.[2] As various accounts, both written and oral, tell it, a large group of Indians had gathered at the outskirts of the village and were preparing to overrun it in the middle of the night. Yet as they approached, they were stopped by the image of a huge figure in gleaming armour seated on a horse with sword drawn. By his side was a snarling dog. So startling was this image that the Indians fled in fear. To confirm what had happened, they returned to Caicara the next morning. Finding the village asleep, they timidly entered, arriving at last at the church. When they entered, they found a statue of Santo Domingo with his dog and immediately recognized that a miracle had happened. The date was 4 August, and from that moment on was celebrated as the official Patron Saint's Day of Caicara.[3]

The town grew slowly and more than fifty years after its founding still had only 400 inhabitants (Vila 1978: 97). But its location at the crossroads between larger commercial centres such as Maturín in the south and Cumaná and Barcelona in the north helped establish it as an important stopping point for mule trains and travellers. Even more important was its access to the rich farmlands of the Guarapiche valley, which soon began to attract large numbers of settlers. Cotton, corn, indigo and tobacco were the earliest crops, but as farms were broken up into smaller holdings vegetables such as tomatoes, cucumbers and cabbage became even more important.[4] By 1961 there were over 4,700 people living in Caicara and an equal number in the smaller surrounding communities and *caceríos* (hamlets) (Ramírez 1972: 7). Almost none of them could be identified as Indians.[5]

Then as now, the festival cycle revolved around two main holidays, the Fiestas de Santo Domingo de Guzmán or Patron Saint's Day of 4 August, and the Día del Mono on 28 December. While they have some similarities, they are in most ways structurally opposite. For if the Mono, as many of its participants claim, is an expression of all that is indigenous, the Festival of Santo Domingo commemorates the

miraculous triumph over it. During the Patron Saint's Day, all activity emanates from the church. While there are various diversions,
from local rodeos to travelling carnivals, the principal events remain
the mass and the lengthy procession following it in which the image
of Santo Domingo is carried throughout the town. In recent years
there have also been enactments of Santo Domingo's miracle wherein
children dressed up as Indians are first vanquished and then converted by the sudden appearance of the saint. Throughout the celebration, the message remains the same – the triumph of order over chaos
and faith over paganism. The Día del Mono, however, is an inversion
of this triumph, and rather than emanating from the church begins
in the small outlying communities and farms surrounding Caicara.
Yet in a sense it is also a re-enactment of the battle waged against
Santo Domingo; only in this version, the outcome is reversed.

The performance of the monkey dance is remarkably simple.
Sometime before dawn on 28 December, groups, referred to as
parrandas, begin to gather in various parts of town as well as in the
smaller, outlying *caceríos*. Most of these groups have danced together
for years under names such as Garibaldo, Zanjón, Gavilán, Eufracio
Guevara, and Viento Fresco. Some of these are place names,
indicating the village or section of town where the group comes from,
while others derive their names from famous figures, most often well-
known *moneros* (monkey dancers). Many are wearing costumes with
monkey masks while some have simply painted their faces blue with
indigo. Ideally, they will be led by a woman in a long flowered dress
or a white *liquiliqui*.[6] This is the '*mayordoma*' or '*capitana*' who,
wielding a large machete, keeps order amongst the group. But some
are not led by women and instead have men parodying a *mayordoma*,
dressed in skirts, with oversized breasts and exaggerated wigs. The
most famous of these transvestite figures is Chilo Rojas, a 70-year-
old *monero* who has been dancing for over fifty years. Like other
groups, his is a mix of men and women. Yet as he leads his dancers,
clothed in an elegant dress with purse dangling from his arm, a young
woman advances ahead, waving a banner with the group's name and
the number 28 painted on it. Equally important to each group is its
band, for as the *parrandas* wind through the streets on their way to
the main square, they dance and sing improvised verses:

Allá viene el mono
por el callejón
Abrele las puertas
a ése parrandón[7]

Arriving at different times and from different directions, the *parrandas* enter with a flourish, parading in front of the review stand, and then finally mounting the stage to perform. The order of the parrandas' entrance is anything but random and, although it does not remain the same each year, still retains a clear symbolic importance. In 1990, the first group to enter was the Parranda de San Pedro, a group which had not marched for several years and, as Padre Freites, Caicara's priest, claimed, 'had required a superhuman effort to bring'. In reserving this privileged position for this group, festival organizers were able to emphasize the Día del Mono's traditional character as well as its indigenous roots. For not only is the Parranda de San Pedro considered the oldest remaining group, but it is also the only one composed of Indians. It is also one of the only *parrandas* still organized around a small rural community in the hills outside of Caicara. Following the Parranda de San Pedro was the Parranda de Gavilán, also known as the Negros de Chilo Rojas.[8] As with the San Pedro group, the placement of Chilo, the oldest *monero* still dancing, was both symbolic and honorific.

But the entrance of the *parrandas* is not a system of ranking. Many of the larger groups, for instance, prefer to come later in the morning when there are bigger crowds gathered. With much larger bands, such groups as Garibaldo and Zanjón can also remain on stage much longer. Yet eventually each is replaced by the next and leaves the stage to be swallowed up by the mass of revellers that has been steadily growing since dawn. It is this much larger group, uniting both the public and the *parrandas*, which is doing the monkey dance. Spiralling and swaying back and forth, long lines of dancers are whipped about, hanging desperately onto the belts or shirt-tails of those in front. The leaders of these long columns swing belts which they periodically use on any bystander they happen to pass. Others carry paint cans of blue indigo or skins of wine and rum. By dusk, the plaza is entirely filled with an increasingly chaotic and inebriated mass of dancers. And then as suddenly as it started, the groups begin to drift off one by one, and the festival, without any pomp or ceremony, fizzles to an end.[9]

It may be difficult to see at first glance what this apparent free-for-all has to do with the indigenous traditions preceding the arrival of the Spaniards. Yet many Caicareños are quick to insist that the Day of the Monkey represents the same ritual behaviour that Carib-related peoples of this area have practised for hundreds if not thousands of years. As evidence, they point to the style of dancing, claiming that while Europeans hold hands and move in pairs, indigenous peoples, in a more collective manner, form long lines. They also point out that the musical form is a *marisela*, derived from the traditional Carib or Kariña *mare mare*, and that the instruments used are of predominantly native origin.[10] The *ciriaco* and the conch, the pan-flutes and the maracas, all of them are the same played by the original inhabitants of the area. A further indication of the dance's indigenous origin is the use of face paint, even if somewhat chaotically applied. But the most important link connecting this dance to an Indian predecessor is the figure of the monkey itself. For underlying all of this activity is the widely held belief that the dance is actually a harvest celebration honouring an ancient simian deity. As one young man explained it:

> It happens that the monkeys protected the harvests that the Indians here in Venezuela had, basically corn, which originated here in Latin America. The monkey was the one that frightened the birds away from the harvest. The birds would drive those monkeys crazy. And so this is what happened. They turned the monkey into a god. In gratitude, the Indian made him a god. And they would dance. El Baile del Mono. The Dance of the Monkey. You know how the monkey swings from branch to branch in single file. And the monkey dance . . . the monkey walks holding on to the tail of the monkey in front. And so that's the way the Caicara monkey dances. Understand? Because the Chaima Indians from here used to participate in that harvest. And we're *culturistas*, followers of the Caicara culture. And we're not going to let anyone from outside come in here and change our tradition.

What explanations such as these resolutely deny is that the Day of the Monkey might also share its origins with an African or European past. And yet it is not difficult to discern how elements from these cultural traditions have also contributed to the festival. In fact, in many ways, it is the African and European influence which initially impresses the observer. The *parrandas* with their marching bands and masked dancers are much closer to the African-derived Carnival tradition from nearby Trinidad than anything that existed among Venezuela's native peoples. In fact, as Corradini correctly observes (1976), indigenous dance was usually circular and inward, unlike the *parranda* style with its long lines moving from place to place. Even the long bamboo *ciriaco*, the emblem *par excellence* of 'Indianness', can be traced back to its origins in the West African *carángano* (Hernández and Fuentes 1992: 96; Mendez 1978: 11; Ramírez 1986: 60). Yet equally if not more pronounced is the relationship of this festival to one of Europe's oldest church celebrations – the Day of the Holy Innocents.

Known also as Childermas, the Day of the Holy Innocents was established to commemorate King Herod's slaughter of every male child in Bethlehem under the age of two. While the Bible gives no date for this event, the early Church fathers established it as 28 December, thereby associating it with the four-day Roman Saturnalia concluding the year. In many parts of Europe, it was considered the unluckiest day of the year and was commemorated by giving children (in order to recall Herod's deed) a sound thrashing (Hatch 1978: 1157). Called Cross Day in Ireland and other parts of the British Isles, it was an inauspicious day on which no major event, such as a wedding or coronation, was ever scheduled. A more common tradition, however, did not punish children but rather elevated them into a position of power. It is quite likely that this latter custom began in abbeys and monasteries where the youngest cleric or nun was placed in charge for the duration of the holiday. This inversion was soon to spread, however, into a more generalized burlesque of all power. In England and France, young boys were chosen to be bishops with all the authority that position entailed (Mackenzie 1987). In Belgium, children locked up their parents, requiring them to pay a ransom before they could be freed. But it was not only children who joined in these games. Peasants, women and other disenfranchised groups took advantage of this holiday to not only assume power but to mock it. What was once the unluckiest day of the year was now the most absurd, and so 28 December also became known as the Feast of Fools.

The church, it should be noted, did not appreciate becoming the target of its congregants' humour, and as early as the seventh century began an active campaign to prohibit it. But it was nearly a thousand years before the Feast of Fools finally began to disappear in Europe (Bakhtin 1984: 77). In the New World, however, it had already taken hold, and in countries like Venezuela was extremely widespread. There 28 December was a type of April Fools' Day in which newspapers ran false headlines, wives put salt in their husband's coffee, and children were sent on pointless errands. In the coastal towns of Barlovento 'governments of women' were set up, parodying male authority with absurd decrees and other actions (González 1991; Hernández and Fuentes 1992; Lecuna 1985; Pollak-Eltz and Fitl 1985), while in the highland communities of Lara, masked figures known as Zaragozas danced through the streets behind miraculous images of the Holy Innocents' massacre. And in Caicara workers from the outlying haciendas paraded into town, singing and dancing in the homes they passed, until finally arriving in the plaza where the landowners had set up tables covered with liquor and food. At least this, according to some accounts, was the way the Día de los Inocentes was celebrated until around 1925.

It was at this point, elderly Caicareños say, an innovation in the dance occurred. Indians arriving from the community of El Cerezo suddenly grabbed onto each other, forming a long line of hopping figures. One man, who claims to have witnessed the event, says it was in fear of getting separated from one another. In fact, Jacinto Guevara says it was Balbino Blanco's daughter Veronica who first clutched onto her father, giving the dance its distinctive step. It was at this point that a bystander, perhaps Celestino Palacios, screamed out, 'Allá viene el mono' ('Here comes the monkey'). Although he meant it derisively, others took up the dance, and within several years, it was the only step being done.

While Chilo Rojas also insists that the Monkey Dance is a recent innovation, he remembers its origins somewhat differently:

How did that begin? There was a family around here named Palacios who lived around El Cerezo. They lived up around the Rio de Oro. Okay, and on the Calle de la Casualidad there was a man named Jorgito Taylor who had a business. And he sold ponsigué rum, rum. A Mr Peña Guzmán lived over there as well. And Felix Díaz. And those people, because that was the main street here, the Calle de la, de la . . . that was the town . . . the Calle de la Casualidad!

Okay, they, well, they began to drink rum over there. That was an enormous family that Palacios family. Incredible. There were, no shit, at least fifty. And they were living in the farmworkers' camp. There are still a few old guys living over there on Calle Tracadero. They began to drink rum, and they bought a carafe of rum. They're an enormous family. And so they began to drink rum. And the old man said, 'Hell, whoever doesn't leap from there to here, doesn't get a drink!'

They were all over there crowded into the middle of the street. I was just a kid then, around 17 years old.[11] And so they began coming. One would leap and grab onto the bottle and take a drink and then stay in front. And then the next. And they started in with that and before you know it they were just about at Felix Díaz's corner with the carafe of rum. They went on grabbing one another and then they really got going with that. They grabbed onto one another's belts. Jesus! They belted one another. They'd jump, grab the carafe, take a drink of rum, and keep on going. No shit, they took over the whole street. They held onto one another's belts and just kept on dancing. And monkey, by God! And drinks, no shit . . . And I took off my own belt because that stuff . . . That's the problem.

And that's the way the monkey began. But they didn't dance the monkey before that. I remember . . . Look, it's as if I were watching it today.[12]

What is clear from these multiple versions of the festival's origins is that Caicareños do not agree as to what the celebration represents. For even upon hearing the first-hand accounts of such respected elders as Jacinto Guevara and Chilo Rojas, many still claim the festival has absolutely nothing to do with the Day of the Holy Innocents. In order to understand these differences, it is helpful to see who is making each of these claims. Those stating that the Monkey Dance was simply a craze, taking over in the 1920s and eventually silencing any reference to the Day of the Innocents, are predominantly older people with strong ties to Caicara's agricultural past. However, those insisting that the Day of the Monkey is a completely indigenous celebration, with no link whatsoever to any European or African tradition, are for the most part young men who have left Caicara in order to study or work. For this group, which continues to grow with the changing face of Venezuela's economy, the Day of the Monkey is a homecoming celebration, or as they themselves say, '*un día de retorno*'. It is on this day, conveniently situated between Christmas and New Year, that every Caicareño, no matter where he or she is, will make every attempt possible to return to the village. For them the dance is a symbol of identity, distinguishing them from (rather than joining them to) a larger national tradition that continually threatens to engulf them. The 'Indianness' of the Day of the Monkey is the quality of being native and rooted. It is the ability to localize the no longer local. Or as a young dentist dressed as a priest, who was also a Caicareño living in the Andes, claimed: 'For me the Monkey represents the beginning, the essence. Why? Because it's my identity as both a Caicareño and a native of this community.'

The use of 'native' here ('*indígena*' in Spanish) is intentionally ambiguous. It indicates that he is native because he does the dance and a Caicareño because he is native. The fact that since the 1920s 'indigenous' aspects of the festival have been selected as the most characteristic and meaningful is no doubt a response to the socio-economic changes that have been occurring throughout this area. It is little surprise therefore that the appearance of the Indians dancing in from El Cerezo should coincide with the sudden appearance of another band of strangers – Standard Oil of New Jersey, who at the same moment was drilling its first wells in Monagas.

Although the oil there is well below that extracted in the western-most state of Zulia, Monagas is still one of Venezuela's main oil-producing areas.[13] The effect upon the economy of this state has also been tremendous. It is significant therefore that Jesús Guevara begins his monograph on the Mono, *Sobre las huellas de El Mono* (1974), with an analysis of the impact the oil industry has had upon Caicara and other rural communities in Monagas. After describing the original irresistibility of working in the nearby oil fields, he tells of the tragic results when mechanization arrived and this new labour force was suddenly unemployed.[14] Unfortunately, they were unable to return to their agricultural work and thus became part of a growing underclass in such exploding urban centres as Caracas and Puerto Ordaz. What is particularly revealing is the illustration Guevara includes in his study to dramatize this. It is a picture of oil fields and refineries with a long row of hopeful *campesinos* (identifiable by their straw hats) entering them. One of them has his hand raised as if to signal 'onward'. Yet on the other side is the same row of men (now wearing hard hats) coming out. Instead of *campesinos*, they are now workers, despondent, unemployed, and with their hands in their pockets. Above this whole scene and filling the sky is the God-like figure of the Mono, arms outstretched in an embrace of the entire landscape (Guevara 1974: 7). The symbolism of this image is both powerful and clear. The oil industry has been a factory for the production of urbanism, unemployment and destabilized social rela-tions. And in such a world, it is tradition alone (and particularly that of the Mono) that can hold these various disintegrating elements together.

The illustration reproduced by Guevara indicates another powerful explanation for why this festival suddenly became a celebration of indigenous values and what exactly those values signify. For in addition to being native, as suggested above, the 'indigenous' is also being used to indicate an edenic pastoral past which no longer exists. It is a reminder of another festival and another era in which the dancers did indeed come from the surrounding haciendas and *cacerios*. They were *campesinos* who worked the land and used the festival as an important occasion to join together on an annual basis.

Yet today the *parrandas* almost all come from the town and are largely composed of urban workers who return simply for this day. As the man who claimed the Mono was a celebration of his 'nativeness' also admitted: 'The San Pedro Parranda is the only native one left that comes from outside. The others now are all from town, and they're like us. We're mestizos, but they aren't.'

If it is true that the Mono is being used to invoke the memory of another, less-industrialized reality, then it is one which many Caicareños insist was a much more prosperous one for their town. Caicara before 1920, before the arrival of cars and the oil industry, was still a rural hub for traders and travellers, a town with restaurants and hotels, none of which it now has. As Freddy Natera, a long-time Caicara resident, said:

> Look, Caicara was even more important than Maturín [the state capital]. Caicara had an ice plant. It had a soda bottling plant. Caicara de Maturín, that's the way it was known. And why? One simple reason, it was the agricultural capital of Monagas.[15]

But economic realities are always bound to social ones, and if the 'Indianness' of the Mono celebration is being used to indicate an era of pastoral plenty and wellbeing, it also resituates the participants who wish, at least for the day, to recover that reality. In this sense, 'Indianness' may be seen as a classic instrumental use of ethnicity to restore relations which have been ruptured or destabilized.[16] It resuscitates the memory of a forgotten 'tribe' long dispersed throughout Venezuela's various urban centres. It creates distinctions where distinction has been lost, and makes Caicareños unique among all others. Or as Caicareños continually proclaim about their Mono: 'It has nothing to do with the Día de los Inocentes or any other holiday, because the only place where it is danced is here.'[17]

The 'Indianness' of the Mono, however, is not simply an oppositional strategy used to distinguish one group of mestizos from another. It is also a powerful symbol of subversion which, when joined to the anti-social character of the monkey, succeeds in redefining the Día de los Inocentes in a way which is indeed unique to Caicara. Like every Feast of Fools celebration, it maintains inversion as its most important element, mocking all symbols of authority and power with equal abandon. Yet it does so in a way that evokes Caicara's own history. Now, more than 260 years after its founding, the Indians succeed in overwhelming the city. They finally triumph over Santo Domingo and the power of the church he represents. And what is most significant is that they do so in a way that is indeed Carib, that celebrates the triumph of nature over culture and elevates above all that most enduring symbol of anti-culture, the monkey.[18]

NOTES

1 While Boas may not have used the term 'syncretic', his theory of historical particularism was clearly based upon a syncretic model. It was impossible to study any culture in isolation, Boas claimed. And while a particular environment, psychology and even 'genius' might unlock many of the mysteries of a specific culture, it was only through understanding its history of contact and exchange that one could ever come to comprehend it. Or as Boas stated in article after article: 'the whole question is decided only in so far as we know that independent development as well as diffusion has made each culture what it is' (Boas 1982: 436).

2 Caicareños are equally divided over the origin of the name Caicara. Some claim it derives from an Indian chief named Caicuara while others say it comes from an indigenous, yuca-like plant called caracara. The British botanist Robert Schomburgk wrote that 'Kaikara' was a native term for the three stars in Orion's belt (cited in Ramírez 1972: 11). But the most thorough study of the term was done by Juan José Ramírez, who concluded that, while it is impossible to ever be certain, Caicara is probably a Carib-derived word meaning 'Ceiba creek' from *cai*, or *ceiba* (*Bombax sp.*) and *cuara*, 'creek' or 'brook' (1972: 9–11).

3 Most Caicareños seem capable of recounting at least some version of this story. For the most fanciful written account, see Ramírez (1972: 71–3), in which he not only identifies the Indians as Pariagotos but names various chiefs. The following version was told to me by Mariá Maita de Guevara in 1990:

> That was when Caicara was founded, after all of that. There was a church put up by the Spaniards and the bells were in front in a huge tree. One day they said the Indians were about to attack the village. And then the people were frightened and went into the church. And the people all gathered together praying to God and in the night on the 3rd of August when Santo Domingo appeared, there in the gully they call Santo Domingo. And when the warriors came in the night they saw a man mounted on a horse and a dog at the feet of the horse and a huge army and they saw how the gold and silver from his buckles and buttons glowed. And when the Indians saw that they became frightened and ran away. And they told the other chiefs: 'There was an enormous army there at the edge of the village guarding it and we couldn't get by.' Then the other Indians crept up very slowly. But they didn't find anything. They were frightened by what the others had told them. They didn't go any further but stayed where they were till dawn. And you know the Indians are very brave so a group of the brave Indians dared to enter the village to see what exactly had happened. They came in little by little, and among them were some of the ones who had seen Santo Domingo when he was riding his horse. They saw the people who

were in the plaza and the bells were ringing and so they went into the church and what was their surprise, their terror when they went in and saw the man who had danced upon his horse on a pedestal in the centre of the altar. And they all ran out terrified. And it was from that moment on, from the apparition of Santo Domingo that the Indians became more religious. Ever since then every August 4th, the Indians come with their *parrandas* and things, dancing, to make offerings and pay homage to the church.

It should be noted that while Caicareños claim that 4 August was the date of Santo Domingo's miracle and thus the reason for their holiday, it is also the Catholic Church's official day for this saint. Known in English as Saint Dominic, Santo Domingo de Guzmán was a twelfth-century monk who founded the Dominicans or Order of Friars Preachers. Born in Calaruega, Spain, he rose to prominence for his success in combatting the Albigensians in southern France.

4 The shift in crops can be attributed to a number of causes including access to markets and changing settlement patterns. Nevertheless, one important factor has been the agrarian reform movement begun in 1959, which sought the redistribution of arable land into smaller holdings. The most detailed analysis of this area's economic and agricultural history is to be found in Arzolay *et al*. 1984.

5 Caicara and the surrounding communities form an administrative entity called the Municipio of Caicara which in turn joins two other *municipios* to create the Distrito Cedeño. While the population for the Municipio of Caicara did not increase substantially between 1961 and 1971 (from 9,384 to 10,804), the proportion living within the village of Caicara itself nearly doubled to between seven and eight thousand. Unfortunately, it becomes more difficult after this date to obtain specific data for the village of Caicara as subsequent censuses report only the populations for the *municipio* and *distrito*. This may be an indication of how much the *municipio* is now identified as the town. In any case, the 1981 population for the Municipio of Caicara was 13,638 and for the Distrito Cedeño 21,909 (Arzolay *et al*. 1984: 313; Ramírez 1972: 7). A reasonable estimate is that the present population of Caicara is between nine and ten thousand. There are no statistics for the indigenous population of either Caicara or the *municipio*. However, in 1981 the indigenous population for the State of Monagas was 2,142, up from 515 in 1950 while less than half that first reported in 1783, when it was 5,451. The 1981 population for all of Monagas was 390,071 (Arzolay *et al*. 1984: 104, 313).

6 The *liquiliqui* is a white linen or cotton suit with a high, upturned collar. While there are various theories as to its origins, it is generally assumed to have come from the southern *llanos* or plains and is considered by many to be the *traje tipico* or 'typical dress' of Venezuela. Another important aspect of the *mayordoma's* costume is a large straw hat decorated with flowers and fruit.

7 Although improvisation is most often based on both the people and locale immediately surrounding the singer, there are popular verses which are commonly repeated each year. The one cited here is among the most famous and may be translated as:

> Here comes that monkey
> down the narrow street
> Open up your doors
> to those dancing feet

8 Gavilán is the area in Caicara from which the Rojas group comes. However, they are also known as the Negros de Chilo Rojas because the group marches with their entire bodies and faces blackened. It is Rojas' contention that the use of blue indigo is a recent innovation and that formerly all celebrants were covered in black.

9 For the last several years, festival organizers have held a large dance on the evening of 28 December in order to raise funds for the celebration. These dances, with *salsa* or *merenque* groups brought in from either the capital or Puerto Ordaz, are held in a large hall where an admission fee is charged. Because of this dance, the Mono usually winds to a close between six and seven o'clock.

10 For more on this slow, liturgical music, sung in quatrains and most commonly identified with the Kariña or Carib Indians of Venezuela's eastern plains, see Acosta Saignes 1952; Carreño and Vallmitjana 1967; Corradini 1976; and Dominguez and Quijada 1969.

11 Rojas was born in 1920 and so must have been a good deal younger if this was the late 1920s.

12 In another statement concerning the recent invention of the Monkey Dance, Rojas was even more candid in his disdain. This statement also explains Rojas' belief that formerly all participants painted themselves black, hence the alternative name for both his group (the Negros de Chilo Rojas) and the festival (Día de los Negros or 'Day of the Blacks'):

> The 28th of December? The Day of the Holy Innocents. And that's that! Day of the Blacks. It was later that . . . My thing is black. Simple. That, that's not indigo. They never used that here. Here they used kettles from the store or grills . . . Here is is [referring to the soot].
>   Día de los Negros, Día de los Santos Inocentes. They didn't talk about Monkeys. That stuff about monkeys they invented. Like now, if I grab that drum and we say, 'Shit, let's invent the dance of the rooster, the dance of such and such.' And we go out dancing some thing, hopping around.

Because of Rojas' belief that the current Día del Mono celebration is a corruption of the earlier holiday, he has refused to take his turn performing on stage as all other groups do when they enter the plaza.

13 In 1981 Monagas was responsible for 7.8 per cent of the total oil produced in Venezuela, which is a tremendous amount for a nation whose foreign exports are nearly 98 per cent oil dependent. Almost all the remaining oil comes from the Lake Maracaibo area of Zulia (Arzolay *et al.* 1984: 249–77).

14 The main part of this irresistibility is the fact that in the 1920s when Standard Oil first arrived, farm workers could increase their salaries from 30 cents a day to $2.50 or more (Guevara 1974: 5). See Arzolay *et al.* for a well-documented analysis of the shift in Monagas' population from rural to urban. In 1950, the population was 42.5 per cent urban and 57.5 per

cent rural. By 1981 this ratio had shifted to 66.4 per cent urban and 33.6 per cent rural. Their estimate is that by 2001 the ratio will be 85.1 per cent to 14.9 per cent (1984: 73).

15 A more probable explanation for why Caicara is referred to as Caicara de Maturín is to distinguish it from Venezuela's other Caicara which is located in the state of Bolivar and known as Caicara del Orinoco.

16 It is worth noting Bentley's 1987 discussion on the difficulties of categorizing ethnicity as either instrumental or primordial, and particularly his warning against interpreting the motives of individuals' actions on the basis of their results:

> In ethnicity studies this meant that if ethnic groups act in ways that appear strategically advantageous, then strategic advantage must be the raison d'etre of those groups; if ethnicity increases in visibility during times of disorienting change, then it must be because people seek in ethnicity an emotional refuge from change. The theory of practice avoids this fallacious reasoning because it does not identify the systematic consequences of collective action with individuals' intentions.
>
> (1987: 48)

In relation to these observations, it must be noted that there are other interests, political and economic, which are achieving strategic advantage through the promotion of the Mono's purportedly unique indigenous status. As the Mono gains more national attention, tourism increases along with government grants and stipends for those promoting the festival. Along with such financial support can come an important power base. And indeed, both major political parties, COPEI and Acción Democrática, have their own culture centres with their own *parrandas*.

17 While Sollors has insisted that ethnicity be viewed as a modern phenomenon integrally linked to the rise of the nation-state, it may also be seen, particularly as a strategy of opposition, as a contemporary articulation of syncretism:

> Ethnicity is not so much an ancient and deep-seated force surviving from the historical past, but rather the modern and modernizing feature of a contrasting strategy that may be shared far beyond the boundaries within which it is claimed.
>
> (Sollors 1989: xiv)

18 For a discussion of the role of the monkey as a Carib symbol of anti-culture par excellence, see Guss 1989. For an interesting comparative view of the monkey's symbolism in another cultural context, see Ohnuki-Tierney 1987.

REFERENCES

Acosta Saignes, M. (1952) 'El Maremare: baile del jaguar y la luna', *Archivos Venezolanos de Folklore* 2: 3–19.

Arzolay, C., Loreto, C., Marcano, E. and Morales, O. (1984) *Geografía del Estado Monagas*, Maturín: Ediciones Gobernación del Estado Monagas.

Bentley, G. Carter (1987) 'Ethnicity and practice', *Comparative Study of Society and History* 29, 1: 24–55.

Bakhtin, M. (1984) *Rebelais and his World*, Bloomington: Indiana University Press.

Boas, F. (1982 [1940]) *Race, Language, and Culture*, Chicago: University of Chicago Press.

Carreño, F. and Vallmitjana, A. (1967) 'Comentarios sobre el origen indígena del Mare Mare criollo', *Archivos Venezolanos de Folklore* 8: 327–35.

Chitty, J.A. de Armas (1982) *Historia de la Tierra de Monagas*, Maturín: Ediciones Gobernación del Estado Monagas.

Corradini, H. (1976) 'Divulgación de las culturas indígenas: Maremare, cantos sagrados de los indios Kariña', *El Luchador* (Ciudad Bolívar), December 28, 29, 30.

Dominguez, A.L. and Quijada, A.S. (1969) *Fiestas y danzas folklóricas de Venezuela*, Caracas: Monte Avila Editores.

González, E.A. (1991) 'La festividad de los Santos Inocentes en Osma'. *Anuario FUNDEF (Fundación de Etnomusicología y Folklore)* 2: 60–5.

Guevara Febres, J.A. (1974) *Sobre las huellas de el Mono: Caicara de ayer y siempre*, Puerto Ordaz: Diego de Ordaz.

Guss, D.M. (1989) *To Weave and Sing: Art, Symbol, and Narrative in the South American Rain Forest*, Berkeley: University of California Press.

—— (1993) 'The selling of San Juan: the performance of history in an Afro-Venezuelan community', *American Ethnologist* 20, 3: 451–73.

Hatch, J.M. (1978) *The American Book of Days*, New York: H.W. Wilson.

Hernández, D. and Fuentes, C. (1992) *Fiestas tradicionales de Venezuela*, Caracas: Fundación Bigott.

Lecuna, Y. S. de (1985) 'La inversión simbólica de lo sagrado y secular en las Locainas', *Montalbán* 16: 47–70.

Mackenzie, N. (1987) 'Boy into bishop, a festive role reversal', *History Today* 37: 10–16.

Mendez, Doris Ruíz de (1978) *Trabajo monográfico sobre el Baile de 'el Mono' de Caicara de Maturín*, Caracas: Instituto Nacional de Folklore, Centro de Formación Técnica.

Ohnuki-Tierney, E. (1987) *The Monkey as Mirror: Symbolic Transformations in Japanese History and Ritual*, Princeton, NJ: Princeton University Press.

Pollak-Eltz, A. and Fitl, R. (1985) 'La Locaina en Venezuela y sus antecedentes en el Medio Oriente y en Europa', *Montalbán* 16: 71–104.

Ramírez, J.J. (1972) *Remembranzas Caicareñas*, Caracas: 'La Bodoniana'.

—— (1985) *Monagas y su saber tradicional*, Maturín: Ediciones Gobernación del Estado Monagas.

—— (1986) *Diccionario folklórico ilustrado*, Maturín: Ediciones Gobernación del Estado Monagas.

—— (1988) 'El Mono de Caicara: una tradición monaguense que se pierde en el abismo del tiempo', *Folklor Oriental*, December: n.p.

Sollors, W. (ed.) (1989) *The Invention of Ethnicity*, New York: Oxford University Press.

Vila, M.A. (1978) *Antecedentes coloniales de centros poblados de Venezuela*, Caracas: Universidad Central de Venezuela.

8 Manipulated identities

Syncretism and uniqueness of tradition in modern Japanese discourse

Klaus-Peter Koepping

CONCEPTUAL PRELIMINARIES

The problem of the emergence of national or ethnic identity has been brought once more into sharp public focus through a number of violent struggles for self-determination. These began after the First and Second World Wars and led to the rise of new nation-states which were largely couched in terms of anti-colonialism, anti-imperialism and national independence, while the more recent movements which we are witnessing seem rather to be directed against the existence of these very nation-states in their multi-ethnic, multireligious and multicultural composition.

Earlier struggles created a dilemma for anthropological concepts and theories, for movements such as Cargo cults, while clearly syncretic, were directed against those powers from which parts of the syncretized cultural ideas derived. This left such concepts as 'syncretism' and 'anti-acculturative' movements in an ambivalent relationship in terms of explanatory power, as is shown in the debate between Worsleyites, who claimed these movements as new ideologies, and Lawrencians, who pointed to the tradition-laden epistemological base-line (Worsley 1957; Lawrence 1964). It became clear in the anthropological debate on culture change processes that Thurnwald's 'acculturation' can never be a neutral term. Not only were the processes of innovation through borrowing enmeshed in political power constellations, but the very process of adopting the innovative ideas or techniques was frequently accompanied by violent and nativistic struggles against the donor-culture, which found their outlet in what Mühlmann called 'pre-political' movements of millenarian, utopian and charismatic–messianic character (Mühlmann 1964). These 'anti-acculturative' movements – often the forerunners of political revolutions and nation-states – were profoundly ambivalent,

assimilating foreign ways of thinking while resisting foreign domination, taking the very legitimacy for resistance from foreign, mostly
Western, ideas of self-determination or freedom, while casting the
image of the 'new society' in terms of real or imagined traditional
values unsullied by foreign influences.

As much as anthropological theory – in its discussions on processes
of exogenously induced culture change – retained the essentialist
concept of culture, as if clearly discernible and discrete units were in
pristine contact situations, so too did the revivalistic movements
assume a pristine and definable cultural entity as the base-line for
their identity formation. Thus on both discourse levels, the anthropological and the social actor's, the very notion of 'syncretism' was
elided from discussion.

The more recent movements of 'ethnic self-determination' seem to
threaten anthropological self-understanding and conceptualization
on an even more basic level, for it is not syncretism itself but the
'invented tradition' of separateness and uniqueness of cultural self-
understanding which challenges the notion – dear to the anthropological enterprise – of describing the culture of an ethnic group in
the way it sees itself and thereby eliminating any use of a comparative
yardstick. The challenge is to the notion, first clearly enunciated by
Herder from the 1770s onwards (see Barnard 1969: 325), that each
cultural and historical period and entity has to be judged by its own
standards. The problem behind this requirement was clearly perceived by Leach when he stated that we should be careful lest we
endorse the claims for the rights of a national minority, for the
ensuing fragmentation often leads to violence: 'It is nationalism, not
technology, which is our contemporary disaster, the lamentable
delusion that only the separate can be free' (Leach 1967: 809). The
experience of the generation after Herder, when from the 1830s to
the 1850s a whole range of identity formations on Herder's principles,
such as Panslavism, became politically powerful, is being repeated.

Anthropology's task has not been made easier because the current
consciousness of what Said has called 'overlapping territories, intertwined histories' (Said 1993: ch. 1) is being acknowledged as
the norm of cultural developments. If anthropological discussion
continues to parrot the catechism of 'culture' as if it were a given
reality outside of time and space at each particular moment, we
should not be surprised if this very concept of the uniqueness of each
culture is taken from anthropological discourse, used, and redefined
by any social unit to create ever more discrete units which in turn
clamour for their place in the sun, leading to what Said has called

'the awful din of unending strife, and a bloody political mess' (Said 1993: xxiii). However, with the readmission into the scholarly vocabulary of the term 'syncretism' as descriptive shorthand for cultural realities, we may have taken a first step in avoiding that essentialism which, through the assumed unsullied pristineness and objective reality of such things as 'Germanness', 'Japaneseness' or 'Africanism', has become the tool of that struggle in which everyone insists on the 'purity or priority of one's own voice' (Said 1993: xxiii).

The path between the acknowledgment of unique configurations of cultural self-perception and the criticial assessment of the claims for such self-fashioning is the difficult one that anthropologists in their meta-narratives have to tread. The Japanese have had long experience of this tightrope, and in the following I shall therefore show how the Japanese elite as well as popular movements have, since the latter third of the nineteenth century, coped with the conundrum, steering between their belief in cultural uniqueness and the attempt to universalize their own attitudes in the world.

THE PRESENT-DAY DISCOURSE ON CULTURE IN JAPAN

For more than a decade now, the term 'internationalization' (*kokusaika*) has appeared conspicuously in public discourse in Japan, in newspaper editorials as well as in executives' meetings. It encompasses two elements: how to become international, learning more about foreign business customs or raising foreign-language competence, and – for the large companies – how to blend better overseas in order to sell more. While these pragmatic concerns are driven both by the scale of Japanese international economic involvement and by the perception, especially in the USA and in Europe, of Japanese power and export surplus, they also touch upon anxieties and reflections about cultural identity: what does it mean to be Japanese? The current public discourse and the intellectual reflections of the Japanese have thus shifted but slightly from the nineteenth century, yet there is one major difference apparent to the long-term observer. Formerly, the problem was 'How can we preserve Japanese uniqueness at home under the onslaught of foreign institutions?'; now it is rather 'How do we sell Japanese uniqueness overseas?'.

This almost obsessive concern with the uniqueness of their culture, which finds its present-day expression in the newly coined term *Nihonjinron* ('theories of Japaneseness'), used in inside as well as outside discourse on Japanese culture, is, as Sydney Crawcour has cogently pointed out, neither a scientific description nor an analysis of the reality of Japanese society but rather a 'normative ideological system' (Crawcour 1980: 187).

The *Nihonjinron* craze in Japan has fostered such ideas as the specific uniqueness of the Japanese brain, which makes Japanese thought processes and linguistic expressions incomparable (see Tsunoda 1978) and therefore incomprehensible to and unlearnable by foreigners, or the uniqueness of Japanese stomachs, which prevents them digesting Australian beef (the *wagyu*, 'our beef', issue of the late 1970s). While such modern excrescences of the myth of uniqueness as superiority can either be refuted with scholarly arguments with a dash of sarcasm (see Miller 1982) or dismissed as passing fads of the pulp press, we cannot avoid pointing to the potential influence on the mass readership who recognize in these idiocies their own deepest anxieties and find in them 'scientifically' constructed palliatives. As Dale pointed out: 'the Nihonjinron have become a force in society conditioning the way Japanese regard themselves' (Dale 1986: 15). Not surprisingly, the wholesale and uncritical adoption by some Western management theories of 'the Japanese way' has strengthened in a complex feed-back loop the Japanese self-perception of their superiority, for the very Western cultures from which one learnt the scientific way toward modernization, and which covertly are always taken as the yardstick for the measuring of one's achievements, now need to adopt Japanese techniques of managing social relations within the economic realm (see Mouer and Sugimoto 1986).

Behind those popular issues are serious scholarly debates which show a variety of attitudes toward syncretism. The famous Sanskritist and historian of Japanese modernity, Nakamura Hajime, tries to make the point that modernization and Westernization are two distinct processes, and that premodern Japan was politically and economically comparable with the Renaissance or Reformation period of the West (Nakamura 1986). Nishitani Keiji in turn puts forward the very 'anthropological' proposal that a renewal of the West can only come about through an encounter with a 'completely different foreign culture or religion', thus inverting the position of the parties of the interaction in syncretic encounters which was assumed to hold for the nineteenth century (Nishitani 1986: 196–7). As no other Asian or Third World nation except Japan achieved any form of economic, social or power parity with the imperial powers of the nineteenth century or the economic powers of the late twentieth century, the issue of Japanese attitudes to foreign intrusions has become one of international debate. If Japan is such an exception in historical times, how has it achieved this counter-hegemony? We cannot unequivocally decide this issue from the available historical and socio-political data, for these allow one to argue either that the Japanese succeeded because of their isolation and their rejection of foreign intrusions during the major period of the shaping of modernity (from 1600 until 1868) or, taking the opposite view, that it is the Japanese 'genius' for syncretism – and indeed their successful synthesis of different cultural traditions – over the last 1500 years of recorded history which enabled them to take over selectively what they thought would not only fit their culture, but also counter the hegemony of Western imperial powers. More important than this chicken-and-egg issue is the need to deepen our understanding of the discourse the Japanese have conducted about their selective strategies and thus to understand what may lie behind certain prejudices or attitudes of seclusion, of rejection, or of acceptance of particular outside influences, and how the Japanese manage to swing between uniqueness and universality in their quest for self-identity.

It is only with knowledge of this discourse in different social strata in Japan, and with insight into the narratives on Self and Otherness, that the anthropologist is able to build the meta-narrative of the interplay between the inside and outside visions of Japan's role in the world community. The present chapter can only be a preliminary attempt at such investigation, but it is apparent that these discourses on identity, on Self and Otherness, have more than academic importance: each move by the economic powers of the world or by GATT with regard to Japanese export policies finds a considered response couched in terms of the 'specific cultural constraints' of Japan, and each Japanese response is taken as the base-line for a reassessment of the outside's view of that culture. By concentrating on the competing discourses internal to Japan, anthropologists at least remain true to their professional aim of soliciting the inside view, and may thus avoid the pitfalls of either distorting these through the imposition of a priori theories from the outside, or of exoticizing the other's view. This can only be done by rejecting the Japanese delusion of superior uniqueness, in referring back to some comparative universal tendencies found in discourses on identity formation in other societies: only then can one retain a critical edge in the meta-narrative.

The main focus of the following sections is therefore on the Japanese theory and practice of modernization through syncretizing efforts, and this on two levels: how the late nineteenth-century literary elite reflected on the syncretism resulting from the import of Western institutions engineered by the ruling oligarchy after 1868, and how the response of the masses to this syncretism finds expression in popular charismatic and millennial utopian movements, which, while trying to universalize a world-saving message, built on precepts that are similar to, though more nativistic than, those of the nineteenth-century elite, without the latter's Confucian influences. I shall mention some historical ideological antecedents of this modern discourse and point out the diversity of Japanese views, though I cannot here delineate and define universal tendencies of syncretism or discourses on syncretism, as this needs a further, meticulous, comparative analysis.

NISHIMURA SHIGEKI: A MEIJI REFORMER AS ANTHROPOLOGIST BEFORE ANTHROPOLOGY?

Shortly after the Meiji Reformation of 1868, and under the guidance of powerful court officials, bureaucrats and intellectual advisors, Japan revamped its major institutions along Western lines: the prefectural system, the postal system, modern coinage, the Gregorian calendar, a railway system, national banks and a Western education system were set in place by 1873. The political intricacies of the rise of the Meiji emperor will not be dealt with here, but it is important to remember that the return of the imperial institution to real government and symbolic power rested on similar premises to those of the rise of German and Slavic nationalism in the nineteenth century, namely on the works of philologists and a scholarly elite who stressed the uniqueness of specific cultural traditions. *Kokugaku* writings (works of 'national learning') powerfully reinterpreted Japanese history from the end of the seventeenth century to the middle of the nineteenth century, in order to rid ancient Japanese Shinto sources of foreign accretions (see Hammitzsch 1939). This originally purely philological movement took on strong political overtones, being directed against syncretic mergers of Shinto and Buddhist ritual practices and theology, and against everything Chinese, which stood for degeneracy and alienness. While this nativistic movement may have been critical of the Tokugawa rule, as the recent in-depth analysis of the works of the protagonists by Harootunian indicates (Harootunian 1988), it nevertheless strengthened the myth of imperial descent and the central position of the emperor as 'soul of the nation'. The emperor's power, supported by soldier and politician alike, rested on the socially binding force of the traditional family system through reinterpreted and indigenized Confucian values.

The main proponents of the new 'non-syncretic' beliefs were as varied as those of the modernized state bureaucratic syncretism, ranging from the scholarly elite of Confucian persuasion to their equally learned collaborators in the bureaucratic administration of feudal fiefdoms, and from the small followers of military leaders of particular clans to the economic entrepreneurs (see Dore 1969: 121). I shall concentrate here on the personality of one of the foremost educational specialists, Nishimura Shigeki (1828–1902), for through his deep historical understanding and training in Confucian thought he provides us with an excellent insight into the complex reflections and rationale behind the nineteenth-century syncretic push and its limits.

Nishimura began his career as advisor to a powerful Tokugawa provincial ruler; in his youth he studied Dutch books, and learnt some English after 1861. On the restoration of the imperial government in 1868, he was one of the best-informed experts on Western affairs, and though he had never himself travelled abroad, he became a major interpreter of Western learning to a broad spectrum of the Japanese ruling elite. In 1875 he was appointed Lecturer on Western Books to the Meiji emperor and was in addition the teacher of four princes from 1877 to 1880. After major appointments at the Ministry of Education as compiler of textbooks and editor for translations, in 1886 he moved full-time to the court (see Shively 1969: 211). Through his long influence in key positions as advisor to the imperial family (also compiling a book on women's role and learning, upon the request of the empress) and through his years in education, Nishimura is a fitting example to elucidate the diversity of concurrent positions on foreign institutions and practices which a single individual may hold.

Modernization through assimilation of foreign social and cultural institutions, from law to education and from defence to international affairs, was officially sanctioned and promoted as an active goal by the Charter Oath of the Emperor in 1868, the last paragraph of which reads: 'Knowledge shall be sought throughout the world, so that the welfare of the Empire may be promoted' (for different translations see Sansom 1965: 318). While the aim of this policy was clearly to bolster the recently imposed central imperial rule as well as to put Japan on a par with other imperial powers, after the humiliation of the treaties in 1853 and the opening of Japan's ports to world trade, its interpretation was open to debate: whether wholesale or piece-meal, *which* institutions should be taken over and *how* should they be integrated into traditional indigenous systems of thought and administration?

Nishimura's discernment becomes very clear when one compares his writings with the prevailing slogans which governed public opinion in the period until the end of the 1880s. The slogans ranged from 'Repel the barbarians' (*jôi*), to 'Reject Buddhism' (*haibatsu*), and, supported by the central administration and propagated among the people, fed the twin aims of 'Enriching the country, strengthening its arms' (*fukoku kyôhei*) and 'Civilization and enlightenment' (*bunmei kaika*). This last principle builds on the phrase in the Charter Oath of 1868: 'evil customs of the past shall be broken off and everything based upon the just laws of Nature.'

At the height of the controversy between those advocating 'Revere the emperor, repel the barbarians' and those proclaiming 'Civilization and enlightenment', Nishimura stated in 1875 that the first goal would result in admiring antiquity and despising the present, holding one's own country in high esteem and detesting others, while the second would entail discarding the old and taking the new, and developing friendly relations with other countries (Shively 1969: 198). He was firmly against the attitude which we generally label as nativistic, stating that 'When Asians reform the government they call it "restoring antiquity" [referring to the popular slogan around 1868 of *fukko*], and when they discuss morality they call it "revering antiquity"' (see Shively 1969: 206). While he did not reject the myth of the imperial descent, he seems to have disliked the recourse to antiquarian scholarship to prove the 'Japaneseness' of all kinds of invented customary forms of behaviour.

But Nishimura did not want to introduce Western philosophy wholesale either, as it places great stress on knowledge but little on personal conduct. Nishimura's solution was to take the best from Confucian and Western philosophies, as he felt Japan was uniquely able to combine Eastern and Western philosophies (1882; Shively 1969: 235). He acknowledged that Japan had always introduced its moral systems from abroad, but he also stressed that the selection of the elements must be made according to the suitability to one's own customs (Shively 1969: 234). While he sometimes prevaricated in his position about the introduction of Western practices, Nishimura's wish to adopt the best of two worlds was also clearly governed by fear of the Western colonial powers, even in the late 1880s; if both enlightenment and strong arms could not be secured at the same time, he would opt for the second before the first.

In many ways the main theme of Nishimura, the establishing of a code of moral precepts for national identity, was finally implemented by the government in the Imperial Rescript on Education of 1890, which not only listed the five moral relationships of traditional Confucianism but contained the phrases 'pursue learning and cultivate arts, and therefore develop intellectual faculties and perfect moral powers; . . . advance public good and promote common interests', ending with a reference to the mythical legitimation of Imperial rule, 'thus guard and maintain the prosperity of Our Imperial Throne coeval with heaven and earth' (Sansom 1965: 464).

It is clear that this is the point at which the message of the Meiji innovators, who had grappled so arduously with the question of syncretism and learning from the West, was lost amid the rhetoric of the mysticism of the emperor. The rise of the imperial myth and its legitimation through the invented culture of the past, with its apotheosis of Shinto as the national belief system of the Meiji oligarchy, paved the way for the rampant nationalism of the 1930s, the remnants of which can be discerned as echoes in what Harootunian has called the 'shrill pronouncements' of the current discourse on *Nihonjinron* (see Harootunian 1988: 438). These strident, jingoistic phrases are certainly not the direction which the Meiji enlighteners wanted Japan to pursue, for they unanimously subscribed to the main Meiji slogan – 'Western technology, Eastern spirituality' (*seiyô no gakugei, tôyô no dôtoku*) – coined by the Neo-Confucianist Sakuma Shôzan (1811–64), Nishimura's teacher.

The case of Nishimura is of interest for modern comparative anthropology, for he raised – long before professional anthropologists dealt with this problem – the question of how one can remain true to one's own culture while adopting the practices and ideas of another, or, to put it into anthropological terminology and experience, how one can speak with the voice of other cultures in one's own idiom without losing either or both. Nishimura, like the rest of the Japanese scholarly elite of the nineteenth century, ended up splitting the essentialist concept of culture into two abstract entities, a material and a spiritual side (much as modern anthropology after Friedrich Ratzel divided 'material' from 'ideational' culture). The issue is as much with us today in anthropological discourse (see Geertz's invectives about ventriloquism, 1988: 133) as it was and is in Japanese intellectual circles. That this is no mere intellectual pastime for the Japanese I shall make clear in the next section, providing a short overview of a religious mass movement which shows similar anxieties about cultural uniqueness and the concomitant desire to universalize the Japanese message.

SYNCRETISM IN RELIGIOUS MASS MOVEMENTS

The group whose major value premises I shall present[1] is one of the four hundred or so officially registered 'New religions' (*shinkô shûkyô*), most of which sprang up after the promulgation of the Religious Freedom Clause in the Constitution after 1946, though some of the most famous and stable organizations began in the middle of the nineteenth century (see Hardacre 1984, 1986). The common features of all the groups or movements are the founding by a charismatic individual and the aim of personal salvation, ranging from the promise of the alleviation of physical or psychic afflictions to the solving of personal problems of unhappiness, poverty or family strife through either ritual performances (such as prayers, songs, pilgrimages and dances) or an inner change of attitude among believers in the form of good works such as neighbourly help, mutual aid, caring for the sick, giving donations or performing voluntary labour. The groups display a variety of value orientations which may be labelled millenarian, messianic or nativistic (see Koepping 1967, 1974, 1977, 1980, 1990). In their stress on the personal as well as collective level, these movements thus fall into the category of revitalization movements defined by Wallace as those which 'provide personal salvation to the presently afflicted and . . . reorganize the culture in such a manner that a better way of life is brought into being' (Wallace 1966: 164). While some of these groups attract millions of adherents, like the internationally known Sôka Gakkai ('Value Creating Society') with its political offshoot, the Komeito ('Clean Government Party'), others are only regionally influential with between 30,000 and 200,000 members.

I have chosen the specific group Sekai Mahikari Bummei Kyodan ('Religion of the True Light Civilization for the World'), which was founded in 1959 by a Mr Okada Kotama (the second, personal, name having an intended affinity with the word for the historical Buddha, *Gautama*), because the teachings of its founder are avowedly syncretic, aiming to represent a 'universal truth' while consciously referring to Japanese traditions and in particular to the Japanese language as the legitimating feature for the claim of universal truth.

The foundation story goes back to Okada's revelation, which came from the universal God, introducing a 'new era of human history'. Okada considered himself as the trumpet, channel or voice of the divine will for humanity's future, without speaking with the voice of the deity itself (Koepping 1967; Davis 1980). The revelations amount to the following teachings: the modern world is on the way to destruction by a 'baptism of fire' which can only be avoided by a return to the true nature of humanity. Originally, human beings were of divine substance and nature, communing with the deities directly (*kami*, the Shinto term for deity). It was through the introduction of science that the original 'civilization of light' (*bunmei*) turned into what we see as modern culture, a culture of separation and dissent (*bunka*). Release from personal affliction and alienation is possible by remembering the 'way of the gods' (*kannagara no michi*, an indigenous reading of the Sino-Japanese term Shinto) and the era of divinity, when humanity, animals and plants lived together in harmony on Japanese soil. Japan is the source of all species, all languages and all religions, and thus a return to these truths contained in the written Shinto sources of the eighth century is of paramount importance.

Shinto contains the final truth of all religions, while other religions and other scriptures only faintly remember this truth of the 'true light' (*mahikari*): the founder quotes the gospel of St John in corroboration, 'In the beginning was the Word and the word was with God and the word was God.' These revelations of St John are parts of the truth of the baptism by fire, and the ultimate correctness of this interpretation derives from the peculiar linguistic hermeneutics of the founder. Okada insists that the Japanese language and its sounds contain the original divine tongue, other languages and religious texts containing this truth only in a muddled way. Thus the name of St John in its Greek form of Ioannes is read in Japanese phonetics as *Yohane*, which can mean *Yo* = four, *Ha* = eight, *Ne* = sound; there are 48 sounds in the Japanese syllabary. The truth of divine teachings is taught apparently in Japanese, thus making the words of the gods as recorded in Shinto, sources the true divine revelation of the condition of humanity in the past and future.

These religious precepts, which appear in more or less modified form in many of the other four hundred or so existing new religious movements acknowledged by the Ministry of Education in Japan (for variations see Koepping 1990), seem to concentrate on the ethnocentrism, superiority and originality of the Japanese culture. One is tempted to suggest that it sounds as if the imagined, constructed and invented past of the Japanese culture had been deified into an item of worship, and this is certainly not far from the truth. Indeed the legitimation of these teachings through Okada's recourse to the sacredness of the Japanese language puts the historical scholar on the right track. Many of the precepts about the sacredness of Japanese, which, as Okada also points out, embodies the 'soul of things' (*kotodama*), hark back to their intellectual forerunners, the above-mentioned philological scholars of the nativistic *kokugaku* tradition.

The word *kotodama* is as good an example as any through which to explain Okada's manipulation of Japanese phonetics and his knack of creating in his Japanese audience echoes of cultural semantics which reverberate back through several centuries. His reading of the phonetics of *kotodama* is possible through the underlaying of the sound with different Chinese ideograms which have a similar sound. *Kotodama* originally meant the 'soul of language', but through the substitution of the sign for 'matter' for the homophone *koto* ('language') Okada's reading can imply that the 'soul of things', their essence, their true meaning, is expressed and revealed by the 'soul of language', which, since the writings of the nativistic advocates from the seventeenth to nineteenth century (Kamo Mabuchi, Motoori Norinaga and Hirata Atsutane), is meant to encompass the specific sacredness and ineffability of Japanese. It was and is a divine tongue, somehow only comprehensible to Japanese speakers as it reverberates within their soul, understood not as the spiritual essence of an individual but rather as the spiritual essence of the collectivity, of what since the 1930s is circumscribed as the sacred entity of *kokutai*, the 'state structure', 'national government', the 'national body politic'. This is made up of the unity of folk and ruler, but is symbolically and bodily realized in the person of the emperor who, as a living person, is also a 'living deity', an *ikigami*, descending in unbroken bloodline from the sun-goddess Amaterasu Omikami.

These are the implications and resonances of the word *kotodama* for Japanese, and this teaching of the religious founder therefore connects with the recent craze in the public discussion of *Nihonjinron*, which largely centres on the question of Japanese language (*Nihongo*), its uniqueness, its superiority, its incomprehensibility to foreigners and such like. (For a deeper discussion of the meaning of *kotodama* in the works of the nativists see Harootunian 1988; for a critical assessment of its 'fascist' undercurrents see Miller 1982.)

Without going into the hair-raising intricacies of refashioning Japanese phonetics and writing through Okada's teachings (for details see Koepping 1967, 1974), it is clear that we find here in the religious garb of a millenarian movement (with strong faith-healing rituals) the clear re-emergence of the notion of uniqueness, albeit in a form which claims foreign accretions as deviations from the original Japanese language. Foreign words and foreign religions are not expelled, but taken to retain a grain of a 'hidden truth'. The only outside Western influence which is utterly rejected is science, as the paramount destructive element of modernity. In many ways, this form of refashioning of tradition deals quite differently with foreign intrusions than did the forms of the Meiji elite, who adopted the technology and science of the West while retaining the ideal values of Japan in its Confucian, interpersonal morality rather than its mystic-mythic Shinto ideology.

ON SYNCRETISM AND TOLERANCE: TENTATIVE CONCLUSIONS

In the Japanese context of culture change through the elite-directed appropriation and dissemination of Western technologies, the question of the merging and selectivity of worldviews and of philosophies to guide interpersonal relations or political decisions, work ethics or educational praxis did, as I have tried to show, raise considerable debate within the intellectual circles around the ruling oligarchy of the nineteenth century. At the same time, popular mass movements with millennial aspirations show a similar dichotomizing of the essentialist concept of culture as an assumedly shared pool of standards by separating values from science. In both cases we see the implications of syncretism in action. The term, though, is as ambiguous for the participants in Japanese culture as for anthropological observers, for it encompasses multiple possibilities for interpretation of those actions and attitudes aiming to appropriate foreign knowledge and maintain indigenous traditions. The intellectual Neo-Confucianist Nishimura felt that the uniqueness and authenticity of Japanese culture (thus reified) lay in Confucian moral values, whose prestige he tried to bolster through reference to and comparison with the scientific ethics of Comte, Spencer or Pestalozzi, thus denying the need to import morals together with technology. Many utopian movements in Japan since the middle of the nineteenth century, however, as an example of which I took the recently founded Mahikari, have attempted to reduce foreign religions and morality to original Japanese concepts via reinterpreted Japanese myths and language.

What is of interest in this context is not so much to show that the new religious movements may be little but a reaction against the disorganizing effects of elite-directed modernization (Koepping 1974), but rather that their understanding of syncretism is not the same and that an insistence on uniqueness and a grounding of one's collective identity can be understood in diverse ways. The examples also show that the whole notion, still prevalent in modern Japan, that Japanese culture is unique because it is tolerant of different value systems has to be scrutinized.

The above cases clearly show that neither the elite nor the mass movements are truly tolerant in regard to the introduction of unmodified foreign value systems. Both phenomena are close to the attitude of the eighteenth-century philologists, as illustrated by a quotation from Mabuchi from the 1760s:

> When Confucianism was first introduced into Japan, the simple-minded natives, deceived by its plausible appearance, accepted it with eagerness, and allowed it to spread its influence everywhere. The consequence was the civil war which broke out . . . in 671 . . . In the 8th century the Chinese costume and splendour were adopted by the Court. This foreign pomp and splendour covered the rapid depravations of men's hearts, and created a wide gulf between the Mikado and his people.
>
> (Quoted after Satow 1927: 177)

Modern scholarship finds itself in a similar quandary with the assumption, still reiterated by Colpe in comparative religious studies, that syncretism requires an attitude of tolerance as its precondition (Colpe 1987: 226). While as anthropologists, members of a syncretizing profession as well as analysts of syncretism (Shaw and Stewart, this volume), we may acknowledge syncretic phenomena as authentic expressions of indigenous identity formation in contest with other cultures of the world, in the Japanese clash with Western cultures in modern times we should be free to point to possible self-delusions to which the promoters of such ideological movements may have fallen prey. As Appiah put it in a strongly worded critique of the self-understanding of Afro-American ideologies, with their blatant anti-Semitism, anti-feminism and homophobia: 'The proper response to Eurocentrism is surely not a reactive Afrocentrism, but a new understanding that humanizes all of us by learning to think beyond race' (Appiah 1993: 25).

Japanese histories of religion still hark back to the much-loved illusion that Shinto Japan in the seventh century, during the introduction of Buddhism, was a tolerant society (Anesaki 1963: 9). While there can be no doubt that centuries later the three value systems of Shinto, Buddhism and Confucianism coexisted by ruling different spheres of life, the initial reaction was quite the opposite, for diverse political factions used religions as weapons in the contest for supremacy, as the same writer later acknowledges: 'Strife continued and became finally so vehement that the succession to the throne and other important State affairs became involved, and even the life of the sovereign was threatened' (Anesaki 1963: 55).

Anthropologists, as translators of and between cultures, should also have enough reflexive insight to acknowledge that such reactions are in themselves new forms of manipulation of existing hegemonies of discourse (West versus East, North versus South etc.), in which Western and Eastern ideologies and values are in a constant interplay of contested identities, where nobody can ascertain the beginning of the flicking of the shuttle on the final cloth of syncretic self-understanding. I would argue that anthropological meta-discourses are not necessarily more convincing than those developed by the Japanese intellectual elite or by messianic leaders of mass movements, as both are only meaningfully interpreted in specific contexts; or, as Leach long ago put it in regard to the controversy about virgin birth, we should be careful not to take theological utterings as expressions in a biological discourse on procreation. Yet, I would add, we should be free to spell out those dangerous tendencies which syncretism and reactions toward it entail when contests about collective identities and about the hegemony of different discourses veer toward assuming that the uniqueness of difference means 'superiority' in an absolute and universal sense. This forecloses any critical dialogue by moving the discourse to a religious rather than a rational plane.

NOTE

1 The empirical data were collected during fieldwork periods from 1966–9, 1974, 1978, 1986 and 1988.

REFERENCES

Anesaki, M. (1963) *History of Japanese Religion*, Vermont and Tokyo: Tuttle Co.

Appiah, K.A. (1993) 'Europe upside down', *Times Literary Supplement*, 12 February: 24–5.

Barnard, F.M. (1969) *Herder on Social and Political Culture*, Cambridge: Cambridge University Press.

Colpe, C. (1987) 'Syncretism', in M. Eliade (ed.), *Encyclopaedia of Religion*, vol. 14, New York: Macmillan.

Crawcour, S. (1980) 'Alternative models of Japanese society: an overview', *Social Analysis* 5/6: 184–7.

Dale, P.N. (1986) *The Myth of Japanese Uniqueness*, New York: St Martin's Press.

Davis, W. (1980) *Dojo: Magic and Excorcism in Modern Japan*, Stanford: Stanford University Press.

Dore, R.P. (1965) 'The legacy of Tokugawa education', in Marius B. Jansen (ed.), *Changing Japanese Attitudes Toward Modernization*, Princeton, NJ: Princeton University Press.

Geertz, C. (1988) *Works and Lives*, Cambridge: Polity Press, and Princeton, NJ: Princeton University Press.

Hammitzsch, H. (1939) 'Kangaku and Kokugaku', *Monumenta Nipponica* II: 1–24.

Hardacre, H. (1984) *Lay Buddhism in Contemporary Japan: Reiyukai*, Princeton, NJ: Princeton University Press.

—— (1986) *Kurozumikyô and the New Religions of Japan*, Princeton, NJ: Princeton University Press.

Harootunian, H.D. (1988) *Things Seen and Unseen. Discourse and Ideology in Tokugawa Nativism*, Chicago and London: University of Chicago Press.

Hori, I. (1968) *Folk Religion in Japan*, Chicago: University of Chicago Press.

Ishida, T. (1993) 'The changing intellectual climate in postwar Japanese social sciences', *The International House of Japan* 12, 5: 1–5.

Koepping, K.P. (1967) 'Sekai Mahikari Bunmei Kyodan', *Contemporary Religions in Japan*, 8: 101–34.

—— (1974) *Religiöse Bewegungen im Modernen Japan*, Cologne: Wienand Verlag.

—— (1976) 'On the epistemology of participant observation', *Occasional Papers in Anthropology* 6: 159–77.

—— (1977) 'Ideologies and new religious movements', *Japanese Journal of Religious Studies* 4, 2–3: 103–50.

—— (1980) 'The semiology of revolutionary movements', *Anthropological Forum*, 3–4: 21–40.

—— (1989) 'Mind, body, text: not quite satirical reflections on the anthropology of the trickster', *Criticism, Heresy and Interpretation* 2: 37–66.

—— (1990) *Die Neuen Regionen Japans*, vol. 44, Tokyo: OAG.

Lawrence, P. (1964) *Road Belong Cargo*, Manchester: Manchester University Press.

Leach, E. (1967) 'Reith Lectures', *The Listener*, 7 December – 11 January: 747–9.

Miller, R.A. (1982) *Japan's Modern Myth*, New York and Tokyo: Weatherhill.

Mouer, R., and Sugimoto, Y. (1986) *Images of Japanese Society*, London: KPI Publications.

Mühlmann, E.W. (1964) *Rassen, Ethnien, Kulturen*, Berlin: Reimer.

Nakamura, H. (1986) 'Der religionsgeschichtliche Hintergrund der Entwicklung Japans in der Neuzeit', in C. von Barloewen (ed.), *Japan und der Westen*, Munich: Fischer.

Nishitani, K. (1986) 'Modernisierung und Tradition in Japan', in C. von Barloewen (ed.), *Japan und der Westen*, Munich: Fischer.

Said, E. (1993) *Culture and Imperialism*, London: Chatto and Windus.

Sansom, G.B. (1965) *The Western World and Japan*, London: Cresset Press.

Satow, E. (1927) 'The revival of pure Shintau', *The Tradition of the Asiatic Society of Japan* II: 165–253.

Shively, D.H. (1969) 'Nishimura Shigeki: a Confucian view of modernization', in Marius B. Jansen (ed.), *Changing Japanese Attitudes toward Modernization*, Princeton, NJ: Princeton University Press.

Thurnwald, R. (1932) 'The psychology of acculturation', *American Anthropologist*, 34: 557–69.
Tsunoda, T. (1978) 'Nihonjin no No' (The Japanese brain), excerpted into English, *The Japan Foundation Newsletter* 6, 1: 3–7.
Wallace, A.F.C. (1966) *Religion*, New York: Random House.
Worsley, P. (1957) *The Trumpet Shall Sound*, London: MacGibbon and Kee.

9 Are fireworks Islamic?
Towards an understanding of Turkish migrants and Islam in Germany

Lale Yalçın-Heckmann

Five Turkish women and children were murdered through arson on the night of 29 May 1993, in the city of Solingen. There were subsequent protests, largely by the Turkish community, all over Germany. A Turkish columnist from *Hürriyet Daily* wrote his impressions of the protesting Turkish youth in an article entitled '*Tekbir*, the flag and punks' (Uluengin 1993). The behaviour and mood of these young people, according to the journalist, not only defied Turkish law because they were using the Turkish flag as a scarf or skirt, but it also defied the Islamic code of behaviour. They were saying *tekbir* (the religious formula '*Allah-ü Ekber*' in Arabic, which means 'Allah is great and omniscient') without the due ritual ablutions. The author interpreted the hybridization of symbols and symbolic acts (for instance blue-haired young Turks with punk-style earrings, dancing to rock music and shouting nationalist slogans like 'Turkey is the greatest', a common slogan for soccer fans, or 'Allah is great', a slogan used mostly by religious fundamentalist Turks), as characteristic of 'new Turks' in Germany. He praised their cultural expression, which differentiates them from their contemporaries in Turkey, and indicates the multicultural and multivocal nature of society in Germany.

The manifest hybridization attributed to the migrant culture probably reflects rather more the enthusiasm and political position of the Turkish journalist in the debate on multiculturalism in Germany than an exact depiction of the ethnographic reality. His plea for an acknowledgement of multiculturalism among the Turkish migrant community, as exemplified by the coexistence of multiple religious, national and ethnic symbols, contributes to the general effort to recognize the multicultural reality of Germany. These political statements contrast, however, with the sociological and psychological problems posed by Turkish labour migration to Germany. Recent racist attacks on foreigners in this country have led to a renewed public discussion of xenophobia (*Fremdenfeindlichkeit*). It is, after all, not only a problem for foreigners in Germany, but an internal problem, whose roots and solutions are to be sought within the country.

The complex processes of assimilation and resistance to assimilation in the history of labour migration not only produce such postmodern cultural expressions and collages of symbols but also lead to emotional debates about the 'authenticity' or 'mix' of traditions. These debates are conducted by cultural actors, interlocutors, analysts and outsider observers. Social scientific studies of migrants and of their adaptation processes have produced various authoritative diagnoses, which are subsequently adopted by 'cultural practitioners' (*Multiplikatoren*, a term used in general for foreign or German persons who interact culturally or socially with the migrants, ranging from social or community workers to ethnic artists or business people). As Lutz (1991: 6) has argued, social scientific research on migrant women especially suffers from (a) the application of social-work- and social-practice-oriented paradigms, and (b) the uncritical use of Orientalistic assumptions. In these depictions, the 'culture' of Turkish migrants is described by terms such as 'traditional' or 'Islamic' and is focused on the first generation of migrants. The second generation's cultural identity is described by terms such as 'in-between', or with metaphors such as 'sitting between two chairs' (*zwischen zwei Stühlen sitzen*) or 'being (torn) between two worlds' (*zwischen zwei Welten*).[1] These are terms which are used not only by social scientists or social workers studying or assisting the migrant community, but also by the migrants themselves (Lutz 1991: 230). The migrants' own term for adaptation or assimilation is *uyum* (*Anpassung* in German), and the limits and forms of *uyum* are central to debates on Turkish migrant identity and religion.

As with the depiction of the culture of young Turks by the journalist above, 'syncretic processes loom large in such writings' (see Shaw and Stewart, this volume). Yet syncretism is basically a technical term used much more in the context of religion than for culture (ibid.). Nevertheless, discussions about syncretism are largely missing in writings on the Islam of Turkish migrants. The Islamic religion of migrants is discussed either within frameworks of modernity (Thomä-Venske 1981; Schiffauer 1991) or else within the context of political, religious movements and associations (Binswanger and Sipahioğlu 1988), embracing various types of Islam such as 'orthodox'/urban versus rural Islam, which are thought to be transferred to the migrant setting. If there is any consideration of the mixing of different religious traditions at all, it is sought between these various 'types' of Islam and Islamic practices. Hence, urban Islam becomes politicized and develops into a political-Islamic project, led by religious organizations, or it is said that Alevi Islam adapts secularist Turkish republican discourse in order to construct and accommodate a new identity (Mandel 1989a; Wilpert 1988). That Islam existed in Europe before the arrival of Turkish labour migrants and that ideas about Islam and Muslims may have been formed before the arrival of the labour migrants are issues raised mainly by historians, Turkologists and orientalists (see Kreiser 1985; Karpat 1990). The relationship between these ideas on Islam, as they were formed within the context of European history, and the presence of Islam in Germany before the arrival of Turkish migrants is promptly raised by the minority of German Muslims (see Abdullah 1992).

If accepting, refuting or ignoring syncretism in religion are ways of negotiating power on the part of various agencies (see Stewart, this volume), then the recognition of syncretism within migrant culture (by journalists, for example), and its refutation within the context of migrant Islam (by religious leaders),[2] are issues which need to be explored. More specifically, the problem of who has the authority to define the authenticity of 'migrant Islam', how various groups and individuals within the migrant community deal with the question of *uyum* between various religious traditions, where Turkish parents, for instance, draw the boundaries of religious mixing in rituals, festivals and other practices – all these need to be examined. Labour migrants from Turkey are, after all, of various ethnic, social, economic and even religious (Alevi or Sunni) backgrounds. They also have differing views of religion, as will be discussed in the case of the headscarf below. (My discussion is based on thirty randomly chosen families in a German city and the sample group is not statistically representative of all the Turkish migrants in Germany.) Given this heterogeneity, do Turkish migrants show *uyum* in the domain of religion? If so, do they acknowledge it as such, or is 'migrant Islam' categorically closed to *uyum* in public, but more negotiable in private, within the family or for the second generation? If the surrounding Christian German culture poses a challenge for Muslim rituals, their social significance and meaning, what sorts of processes take place in order to meet these challenges and to what degree are these intentional? And if migrant parents are concerned about the influence of Christian traditions, where do they seek resolutions, and where and how do they confront these influences? These are some of the questions which are significant in exploring power and agency in syncretic practices, which may be articulated as cultural in some contexts, but religious in others.

TURKISH LABOUR MIGRATION TO GERMANY

Let us look briefly at the phenomenon of labour migration from Turkey to Germany and the processes of the establishment of the Turkish community as a significant ethnic group in Germany. Turkish labour migration to Germany as governmental policy began over thirty years ago and was stopped in 1973. Turkish migration since the 1960s can be roughly divided into three phases: first came male and female workers as individuals, recruited for certain jobs and living in workers' residence halls. The second phase is marked by the stoppage of new labour recruits, followed by the arrival of family members, husbands, wives and children. The third phase is reached with the third generation of migrants, born and living in Germany. At present the Turks compose a community of nearly 1.8 million people in Germany, the largest group of foreigners there. Foreigners altogether comprise *c*. 7 per cent of the total population. Although the Turkish population was predominantly working-class during the first two decades of migration, the population composition and occupational structure now show considerable changes. For instance, there are about 35,000 Turkish small businesses in Germany, creating jobs for over 125,000 people. This trend is on the increase. Over 40,000 Turkish families have bought houses and property in Germany, strengthening the trend of becoming a permanent ethnic community and minority. With these slow but constant changes in occupational structures and the penetration of Turks into almost all social strata within German society – even if without fundamental rights with regard to political representation due to their 'foreigner' (*Ausländer*) status – the Turkish community in Germany is becoming increasingly integrated into German political discourse, organized through local and nationwide associations,[3] and hence a social and political force to be reckoned with.

The most significant distinguishing characteristic of the Turkish migrant community which defines them as 'other' (in their own view as well as in the eyes of the 'outsiders', the dominant German society) is their religion, Islam (Elsas 1983; Thomä-Venske 1988). The type of Islam to which they adhered back at home was mainly Sunni Islam, with a significant minority of Alevi Kurds and Turks. Due to the historical and political developments of the last seventy years in the Turkish Republic, the politics of Islam had to take particular positions against the strongly secular tradition of the central state (Mardin 1991; Sarıbay 1985). Hence, there were various (pluralistic) traditions of Islam in Turkey, which the migrants could associate with. In migration they relate these traditions to further pluralism(s); for instance, some migrants reclaim aspects of the republican discourse of pre-Islamic culture(s) and their alleged liberal attitudes towards gender roles as being coterminous with modernity, and define 'their Islam' accordingly, adjusting it to their own migration and diaspora experiences.

As suggested above, many studies of Muslim migrants and institutions in Germany or Europe focus on 'political Islam', Islamic organizations and the existence and spread of Qur'an courses. They often use categories such as folk Islam, traditional Islam, or modernist Islam without necessarily questioning the ways these concepts have been taken out of the original context. Moreover, to deal with the changes in Islamic beliefs and practices in diaspora, modernization theories have often been used. According to these models, changes are reactive, being imposed by a necessary adjustment to the 'modern' (Schiffauer 1991). Some authors, like Fischer and Abedi 1990, prefer to use the term 'postmodernism' to differentiate 'late twentieth-century modernism' from 'earlier modernism', and suggest that postmodernism 'invokes the increasing pervasiveness of global interaction. Thus the debates over conflicting moral grounds [brought on] by the shifts from small-scale communities to international networks of migrants and social strata' (Fischer and Abedi 1990: xxxi). Ahmed elaborates on similar dimensions of Islam and postmodernism, and emphasizes that 'the postmodernist age [presupposes] a questioning of, a loss of faith in, the project of modernity' (Ahmed 1992: 10). Postmodernism 'coexists and coincides with the age of media' (ibid.: 11); it is 'metropolitan' (ibid.: 18); and finally, it 'allows, indeed encourages, the juxtaposition of discourses, an exuberant eclecticism, the mixing of diverse images' (ibid.: 25).

These features largely characterize the Islam of migrant Turks, since it is urban, sometimes metropolitan, and closely linked to the media and its products (Islamic media has been flourishing in Turkey; many migrants are buyers of these journals, videotapes and cassettes, which, among other subjects, treat Islamic history and politics). Nevertheless, the debate on modernity is not yet outdated within the Muslim discourse. Even if postmodernity allows for eclecticism and syncretism (as in the first example of young Turks described by the journalist), this mixture of images is by no means collectively and smoothly accepted by the people themselves as the articulation of pluralism(s). The debate on *uyum* is a case in point. *Uyum* is favoured by many migrants, when it means adapting, for instance, to consumption or work habits and taking on the host society's notion of 'time-use'. Nevertheless, when it comes to *uyum* in religious practice, the degree of flexibility has to be carefully negotiated and contextualized. *'Herkesin dini kendine'* ('Each to [has] her/his own religion') summarizes the common concern for maintaining religious domains separate from one another. The concern with authenticity and rules of commensality in religion – how far certain 'new' celebrations are compatible with Islam – these are daily questions for many migrants. Pnina Werbner, who also studied the phenomenon of change in Islamic concepts and practices among another group of migrants, that of Pakistanis in Manchester, suggests that ritual is 'naturalized' in the context of migration. The performance of Muslim sacrifices and offerings, for instance, presupposes the existence of a category of people who can be defined as the 'poor'. As this category is considered to be absent by the Pakistani migrants in the context of Manchester, the migrants are induced to reflect on 'the taken-for-granted features of rites' (Werbner 1990: 154). Like the Pakistani Muslims in Manchester, the Turkish Muslim migrants are compelled to be conscious of rites of commensality, ritual cleanliness and other religious rites within the migration context. They also have to resolve the problem of reconstructing their 'community', which is expected to become the 'significant other' in ritual, and cope with their 'problem of history and their particular part in it' (ibid.: 1). Hence, how changes in religious ritual and meanings are to be interpreted is dependent on how migrants define their migration experience and their relationship to the host society. A very significant marker of this shift in historical and symbolic belonging can be observed in burial rites, when migrants begin burying their dead in the country of immigration instead of their 'home' country (ibid.: 155). This trend is observable among Turkish migrants as well. In their search for a place as Turkish Muslim migrants in German society, they reshape many religious concepts and practices, albeit with ambivalences. An example to illustrate this point may be the interpretations of Turkish Muslims of the 'sacred Christian time' beginning with Advent and extended to Christmas, the New Year and *'Heilige Drei Könige'* (from the biblical story of the arrival of the three wise men, that is, Epiphany).

GERMAN CHRISTMAS AND NEW YEAR'S EVE

New Year is celebrated in Germany, as in other European countries, with huge firework displays beginning at midnight and lasting until the early morning hours. Young and old go out to the streets and let off their fireworks and firecrackers, spending hours outdoors and creating an atmosphere which is sometimes described as being 'warlike'. On the following day newspapers report not only on the glamour of the celebrations and displays of light and sound, but also on the money spent on fireworks, which came to over a hundred million marks in 1991. Church groups complain that so much money should be spent on an event that lasts only a few hours and brings no moral or social benefits. These firework celebrations, however, are very popular with children. Parents find it difficult to refuse to buy fireworks for the children, who would not be able to sleep throughout this noisy night anyway. Children of Turkish labour migrants are no exception. A working-class Turkish father answered my question about how the non-Muslim environment affected the upbringing of his children as follows:

> For instance, *Weihnachten* [Christmas] is a religious holiday; and those rockets, bombs [that is, fireworks and firecrackers] . . . I actually buy those things for my children. Many people say that there's no such thing in our religion! I *know* there's no such thing in our religion, but we don't have the ability to explain this to a 7-year-old child! Even if we had the ability to explain, the child can't understand it . . . When all other children are playing with fireworks, how could you keep your child tied up indoors? This would give exactly the opposite impression, the opposite of what we desire. I am not encouraging my children to participate in this, but when they want ten fireworks I buy five or six for them . . . It is not only me; nobody could reason with a child when his friends are playing with fireworks on the street, telling him 'look, we are Muslims' . . . He will then simply abhor Islam.

Whether firework displays are compatible with Islam or not is a concern for Muslim Turkish parents in Germany maybe once a year. But shifting definitions of proper or improper behaviour among the younger generation, negotiations for flexible religious symbols and meanings (for example, issues such as 'Should one give in to the demands of the children and decorate a Christmas tree at home?', or 'Why fast in Ramadan?'), and the insecurity about reproducing or controlling these meanings are part and parcel of everyday life for

Turkish Muslim labour migrants. In order to understand religion as a component of everyday life, the role of everyday practices and the power of the religious idiom which frames the daily life practices of the Turkish migrants, an analysis of syncretic as well as anti-syncretic discourses is required. This is especially so at the borders where non-religious beliefs and practices are negotiable, where influences are perceived and adopted and where the 'religious' merges with the 'ethnic', the 'humanist' or the 'political'.

Many Turkish migrants conflate New Year's Eve with Christmas. Nevertheless, the meaning and form of Christmas celebrations is significant not only as illustrating the ways of negotiating Islamic religious symbols in the diaspora context, but also because its meaning for Christian Germans is far from unitary. For those in southern Germany, with strong rural Catholic traditions, the period of Advent and Christmas is a religious 'sacred time', although the 'sacred' is latent and the cultural and social meaning of Advent and Christmas more emphasized. It is also a period full of commercially marketed consumer goods. Advent and Christmas decorations and diverse products are of all descriptions: goods such as candles, stars, lanterns, chocolates in the form of St Nicholas and St Martin, angels, pine-tree decorations for '*Adventskranz*' (a wreath made of pine-tree branches and decorated with candles), wall-hangings and wooden figures like temples for Advent candles. The colours white, silver, gold, green and red dominate almost all public space, shops, banks, offices and of course schools, which Turkish children attend. Also private homes have their windows, doors and gardens decorated for Advent and Christmas. These decorations and products are introduced as early as the beginning of November and are put away usually on 6 January. School and kindergarten children spend much time producing (*basteln*) various ornaments and pictures, in which religious symbolism is central even if not explicated.

Turkish children who attend German classes[4] take part in all these activities, as younger Turkish children take part in religiously oriented games, songs and crafts in community kindergartens run by the Protestant or Catholic Church. During my school visits around Christmas time, I saw that the school buildings and classrooms were decorated with Advent and Christmas decorations. Children were drawing pictures showing the '*Christkind*' appearing at the '*Frauenkirche*', the famous church of Holy Mary in the market-place of Nürnberg, a place internationally known for its traditional Christmas market. Turkish pupils were making these decorations themselves, or else (if they attended Turkish 'national classes') they shared their classroom with 'German classes', using the same space. Turkish teachers were somewhat perplexed at my question about how their pupils react to these pictures, ornaments or the cross on the wall. In many schools in classrooms there is a cross on the wall; this was explained to me by Turkish teachers as the classroom having to be shared between Turkish and 'German' classes. When Turkish pupils stay in a room for most of the time, then the cross is often supplemented with Turkish flags, a map of Turkey, and perhaps a picture of Atatürk, the founder of the Turkish Republic.

How, then, are these symbols and practices, from Christmas decorations to religious songs and plays, perceived by, and incorporated into, the religious and cultural order of Turkish migrants? The behaviour and reasoning of the father cited above is typical in many ways; he chooses a practical strategy of 'accommodation within limits'. For him Christian religion and especially the church are dominant and powerful, and their effects on Turkish children should be reckoned with and dealt with. Hence, practical strategies of accommodation are necessary, if one is to avoid overreaction from children. The father would probably not see this solution as religious syncretism, although he would define the confrontation and challenge as occurring between two *religious* domains and not cultural ones.

To the ordinary German this example might raise totally different questions. Based on my raw personal intuition and discussions with friends and colleagues in Germany, I propose that there is a general consensus on the nature of German state and society: that they are basically secularized. Apart from the political and historical justifications for this claim, how this secular society behaves in reality is fairly differentiated, especially when it comes to regional and traditional differences. Strongly Catholic rural Bavaria or North-Rhine Westphalia vary greatly from large cosmopolitan cities like Berlin or Hamburg. The church also has different claims to power in different *Bundesländer*, as exemplified by the practice of having more religious holidays in traditionally Catholic states or the instance of the cross in classrooms in Bavaria. Nevertheless, it is commonly believed and argued by the media that religion has become a secondary issue, and that the church (the Catholic more than the Protestant) is steadily losing its influence. (This is marked by the number of people giving up their church membership). Hence, for many, the celebrations and paraphernalia related to Advent and Christmas have mainly to do with German culture (*ein Stück Heimat*); they are bound up with market forces and consumerism, and have less to do with the 'essentials' of religion. I was told that a parish priest, for example, once criticized the congregation for attending church only at Christmas: children have to leave the house anyway, so that the father could decorate the Christmas tree as a suprise. The children then could find their presents under the candle-lit tree when they come back from the mass on *Heiligabend*, 24 December.

For many Germans *Weihnachten* contains historically syncretic elements, as exemplified by the Christmas tree being an originally 'heathen' Germanic custom. Furthermore, similar to other Western and European Christmas celebrations (Miller 1993), it is dominated by consumerist and family-centred activities. The focus on the materialist (or creative consumerism, according to Miller 1993) and family-centredness during the whole period overshadows the presence of religious symbolism. Many of my friends tend to explain the presence of Christian symbols during Advent and until after Epiphany as the presence of some kind of 'survival' of religious and local/traditional customs (*Sitte*). The ritualistic activities (from shopping to baking or decorating the Christmas tree) are claimed to be performed mainly for children, or else to remember one's own childhood *Weihnachten* (with its smells, lights and tastes), but hardly to invoke purely religious symbols or meanings.

These contrasting views of sacred Christian time by Germans and Turks could be seen as cultural misunderstanding, on the one hand, but also as an effort to preserve the social markers of religious identity, which are themselves ambivalent and multidimensional, on the other hand. Turkish parents tend to adopt or tolerate the adoption of consumerism related to Christian celebrations, and provide functionalist, pragmatic or aesthetic explanations about their behaviour. The father above, for instance, sees it as unavoidable to allow his son to play with fireworks on New Year's Eve, or give presents to his teacher or friends on this occasion. He, like many other Muslims, would also support similar consumerist practices, such as giving children presents collectively in the mosque and celebrating the Muslim religious holidays with food and gift-giving within the mosque. These are events which assign new functions to public religious space.

For some parents, the period of Advent and Christmas is considered to have an unacceptable influence on their children, as children unavoidably learn not only the visual Christian symbols but also Christian songs and prayers related to Advent and Christmas. A mother complained that her daughter sings these Christmas carols all day long at home and that she does not know how to stop her without hurting her feelings or being too harsh with her. 'These songs are actually prayers, they sing them in Church; so I tell her not to sing them all the time at least', she said. Some other parents were hardly concerned about children's games and songs related to Advent and Christmas. However, they knew that their children might have taken a role as the 'shepherd' or the 'sheep' in games enacting the story of the Nativity, but they did not think participation in such games with a religious context had any effect on their children. 'They were just children, they did it as play, dressed up for Christmas or *Fasching* [carnival]', said one mother.

GENERATIONAL DIFFERENCES AND ISLAMIC DISCOURSES

The need to interpret religious and cultural rites in a new environment is closely linked to the social history of labour migration. From the first generation of migrants onwards, processes of reconstructing the 'sacred' (*kutsal*) and the 'religious' (*dini*) show fundamental differences. To begin with, the two generations of Turks in Germany whom I have taken into consideration have encountered religion and Islam differently:

(a) Parents learned Islam and were socialized to become Muslims primarily in Turkey. Islam was mediated to them in different ways, depending on various factors: rural or urban background, the region of origin, the specific socio-economic standing of the family and the educational, professional and biographical history of the individual. The variations ranged from strictly normative or official interpretations of Islam to mystical (for example, Sufi) ones, and from the highly secularist to the rigidly moralist.

What is common to all parents of the first generation is, however, that they all had 'religion' as a subject in primary school at least for two years. Many parents I talked to in Nürnberg grew up in villages or small towns and attended Qur'an courses taught by private persons or the *imam*.

(b) Another common characteristic of the parental generation is the indirect religious socialization. Parents who later became migrant workers in Germany had religion mediated to them not only within the family or at school, but through the larger community, media and institutions, which share and reproduce the common belief system. These indirect ways of mediating Islamic beliefs and values seem to be the most difficult to reproduce in diaspora. Parents miss the influence of the larger social environment, which shares the Islamic idiom. A parent formulated this deficiency as follows: 'Here children can't live their religion fully; if they had been in Turkey, for instance, they would have heard the *ezan* [call to prayer] five times a day, and would have at least remembered religion. But here instead of *ezan*, they hear the church bells.'

(c) In diaspora some of the Islamic prescriptions gain a particular meaning and weight. One of these is the practice of veiling, or rather covering the hair and the body in a particular style dictated by Islamic fashion (*tesettür modası*). Although veiling has become a political issue and symbol of the Islamic revivalists and political activists in Turkey,[5] for Turkish migrants in Germany the headscarf is an index, an indicator, of ethnic and gender identity in a foreign context. Yet what it signifies is debatable for the migrants themselves. Many Turks in Germany see the headscarf as the anti-symbol of 'modernity', 'female emancipa-tion', or 'willingness to integrate or assimilate' into German society. For them it is not solely a symbol of pure religiosity or a straightforward Islamic prescription. This interpretation of the 'headscarf', and that women with headscarves are identified as Turks, is widely known among the younger Turks. This inclina-tion, furthermore, contrasts with the issues of the headscarf debate in Turkey, as it is conducted by various groups of intellectuals, feminists or urban-educated professional women. In this debate, the reasons and types of covering the head are crucial for a classification of political views. In Germany, the salient marker of Turkish women is *the headscarf*. Those women who do not wear it are seen as 'assimilated', as 'Germanized Turks', or else as 'religiously liberal and modern Turks', as it is often formulated by and for Alevi Turks (Mandel 1989b). This disregards the meanings attached to various types of headwear by various generations of women in rural and urban Turkey.

The deeply ironic predicament of the 'headscarf' as a cultural marker and a symbol of 'Islamic repression of women' also has serious implications for ethnic hatred in Germany. A young neo-Nazi, who attacked foreigners and other socially weak people such as the homeless or disabled persons, says he basically 'hates these women with the headscarf' (*Die Zeit* 1993a). A German neighbour of the women and children who were murdered through arson in Solingen believes he had good relations with his Turkish neighbours: 'These Turkish women were well integrated, they did not even have headscarves.'

(d) Another process of adopting the definition of the dominant
discourse in Germany about who is a Muslim involves another
Islamic prescription: the ban on eating pork. The question of
eating or not eating pork is irrelevant in Turkey; the obsessive
preoccupation with it is strictly a migrant problem. Similar to
'the headscarf' having become a symbol of Muslim Turks in
Germany, the ban on eating pork is one of the best-known
Islamic practices accessible to the German public. Although
migrant Turks have organized themselves to solve the problem
of providing *halal* meat for the Muslim Turkish community, it is
not free of conflicts and problems with the German society as
well as with the Turkish community. The general concern with
the ritual cleanliness of meat and other food products is very
widespread and, I argue, partly reinforced through the outsiders'
definitions of what being a Muslim comprises. By the time they
begin school, children are fully aware of the ban on eating pork,
and Turkish parents usually avoid giving salami sandwiches to
their children for lunch at school, in case it be mistaken for pork.
(There is also non-pork salami sold in Turkish shops.) The
concern is that the child not be mistakenly accused by his Turkish
classmates of eating a pork product. Many Turkish adults try to
adopt vegetarian eating habits in public places in order not to be
asked by a German colleague or friend whether they follow the
ban on eating pork or not. Such a question may be awkward
for various reasons: one may be embarrassed about the
German colleague's ignorance about Islam; one may be reluctant
about having to re-emphasize religious differences; or one may
interpret the question as a test of one's own private religiosity.

Mosque organizations demonstrate an obsessive fascination
with detail (Ahmed 1992: 25–6). They distribute lists of food
products, which are commonly found in most of the super-
markets, and which indicate products thought to contain pork,
fat from pork or alcohol. During my interviews with Turkish
families, women especially expressed their frustration and anger;
a mother complained how some of her guests, allegedly 'better
Muslims', refused to eat the meat she cooked. They asked her
where she bought it, implying that it might be mixed with pork,
or simply 'unclean' because of improper slaughtering methods.
She vehemently defended herself, avowing that pork would
never enter her house and that they slaughter their own animals.[6]
Moreover, her parents-in-law were both *hajjis* (pilgrims who had
been in Mecca) and she had prepared the food and the dinner

to celebrate their return from the *hajj*. Therefore, along with the headscarf, the ban on pork and the elaborate precautions to avoid it have become visible markers distinguishing religious boundaries. They underline the visual aspects of identifying a Muslim from invisible and implicit creeds of belief and ethics.

(e) The influence of the non-Muslim environment, and the competition with it, is most clearly visible in the area of religious celebrations and Islamic organizations. Many parents express their helplessness and dismay in having literally to recreate the meaning and joy of celebrating Islamic religious holidays for their children. The dominant Christian culture and the way Christian celebrations address children put pressure on Muslim parents as individuals and on Islamic organizations as groups to take an active stand. Parents admit the lack of atmosphere in religious celebrations, which they believe existed in their childhood at home. Nevertheless, they try to have a minimum standard and way of recreating the importance and meaning of the day. Buying new clothes or shoes for children, cooking meat and special sweets such as *baklava*, visiting older relatives (*büyükler*) and close friends is the minimum practice of almost all families. Many are, for instance, critical of those Turks who do not take a day off on Islamic holidays; 'Even if one does not celebrate it as at home [in Turkey], one should not work as a slave and ignore the religious holidays.' Islamic organizations go a step further and try to develop new forms of celebrations, such as celebrating the *bayram* (*hajj* or Ramadan celebrations) in the mosque, with food, presents, films and games for families, women and children together. More recently weddings have started to take place in mosques. The social centre character of churches is taken as a model by mosques, and they offer services like conference programmes, discussion groups or sewing courses for women, as well as sports activities for children and teenagers.

CONCLUDING REMARKS

I have argued that the culture and religion of Muslim Turkish migrants in Germany is a case in point for studying power and agency in syncretism. On the one hand, syncretic processes in the religion of Muslim migrants are flourishing, but being refuted; on the other hand, syncretism within the dominant Christian religion and culture is framed as postmodernism as well as secularism, but any hybridization between these two main world religions is highly contested and symbolically loaded. The Muslim Turkish community's and the German society's views of one another's religiosity and religion are indexical to various other debates of modernity versus traditionalism, secularism versus fundamentalism, liberalism versus conservatism, integration versus ethnic isolation and finally racism versus multi-culturalism – debates which are indeed particular and global at the same time. Any analysis of syncretic tendencies in migrant culture and religion has to cope with the problem of distinguishing analytic-ally between 'culture' and 'religion'. The discussion above has tried to show that this distinction between the two, that is, migrant culture and religion, is feasible at the level of exploring contact and interaction with another world religion. The migrants' notions of Islam and of its compatibility with Christianity show considerable flexibility as long as this can be alluded to as cultural adaptation, but a direct syncretism is denied by the migrant community. The German society's notions of their own religion, on the other hand, emphasize its syncretism with pre-Christian European cultural elements, ignor-ing any other possible effects from other world religions such as Islam. The German view of any syncretic change within the Islam of Turkish migrants also reflects a concern to maintain religious boundaries, so that this change would be identified as cultural but less so as religious syncretism.

Finally, the analytical and discursive boundaries of religion and culture are most visible in those instances where syncretism in culture (for example, the notion of cultural integration of minorities in Germany) is welcomed and accepted, but syncretism in religion is seen as undesirable (by Muslim migrants) or is paraphrased as being cultural (from the point of view of the German society). These issues certainly need further research and analysis, as they refer not only to the debates on minority–majority relations and multiculturalist politics but also to the very role of religion in 'postmodernity'.

NOTES

The initial version of this chapter was presented at the EASA Conference in Prague in 1992. Subsequent versions have been read by Rosalind Shaw, Nancy Lindisfarne, Ruard Absaroka, Ayşe Çağlar and David Heath, who all made useful criticisms, comments and corrections. Regina von Haller-Beckmann and Gaby Franger have discussed the German Christmas and my ideas about German attitudes towards religion with me. Thanks are extended to all of them, and special thanks are due to Charles Stewart for his very thorough editorial work, suggestions and critical debate on many aspects of this chapter. All errors are of course my own. The arguments in this chapter are derived from a social anthropological research project at the University of Bamberg, on Islamic socialization among Turkish migrant families. The study has been carried out since 1990 in Nürnberg, where I have lived since 1988. It explores the type(s) of Islam being mediated at home and in the larger context of diaspora. Research methods include qualitative interviews with household members (8–9-year-old children, 14–15-year-old teenagers, and parents) from 30 Turkish migrant families, with Turkish teachers and *imams*, as well as participant observation at school and in mosques.

1 For a critical assessment of this type of narrowly defined culture concept, see Çağlar 1990.

2 For a very similar usage of the term 'migrant Islam' see Saint-Blancat 1993, who actually uses 'migrant Islam' and 'Islam transplanté [*en Europe*]' interchangeably.

3 E. Özcan's study quoted in *Die Zeit* shows that there are 3,000 Turkish immigrant organizations (*Vereine*) in Germany, of which 1,000 are political, 600–800 athletic, 500 Islamic-religious, and 500–700 cultural and social. There are also some 28,000 Turkish members of the Social Democratic Party of Germany (*Die Zeit*, 1993b); those who have German citizenship also have the right to be elected as party officials.

4 By 'German classes' here is meant the 'regular classes' (*Regelklasse*), peculiar to the Bavarian educational system, where the classes are composed mostly of German pupils with a minority of foreigner children, and the language of tuition is German. The alternative, which is largely optional, is the 'national class' (*Nationalklasse*), where children are all one nationality (for example, all Italian, Turkish or Portuguese) and the language of tuition is primarily the language of that particular nationality. Turkish children attending 'national classes' are taught by native Turkish teachers. The implications of these two class types for the socialization of children are very significant, especially in terms of establishing early and lasting types of contact and friendship ties among children of varying nationalities.

5 See Göle 1991 for a political and historical discussion of the implication of female dress and its significance for the modernity project of Turkish democracy. See also Kandiyoti 1991.

6 Animal slaughtering is often done by Turkish families in Nürnberg, although it is not totally legal. A few Turks come together and make an arrangement with a German farmer from a village in the vicinity and slaughter the animal there themselves. Alternatively they hire a Turkish Muslim butcher to do it for them according to the religious prescriptions. Various mosque organizations carry out the slaughtering on a larger scale and follow the German regulations; they sell this meat regularly to their members.

REFERENCES

Abdullah, M.S. (1992) 'Islam – nicht nur eine Gastarbeiter-religion', *Das Parlament*, 17–24 April.

Ahmed, A.S. (1992) *Postmodernism and Islam: Predicament and Promise*, London: Routledge.

Binswanger, K. and Sipahioğlu, F. (1988) *Türkisch–islamische Vereine als Faktor deutsch–türkischer Koexistenz*, Benediktbeuern: Rieß–Druck Verlag.

Çağlar, A. (1990) 'Das Kultur-Konzept als Zwangsjacke in Studien zur Arbeitsmigration', *Zeitschrift für Türkeistudien* 1: 93–105.

Die Zeit (1993a) 'Den Haß krieg' ich nicht mehr los', 1 January.

—— (1993b) 'Dossier: Drinnen vor der Tür', 11 June.

Elsas, C. (ed.) (1983) *Identität: Veränderungen kultureller Eigenarten im Zusammenleben von Türken und Deutschen*, Hamburg: E.B. Rissen.

Fischer, M.J. and Abedi, M. (1990) *Debating Muslims: Cultural Dialogues in Postmodernity and Tradition*, Madison, WI.: University of Wisconsin Press.

Göle, N. (1991) *Modern Mahrem: Medeniyet ve Örtünme*, Istanbul: Metis.

Kandiyoti, D. (1991) 'End of empire: Islam, nationalism and women in Turkey', in D. Kandiyoti (ed.), *Women, Islam and the State*, London: Macmillan.

Karpat, K. (1990) 'The *hijjra* from Russia and the Balkans: the process of self-definition in the late Ottoman state', in D.F. Eickelman and J. Piscatori (eds.), *Muslim Travellers: Pilgrimage, Migration, and the Religious Imagination*, London: Routledge.

Kreiser, K. (1985) 'L'Islam en Allemagne et les Musulmans Allemands', in M. Morsy (ed.), *L'Islam en Europe à l'Époque Moderne*, Paris: Editions Sinbad.

Lutz, H. (1991) *Welten verbinden: Türkische Sozialarbeiterinnen in den Niederlanden und der Bundesrepublik Deutschland*, Frankfurt/Main: Verl. für Interkulturelle Kommunikation.

Mandel, R. (1989a) 'Ethnicity and identity among migrant guestworkers in west Berlin', in N.L. Gonzalez and C.S. McCommon (eds.), *Conflict, Migration, and the Expression of Ethnicity*, Boulder and London: Westview Press.

—— (1989b) 'Turkish headscarves and the 'foreigner problem': constructing difference through emblems of identity', *New German Critique*, 46: 27–46.

Mardin, Ş. (1991) *Türkiye'de Din ve Siyaset: Makaleler III*, Istanbul: Iletişim.

Miller, D. (1993) 'A theory of Christmas', in D. Miller (ed.), *Unwrapping Christmas*, London: Routledge.

Saint-Blancat, C. (1993) 'Hypothèses sur l'évolution de l'"Islam transplanté" en Europe', *Social Compass* 40, 2: 323–41.

Sarıbay, A.Y. (1985) *Türkiye'de Modernleşme Din ve Parti Politikası*, Istanbul: Alan.

Schiffauer, W. (1991) *Die Migranten aus Subay: Türken in Deutschland: Eine Ethnographie*, Stuttgart: Klett-Cotta.

Thomä-Venske, H. (1981) *Islam und Integration*, Hamburg: E.B. Rissen.

—— (1988) 'The religious life of Muslims in Berlin', in T. Gerholm and Y.G. Lithman (eds), *The New Islamic Presence in Western Europe*, New York and London: Mansell.

Uluengin, H. (1993) 'Modern zamanlar – Tekbir, bayrak ve punk', *Hürriyet Daily*, 3 June.

Werbner, P. (1990) *The Migration Process: Capital, Gifts and Offerings among British Pakistanis*, Oxford: Berg.

Wilpert, C. (1988) 'Religion and ethnicity: orientations, perceptions and strategies among Turkish Alevi and Sunni migrants in Berlin', in T. Gerholm and Y.G. Lithman (eds), *The New Islamic Presence in Western Europe*, New York and London: Mansell.

10 Syncretism, multiculturalism and the discourse of tolerance

Peter van der Veer

The term 'syncretism' is often used in anthropology and history as if it were a transparent, descriptive term, referring to the 'borrowing, affirmation, or integration of concepts, symbols, or practices of one religious tradition into another by a process of selection and reconciliation' (Berlin 1980: 9). However, like many terms used to describe aspects of religion, indeed like the term 'religion' itself, it has a peculiar Western history. I cannot trace that history in any detail here, but, before looking at 'syncretism' in the Indian context, I would like to point out that the term is hardly a neutral one in modern Christian history, that it is part both of religious debate itself and of the description and analysis of that debate. Moreover, I want to suggest that the term 'syncretism' refers to a politics of difference and identity and that as such the notion of power is crucial in its understanding. At stake is the power to identify true religion and to authorize some practices as 'truthful' and others as 'false'. Syncretism is regarded positively by some, as promoting tolerance and negatively by others, as promoting the decline of the pure faith. Finally, I want to suggest that the role played by the term 'syncretism' in societies with religious cultures is played by the term 'multiculturalism' in societies with secular cultures. While the bulk of this chapter is devoted to the Indian case with which I am most familiar, I want to put this case in a broader framework by, first, looking at these terms in the context of the Christian West.

Syncretism is a term used in Christian theology since at least the seventeenth century. According to the *Oxford English Dictionary*, it denotes an 'attempt to sink differences and effect union between sects or philosophical schools'. While Erasmus of Rotterdam used the term in 1519 in the sense of reconciliation among Christians, the theologian Calixtus of Helmstadt was the first to use 'syncretism' in theological debate to mean the sinking of theological differences, at a church conference in Thorn in 1645 (Kamstra 1970). While syncretism thus sounds like a positive strategy to contain conflict and promote tolerance or, in recent parlance, at least 'dialogue', it is striking how pejoratively the term is often used by the defenders of 'the true faith'. It is seen as a loss of identity, an illicit contamination, a sign of religious decadence (Pye 1971). In theological disputes it was generally regarded as a betrayal of principles, or as an attempt to secure unity at the expense of truth. Syncretism is seen as a corruption of the Truth. I want to suggest that the ambivalence of the term relates to the rise of Protestantism and the ensuing religious civil wars in Europe.

The period in which syncretism comes into theological debate is, interestingly enough, also the period in which Lord Herbert produced a universal definition of religion in terms of what later came to be called natural religion (Asad 1983). It seems to me that the emergence of the notion of natural religion as a belief in and worship of a supreme power which is found among all human beings is related to the emergence of the notion of syncretism. The Deist perspective in the early eighteenth century was that the great truths of religion were all universal and that true religion was ultimately natural religion, open to reason and not bound to particular historical events of revelation which divided one religious community from another (Taylor 1989: 273–4). These notions replace the idea that there is only one absolute Truth and that expressions of that Truth are ultimately authorized by the universal, Catholic Church. Deviations from that Truth were heresies and certainly not alternative, in principle equal forms of expression of natural religion.

Syncretism as the union of different, supposedly equal, theological viewpoints can also only come up when the idea of absolute Truth is abandoned. Of course, there is the whole history of the Christianization of Europe with its unions of different beliefs and methods of worship, but this is not syncretism as in the *OED* definition: it is a triumphant history of religious expansion and conversion which ultimately establishes the absolute Catholic Truth by appropriating religious symbols in the construction of the church. The new understandings of syncretism as union of differences and of religion as natural could, possibly, only arise when the authority of the universal, Catholic Church as the sole source of knowledge and truth had declined, as it indeed had in the seventeenth century. This is not to say that the medieval church imposed total uniformity. Indeed, this would have been totally impossible. What it attempted to do was to establish itself as the single source of authentication.

With the rise of Protestantism the universality of the Truth of the church and of Christendom as the sacred community of believers gives way to a plurality of religious truths and communities. Initially, this caused large-scale civil strife, based on religious differences. One answer to this war of all against all was the rise of the absolutist state and its successor, the secular nation-state (Koselleck 1988). Another response to religious civil warfare was the combined notions of syncretism and religious tolerance. Conversion as an aggressive missionary project among Christians became more and more a marginal phenomenon, often condemned as proselytism.

Natural religion is, then, something everyone has in different forms, but these differences are private matters without political consequence. One can still maintain that religion provides one with an absolute Truth, but this conviction remains private and does not operate on the level of the society at large. Of course, we have to realize that secular nationalism is only an ideological movement and not a global, all-encompassing ideology of modernity. However, in societies in which secularism is a defining aspect of national culture, the debate shifts from religion to national culture, from syncretism to multiculturalism and from conversion to assimilation.

In European and American secular discourse, religious difference is depoliticized. Here it is culture which is discursively salient and not religion. 'Multiculturalism' and 'assimilation' in secular society are discussed along lines very similar to the earlier Christian debates on 'syncretism' and 'conversion'. National culture is unity in diversity, the folkloristic parading of cultural difference as a sign of national unity. On the one hand, there is the positive image of the blending of equal elements. This is clear in the metaphor of the 'melting pot', which says that the USA has a national culture that is the result of the melting of diverse, heterogeneous ethnic elements. The cultures of the diverse ethnic communities which have settled here are portrayed as equal contributions to the national culture: '*E pluribus unum.*' On the other hand, there is the negative imagery of loss and contamination, which emerges most clearly in the separatistic search for pure origins and clear boundaries. Again, while in the case of syncretism there is the failure of conversion, in the case of multiculturalism there is the failure of assimilation. In the first case this is a failure of the church apparatus to authorize social practice effectively; in the second it is a failure of the state apparatus.

That the project of the 'melting pot' was not entirely successful became clear to sociologists in the 1960s (Glazer and Moynihan 1963). While conservatives continue to cling to the 'melting' or assimilation project, liberals now try to go 'beyond the melting pot' not only by allowing cultural difference to be paraded on the streets as part of the celebration of the nation, but also by including it in the curriculum in schools, as a celebration of difference in the heart of the assimilation machinery. That is, of course, the point at which someone like the historian Arthur Schlesinger (1992) starts to worry about what he calls 'the disuniting of America'. As long as cultural difference is, like religious difference, something practised in the margins of social life, as a 'hobby' one might say, it is 'depoliticized', but as soon as difference is emphasized in the curriculum, part of the central assimilation machinery of the modern nation-state, it becomes a political issue of the first order – which it is in the United States today.

The comparison I have made between multiculturalism and syncretism, between conversion and assimilation, is of more than academic interest. It shows that a radical opposition between religious tradition and secular modernity is untenable. Moreover, it shows that the problems of cultural pluralism that have often been portrayed as those of traditional societies in the Third World, the 'transitory ills' of young nation-states, are in fact very much also the political issues of the modern, industrialized societies of the West today. My brief description of the Western development should serve to dispel the common illusion that the rest of the world suffers from problems, such as religious strife, which have already been solved in seventeenth-century Europe. My suggestion is that the debates and conflicts which are in India largely conducted in religious terms are conducted in the West in the secular terms of race, ethnicity and nationalism. This is indeed a significant transformation, but whether it shows the triumph of the Enlightenment is certainly questionable.

HINDUS AND MUSLIMS IN INDIA

Let us now turn to the postcolonial context of India. The issues of 'syncretism' and 'multiculturalism' are crucial for the project of the contemporary Indian nation-state. Since both ethnic and religious identities are important in India, the terms 'multiculturalism' and 'syncretism' are used interchangeably here. That the problems of the West and those of India resemble each other is certainly not surprising. India is not outside the modern world system of nation-states. It has a democracy with its politics of numbers, of majority and minorities.

Arguably, the most important political fact in twentieth-century

South Asia is the Partition, with its aftermath of military violence between India and Pakistan and the continuing violence between Hindus and Muslims in many parts of India. The National Congress Party, the leading political force in the country, has tried to contain this violence by projecting a secular 'multiculturalism', allowing for the possibility of the peaceful coexistence of different ethnic and religious communities under the umbrella of a secular state which does not interfere with the religious practices of those different communities. Difference is institutionalized in the separate civil codes of the Hindu and Muslim communities, in separate educational institutions and so on. In fact, one could argue that the Indian state is a prime example of the institutionalization of difference, especially in its reservation policies for backward and scheduled castes. All this is very much a legacy of the colonial state, and in the colonial period such policies were condemned as 'divide-and-rule' by the same nationalists who continued them after Independence.

Secular nationalism sees the role of the state as that of an arbiter of intercommunal disputes, which transcends the various communities that make up Indian society. Again, this is the same neutrality which the British tried to project, but clearly this is more easily done when Christian Britishers rule India than when the country is ruled by power-brokers who represent, after elections, their own constituencies. Because of the potentially disruptive nature of everyday politics the unifying role of the nationalist imaginary is crucial. Nehru and Gandhi, the leaders of the Indian National Congress during and after Independence, therefore stress the tolerance of Indian civilization. For Nehru (1946: 77–8), Hinduism is 'vague, amorphous, many-sided, all things to all men. It is hardly possible to define it.' It is a 'way of life' rather than a religion. This inclusivist definition of Hinduism as the Indian way of life is tempered by the fact that Nehru always refers to the Buddhist Maurya emperor Ashoka and the Muslim Mughal emperor Akbar as the prime examples of the tolerant nature of Indian civilization. Nehru, interestingly enough, thus links the secular modern Indian state to enlightened rulers who tried to create harmony between the different religions without interfering in their religious doctrines. This is why the symbol of the wheel, taken from the Sarnath Capital of Asoka, was adopted as the symbol on the national flag.

Mahatma Gandhi also stressed constantly the essential tolerance and also non-violence of Indian civilization. Following nineteenth-century reformers, such as Vivekananda, he located those characteristics not in enlightened rule but in a spirituality which is the essence of Hinduism and, in his view, informs all religious traditions. Gandhi's scattered and often contradictory views on the subject have been philosophically systematized by the philosopher and President of India, Sarvepalli Radhakrishnan, who makes a distinction between Religion and religions and equates Religion with Hinduism as the Spirit of India. As the argument goes, this spirituality has as an important characteristic: its non-violent tolerance. Religion in Radhakrishnan's view is a distillation of the essence of all religions and thus allows the unification of diverse religious groups (Minor 1989).

The notion of the pluralist, tolerant nature of Indian civilization is not only held by India's nationalist leaders. It is complemented by the idea that there is a 'folk culture' or a 'popular religion' in India which is at the grassroots level 'pluralistic' and 'tolerant'. This idea is nowadays widely held among Indian intellectuals and in the Indian media. One element here seems to be that the modern, Western, liberal utopia of 'multiculturalism' is projected onto what is seen as 'traditional society'. A good example of this is the work of Ashis Nandy, a leading Indian intellectual. Nandy makes a sharp distinction between faith and ideology. By faith he means 'religion as a way of life, a tradition which is definitionally non-monolithic and operationally plural'. By ideology he means

> religion as a sub-national, national or cross-national identifier of populations contesting for or protecting non-religious, usually political or socio-economic, interests. Such religions-as-ideologies usually get identified with one or more texts which, rather than the ways of life of the believers, then become the final identifiers of the pure forms of the religions.
>
> (Nandy 1990: 70)

According to Nandy, we can find this 'religion-as-faith' among the 'non-modern majority of Indian society' which lives in the rural areas. Despite this neat distinction, Nandy finds a political spokesman for the traditional faith of the masses, of 'the people', in Gandhi, the ideologue of Hindu tolerance:

> Gandhi used to say that he was a *sanatani*, an orthodox Hindu. It was as a *sanatani* Hindu that he claimed to be simultaneously a Muslim, a Sikh and a Christian and he granted the same plural identity to those belonging to other faiths. Traditional Hinduism, or rather *Sanatan dharma*, was the source of his religious tolerance.
>
> (Nandy 1990: 91)

All this may sound somewhat peculiar, but Nandy articulates what is a major element of intellectual discourse in India, namely that the religious violence we see all over the place is the work of shrewd manipulators, of fanatic religious and political operators. This is, of course, a kind of discourse which is very similar to that of the current authorities and their colonial predecessors. The difference is that Nandy and his followers accuse the secular state with its project of modernization and unification of having at least partly destroyed the traditional way of life and thus having made the violence possible. That Indian intellectuals have such a bleak picture of the state is certainly not surprising, when we see the extent to which politicians and police authorities play leading roles in communal violence. Nevertheless, the empirical evidence for this involvement should lead to a demystification of the sharp distinction between a secular state and a religious society.

It can also be appreciated that Nandy's view formulates a certain hope that a more positive image of religion can be salvaged from the contemporary, nasty facts of rising communal violence in India. In 1984 Hindu nationalists launched a political campaign to replace the so-called Babar Mosque in Ayodhya with a Hindu temple. Their claim is that the sixteenth-century mosque had been built on the birthplace of the Hindu god Rama, a site which had previously been occupied by a Hindu temple. In the meantime this has developed into one of the hottest issues in Indian politics today (van der Veer 1988, 1994). Thousands of people have died in riots between Hindus and Muslims over this issue. A major opposition party has very successfully embraced it. In December 1993 the mosque was demolished by a large group of Hindu militants. This has endangered the relations between Hindus and Muslims in the country to an enormous extent. It is against this background that the attempts to find signs of peaceful coexistence between Hindus and Muslims in history or in the rural areas have to be understood.

I fully sympathize with any attempt to stop the communal violence in India, but it might still be important to examine critically the notion of the essentially tolerant and pluralistic character of Indian civilization. The importance of such a critical understanding is underlined by the fact that this notion is used even by the very people who perpetrate communal violence. A good example of this is a large advertisement for the Hindu nationalist movement Vishva Hindu Parishad in the newspaper *The Times of India* (13 February 1988), in which Hinduism is described as the religion of Mankind, as 'a parlement [sic] of religions and the very antithesis of violence, terorism [sic] and intolerance' (McKean 1992: 33).

There are at least two great difficulties with Nandy's view of a tolerant pluralism, projected either onto the 'rural folk' or onto the 'premodern past'. The first is that it denies any agency to the people who are involved either in communal violence, or in voting for religious parties, or even in voting and fighting for a separate state, like Pakistan. They are portrayed as simply misled by their fanatic leaders. A connected difficulty is that it cannot account for communal violence in the precolonial period, of which we have abundant evidence. Its view that it is the secularism of the state which causes the violence cannot account for the fact that it was under the most stridently secularist government of Nehru that communal violence occurred least. The second problem is that this tolerant and pluralistic spirit of India is essentially Hindu. It effectively denies that Muslims have a religion which is different from that of the Hindus. As Nandy says, 'it is religion-as-faith which prompted Indians to declare themselves as Mohammedan Hindus in Gujarat in the census of 1911' (Nandy 1990: 70). However nice this may sound, it has the unintended ring of the demand in Hindu communalist writings that Muslims as converts should realize that they are Hindus first. If they do not realize their true nature, they had better go to Pakistan.

While Nandy uses the term 'pluralism' in connection with tolerance, in scholarly writing on Indian Islam the term 'syncretism' is often used. According to the historian Aziz Ahmad (1969: 44), 'Indian Islam represents a mosaic of demotic, superstitious and syncretic beliefs, which movements of mass reform like that of the Mujahidin in the nineteenth century have tried to erase, but not with complete success.' The historian Asim Roy describes in his book *The Islamic Syncretistic Tradition in Bengal* (1983) how syncretism came under attack by Islamic reformist movements in nineteenth-century Bengal. Finally, the anthropologist Imtiaz Ahmad (1981: 14) has argued that 'the Islamic theological and philosophical precepts and principles on the one hand and local, syncretic elements on the other' are integrated in Indian Islam.

As in the European context, syncretism is not a simple descriptive term in contemporary India. This is clear from the historian Francis Robinson's critique of Imtiaz Ahmad's work on Indian Islam. According to Robinson (1983: 187), Ahmad's argument that high Islamic traditions and local, syncretic customs peacefully coexist in one religious system derives from his wish to show that Indian Muslims have their roots deep in Indian society and that they are therefore good and loyal citizens of India. Robinson develops an alternative view by emphasizing a long-term process of Islamicization by which local customs were infused with new meanings or were eradicated. His interpretation attempts to show the gradual marginalization of syncretic practices and the slow victory of what he calls 'the pattern of perfection' through reform, with some assistance from the modern state 'with all its great coercive force and power of social penetration' (Robinson 1983: 194).

Robinson seems to be accusing Imtiaz Ahmad of deliberately emphasizing syncretism to show the 'Indianness' of Indian Islam. In a sharp reaction to this the anthropologist Veena Das (1984: 299) asks whether Robinson's article perhaps shows support for repressive Muslim regimes that force their subjects to follow the right path. This goes some way in illustrating the extent to which the discussion of Islamic syncretism in India is related to the position of Muslims in India after the Partition. This has become even more pressing today, when Hindu nationalists in the aftermath of the demolition of the Babar Mosque in Ayodhya highlight the equation Indian = Hindu, and ask Muslims who do not accept their Hinduness to leave for Pakistan.

It is not only the Indianness of Muslim practices in India that is at issue here. As Gail Minault (1984: 302) observes, evidence of syncretism is also meant to be a challenge to the idea that the Hindu and Muslim communities have incompatible values, which would be the cause of the violence of the Partition and the ongoing communal strife in India. This relates to Nandy's argument that pluralism implies tolerance and mutual respect, a notion which is also present in the American discussion of multiculturalism. It is a notion which is derived from the historical context of seventeenth-century Europe, in which, as we have seen, the term 'syncretism' came to be used precisely for creating harmony. Nevertheless, it is by no means clear that syncretism in the sense of borrowing from one tradition into another would indeed create harmony and tolerance. In some contexts one would almost be tempted to propose an inverse relation: growth of syncretism implies decline of tolerance.

In a recent analysis of rituals at Kataragama, a centre of Hindu–Buddhist syncretism in Sri Lanka, Richard Gombrich and Gananath Obeyesekere (1988: 163–99) show the extent to which borrowing by Sinhalese Buddhists from Tamil devotional practices in fact is part of a larger social transformation in which ethnic and religious antagonism grows. What happens in Kataragama is the gradual adoption of Tamil Hindu practices accompanied by a denial of their origin in Hinduism. The Tamil presence is subsequently marginalized, as in the rest of Sri Lankan society. Moreover, according to Bruce Kapferer

(1988), the so-called 'syncretistic' adoption of Hindu deities in the context of Sinhalese possession cults is directly connected with the growing demonization of the Tamil population. These practices are very much 'folk cults' with little elaborate, rationalizing theology, but they are increasingly adopted by a nationalistic Sinhalese bourgeoisie, which takes a leading role in the ethnic strife in Sri Lanka. So much for the romanticization of 'folk' practices.

THE SUFI SHRINE

The centre of Hindu–Muslim syncretism in India is the shrine of the Sufi saint. There are thousands of them all over India, and both Hindus and Muslims worship the saints who are buried in the tombs. The syncretism of saint worship has been a subject of debate among Muslims for centuries. The issue in this debate is not whether saint worship promotes harmony and tolerance, but whether it is a correct and orthodox practice. A long-standing argument against the worship of saints is that the imputation of divine powers to the saint and the tomb threatens the monotheistic nature of Islam. It is argued to be *shirk*, polytheism, and *bid'a*, an 'innovation' contrary to *sunna*, the example of the Prophet. In the Indian context, saint worship is often condemned as an imitation of Hindu polytheism. The argument is put forward most forcefully by the sixteenth-century Naqsbandi Sufi leader Shaikh Ahmad Sirhindi, and gains force with the teachings of the eighteenth-century Shah Wali-Allah of Delhi. In the nineteenth century a number of the Indian movements that oppose saint worship are influenced by the Arab reformist movement of the Wahhabis (Gaborieau 1989).

It is important in the genealogy of Muslim debate about saint worship in India that one of the main issues has always been 'syncretism', or 'Hindu influence' and 'Hindu participation'. The charge that saint worship resembles Hindu polytheism is constantly strongly rejected by defenders of the practice. Their defence is based not on the notion that the practice promotes harmony between Hindus and Muslims, but on the claim that it is an orthodox practice, in continuity with the Islamic past (Fusfeld 1987). The defenders deny that saint worship is syncretic. This does not directly imply that saint worship as a practice does not have tolerance and harmony among Muslims and Hindus as a (perhaps unintended) consequence. The only thing which is clear from Muslim debate is that syncretism is rejected as a deviation from the Truth.

From the nineteenth century the arguments in favour of saint worship gradually lose ground under constant attack by a growing reformist movement. Nineteenth- and twentieth-century reformist discourse in one way or another clearly serves as a successful attempt to redefine the boundaries of the Muslim community, and as such is directly related to the discourse of nationalism. This is not to say that saint worship has disappeared in India. On the contrary, the practice is still very much alive. This gives the anthropologist an opportunity to go beyond what the historical sources say about Muslim attitudes towards it. One may try to observe to what extent saint worship by both Hindus and Muslims promotes harmony and tolerance.

It is important to note here that the ethnographic record on Islamic saint worship in India is very limited. The following observations can therefore not be compared to other data sufficiently to yield a conclusive argument.

Recently, I have done fieldwork on saint worship in Surat, a major industrial city in Gujarat, west India. The Sufi brotherhood I worked on is that of the Rifa'i, who came to Surat in the seventeenth century and founded a lodge with a number of subsidiary shrines in south Gujarat, between Bombay and Ahmedabad. The Rifa'i are a prime example of what are called 'heterodox' (*be-shar*) brotherhoods in the literature on Sufism, because of their rather extreme public rituals of tongue-piercing and the like (Herklots 1921). Muslim law (*shari'a*) is a yardstick of orthodoxy, and Rifa'i practices are considered by some Muslims to go against the grain of this law. It should be recognized, however, that the attribution of the term 'heterodox' to Sufis like the Rifa'i is exactly one of the issues in Muslim debate and cannot be taken for granted by non-Muslim observers.

Let me briefly discuss the participation of Hindus in the saint's day of the Rifa'i brotherhood in Surat. I have given a more elaborate description of the brotherhood and its rituals elsewhere (van der Veer 1992). The saint's day commemorates the death anniversary of a saint, that is to say of his mystical union with his beloved God. It is an occasion of great power, since the saint, who is believed to be alive in his tomb, is able to help his supplicants thanks to his direct and unhindered access to God. A procession led by the living descendant of the saint goes to the tomb to replace a cover on the tomb and smear it with sandalwood paste. The distinguishing feature of a procession of the Rifa'i brotherhood is the 'playing' (*khelna*) with swords. Cheeks, tongues and other parts of the body are pierced with swords and iron pins. Hindus are always the majority among the spectators of the procession. They come in large numbers, as some informants expressed it, to see, to take *darshan* (view) and thus to partake in the flow of power by seeing. They also throng into the tomb at the moment of smearing sandalwood paste on the tomb, since they see it as the moment of great power, and ask for the blessing of the saint who is buried in the tomb. Hindus do not use the Muslim term *dargah* for the tomb, but the Hindu term *samadhi* (referring to a Hindu saint in meditation). Hindus therefore do participate, but clearly on their own terms.

It is also important to determine the boundaries of Hindu participation. They do not participate in the *hal* (trance) of the young men and faqir who 'play' with the swords as initiated followers of the living saint. Secondly, they develop no direct relation with the living descendent of the buried saint, but focus on the tomb as a silent icon of sacred power. In that way they are not subjected to the discourse of Sufism which may interpret the ritual in a different way to theirs. Finally, the Rifa'i combine the procession to the tomb with communal prayer in the mosque, with the saint acting as leader of the prayer (*imam*). It is here that the clearest boundary between Hindus and Muslims is drawn. It emphasizes the fact that it is wrong to see the Sufi tomb in isolation from other Islamic institutions, such as the mosque.

How do the Hindus I interviewed see their relation to the tomb and the saint's day? As I have already said, they attribute great power to it, but primarily in relation to illnesses and misfortunes caused by spirits. A number of my informants told me that they see a connection between the impurity of spirits and the fact that Muslim saints have power over them. Muslims appear to be close to the world of spirits and thus are able to master that world. In that sense they appear to be close to untouchables, who also can be specialists in exorcism. Thus there seems to be an incorporation of saint worship as a lower, impure practice in a Hindu worldview. Nandy's notion that there is a relation between this kind of syncretism and communal harmony is not supported by my material.

There is also nothing in my material which points to the gradual conversion of Hindus who are convinced of the power of the tomb. Quite probably, this may have been the case in an earlier historical period, although we do not have any material detailing the process. In contemporary India, conversion of Hindus to Islam is not on the agenda of Sufis. This is not surprising, since the power of the tomb and the saints is, more or less, limited to a fairly circumscribed domain of healing and magic. The Rifa'i brotherhood I studied controls few resources in the larger socio-economic world and this, obviously, diminishes its appeal and power.

Nevertheless, in however limited a way, there is no denying the fact that Hindus do participate in the Rifa'i cult. This does not embarrass the Rifa'i, since they see it as a confirmation of the importance and power of their cult. More striking than this understandable pride is the position of the Muslim opponents of tomb worship. In my many conversations with them they did not once mention the issues of Hindu influence or Hindu participation, which were once so important in Muslim debate.

To explain the avoidance of the related themes of Hindu participation and the influence of Hinduism, one should, paradoxically, realize the enormous political overdetermination of these themes. I would argue that it is hardly possible in contemporary India to separate discussion of them from the political assertion of boundaries between Hindus and Muslims. As I have argued earlier, the theme of 'Hindu influence' in reformist arguments has become linked to Muslim politics in India, since it deals directly with the boundaries between the two communities. There is no doubt that Hindu–Muslim relations are rapidly deteriorating in Gujarat, and communal violence, which was already rampant in places like Ahmedabad and Baroda, has recently hit Surat in a terrible way. Muslims in the city are very much preoccupied with their relation to the 'majority' community, and the dispute about the mosque–temple in Ayodhya has created a great insecurity among them. In Surat I got the impression that Muslims try to distance themselves from radical political assertion and that the theme of 'multiculturalism', 'communal harmony' and 'tolerance' dominates their discourse. I would suggest that this may, at least partly, explain why they do not talk about the sensitive issues of Hindu participation and the influence of Hinduism.

CONCLUSION

Syncretism is a term which in comparative religion refers to a process of religious amalgamation, of blending heterogeneous beliefs and practices. As such, it is an aspect of religious interaction over time. This can be seen as such a broad process that indeed every religion is syncretistic, since it constantly draws upon heterogeneous elements to the extent that it is often impossible for historians to unravel what comes from where. One could therefore argue that it is a useless concept. I agree that it is, when seen as a simple descriptive term. However, I hope to have shown that syncretism is a very interesting, though elusive, concept when seen as part of religious discourse.

Richard Handler (1988) has recently argued in a book on nationalism that boundedness, continuity and homogeneity are not objective aspects of social life, but metaphors used in nationalist discourse to create the 'entitivity' of the nation. The same could be argued about the role of religious discourse in the construction of religious communities. Syncretism is a term within that discourse which acknowledges the permeability and fluidity of social life, but is used to evaluate it. That evaluation depends on the context in which it is made. Syncretism can be seen, negatively, as a corruption of the absolute Truth. It can be seen, positively, as a sign of tolerance. In all these cases it has to be discursively identified.

'Multiculturalism' appears to have replaced the term 'syncretism' in discourse about modern, secular society. Again, it is a term that refers to the openness of social life and is used to judge it, negatively or positively. Those who defend multiculturalism in the United States want to maintain cultural differences by respecting them. In their view the different cultural identities of American citizens should be recognized in a multicultural curriculum. They further claim that this would promote tolerance (see Taylor 1992). Those who reject multiculturalism see it as a deplorable deviation from the Enlightenment project. They continue to value the old ideal of assimilation to Euro-American civilization.

What the debate about syncretism in seventeenth-century Europe and that about multiculturalism in the contemporary United States seem to have in common is that they both try to give answers to situations of civil strife seemingly caused by insurmountable differences in religious or cultural identities. Both terms belong to a discourse of tolerance and communal harmony. This is also true for the Indian case. I see the case made for the pluralistic culture of India as basically a plea for communal harmony, and one would certainly not want to distance oneself from that. Nevertheless, it remains important to examine critically the terms in which the case is made. Both radical Hindus and their opponents claim that Indian culture is basically tolerant, because it is pluralistic. This claim can be used in very different ways, but often it has a distinctively Hindu flavour. As I have tried to show, both in the case of the philosopher Radhakrishnan and in the case of Hindu participants in Sufi saint worship, Hindu syncretism encompasses other religions. It includes Muslim practices on a hierarchically low level. While it is questionable whether Muslims like this inclusion, it is also not immediately clear why it should lead to respect and communal harmony.

In the discussion of Indian Islam, saint worship is often seen as syncretistic and tolerant. I have argued that Muslim worshippers of saints reject syncretism and that tolerance does not immediately follow from this practice. Muslim debate about saint worship resembles Christian debate about syncretism. Some Indian Muslims identify saint worship as 'innovation' and thus a corruption of the Truth. This identification is not accepted by others, who see saint worship as an integral part of orthodoxy. When anthropological outsiders label saint worship as syncretistic, they affirm one position in a Muslim debate about orthodoxy.

NOTES

This chapter is an amended English version of my inaugural lecture for the Chair in Comparative Religion given at the University of Amsterdam on 2 April 1993. I want to thank Charles Stewart for his invitation to join this volume and for his incisive comments.

REFERENCES

Ahmad, A. (1969) *An Intellectual History of Islam in India*, Edinburgh: University of Edinburgh Press.

Ahmad, I. (1981) *Ritual and Religion among Muslims in India*, New Delhi: Manohar.

Asad, T. (1983) 'Anthropological conceptions of religion: reflections on Geertz', *Man* (NS) 18: 237–59.

Berlin, J. (1980) *The Syncretic Religion of Lin Chao-En*, New York: Columbia University Press.

Das, V. (1984) 'For a folk-theology and theological anthropology of Islam', *Contributions to Indian Sociology* (*ns*) 18, 2: 293–99.

Fusfeld, W. (1987) 'The boundaries of Islam and infidelity', in Katherine Ewing (ed.), *Shari'at and Ambiguity in South Asian Islam*, Berkeley: University of California Press.

Gaborieau, M. (1989) 'A nineteenth-century Indian 'Wahhabi' tract against the cult of Muslim saints: *Al Balag al Mubin*', in Christian Troll (ed.), *Muslim Shrines in India*, Delhi: Oxford University Press.

Glazer, N. and Moynihan, D. P. (1963) *Beyond the Melting Pot*, Cambridge, MA.: Harvard University Press.

Gombrich, R. and Obeyesekere, G. (1988) *Buddhism Transformed*, Princeton, NJ: Princeton University Press.

Handler, R. (1988) *Nationalism and the Politics of Culture in Quebec*, Madison, WI: University of Wisconsin Press.

Herklots, G.A. (1921 [1832]) *Islam in India or the Qanun-i-Islam: The Customs of the Musalmans of India*, new edn, rev. and rearranged William Crooke, London: Oxford University Press.

Kamstra, J.H. (1970) *Synkretisme*, Leiden: E.J. Brill.

Kapferer, B. (1988) *Legends of People, Myths of State*, Washington, DC: Smithsonian Institution Press.

Koselleck, R. (1988) *Critique and Crisis*, Cambridge, MA: MIT Press.

McKean, L. (1992) 'Towards a politics of spirituality: Hindu religious organizations and Indian nationalism', unpublished PhD thesis, University of Sydney.

Minault, G. (1984) 'Some reflections on Islamic revivalism vs. assimilation among Muslims in India', *Contributions to Indian Sociology* (ns) 18, 2: 301–5.

Minor, R. (1989) 'Sarvepalli Radhakrishnan and "Hinduism"', in Robert Baird (ed.), *Religion in Modern India*, Delhi: Manohar.

Nandy, A. (1990) 'The politics of secularism and the recovery of religious tolerance', in Veena Das (ed.), *Mirrors of Violence*, Delhi: Oxford University Press.

Nehru, J. (1946) *The Discovery of India*, New York: John Day.

Pye, M. (1971) 'Syncretism and ambiguity', *Numen*, 18: 83–93.

Robinson, F. (1983) 'Islam and Muslim society in South Asia', *Contributions to Indian Sociology*, (ns) 17, 2: 185–203.

Roy, A. (1983) *The Islamic Syncretistic Tradition in Bengal*, Princeton, NJ: Princeton University Press.

Schlesinger, A. (1992) *The Disuniting of America: Reflections on a Multicultural Society*, New York: Norton.

Taylor, C. (1989) *Sources of the Self*, Cambridge, MA.: Harvard University Press.

—— (1992) *Multiculturalism and 'The Politics of Recognition'*, Princeton, NJ: Princeton University Press.

Van der Veer, Peter (1988) *Gods on Earth*, London: Athlone.

—— (1992) 'Playing or praying: a Sufi saint's day in Surat', *Journal of Asian Studies* 51, 3: 445–564.

—— (1994) *Religious Nationalism. Hindus and Muslims in India*, Berkeley: University of California Press.

Afterword

Richard Werbner

These essays breathe new life into the study of syncretism. Syncretism is, of course, full of controversies – some surrounding the very concept itself, others about what is pronounced to be the diabolical sin of mixing religious traditions, still others about the authenticity of reconciling religious differences. The essays disclose a considerable range of such controversies, involving Christians, Muslims, Hindus or Shintoists and their opponents: and the overview in the introduction, 'Problematizing Syncretism', unearths the archaeology of syncretism itself, of a term that is highly contentious, and around which has accumulated a largely pejorative semantic load.

Not suprisingly, the religious politics, as it is discussed in a number of the essays, turns upon the play of the argumentative imagination. It is all about image and counter-image, debate and counter-debate. These essays enable us to understand how that play of the argumentative imagination is realized: how it is enacted in syncretism during the formation of a nation state, foregrounded in situations of colonial and postcolonial dominance or resistance, and glorified in the struggle for expansive imperialism by a world power.

The contributors bring together a theoretical interest in the social history of religious synthesis with the interest in both cross-cultural translation and the politics of cultural difference and social identity. This leads them to address socio-cultural change, whether syncretic or anti-syncretic, by treating its rich specifics as historically sited phenomena. In turn, this also leads to an illumination of the connections between broad problems of personal agency and syncretism. Here syncretism is delineated as the *continually contested* social action which, operating across cultures or traditions, appropriates, reproduces, or re-invents religious belief and practice. The politics of syncretism is a politics of interpretation and re-interpretation.

What becomes obvious is that syncretism is not one but many

processes; the concern of many discourses, not one alone. A number of the essays make this point by focusing their theoretical arguments on the many ambiguities of syncretism. Close attention is paid, and rightly so, to the significance of the differences in participants' perspectives.

An important example is a remarkable case in which, on one side, a local *imam*, as a homecoming pilgrim, foregrounds purist reforms, intended to make local religious belief and practice conform publicly to the perceived universals of Islam as a world religion. On the other side, all of that imported reality is backgrounded by notable women in controversy with the *imam*: they foreground the continuity in their secret – and to the *imam*, *inaccessible* – religious practice. It is their secret practice which identifies the women and their selves to themselves, as they truly are, in their indigenous identity. Here we are made to understand why, as historically situated agents, able to compartmentalize one sphere of social interaction from another, participants disagree among themselves not merely about the desirability of syncretic change, but also about its actuality.

A number of the essays extend the argument further – they elucidate how the management of identity and difference is actively reworked to fit the insistence upon setting apart a sphere of 'religion' as the lasting, the pure, and the authentic. As such, it is shown to be a sphere which is quintessentially definitive of the self in contrast to the Other.

A brief example is enough for an immediate illustration. Living in Germany, Turkish immigrants are drawn into the celebration with Germans of Christmas fireworks. What the immigrants resist is the blurring of the difference between them and their German hosts at the expense of their identity as Muslims. Instead, they do all they can, in the face of the subtle and inescapably intense pressures of the season, to redefine the Christmas celebration – it is made out to be a matter of 'culture' and, as such, wholly secular – 'religion' does not come into it. Islam, like the precious identity which the migrants secure from it, is kept uncompromised in its perceived authenticity.

The slash in the collection's title – *Syncretism/Anti-syncretism* – is a deliberate marker, and so, too, is the relation it represents. Subsumed at its broadest, the relations between the tendencies is what we might call co-implication; it is a mutual involvement, but, according to context, the involvement is an encompassment of one tendency by the other, or their complementarity, or their signficance as cause and effect in a spiral of causes and effects, or the tension between them as conflicting tendencies. And in specific cases, over time, it may be all of these, or a combination of a number. It is, of course, a relation full of paradoxes, which the essays take great care to illuminate, showing how and why the participants transcend or transgress religious boundaries in syncretism, while in anti-syncretism, they defend them.

The study of syncretism has its own Scylla and Charybdis. At one extreme is that hard place packed by much of the chorus of high (or 'post') modernity. There intercommunication across cultural differences is no less than the universal truth. At the other extreme is the sea of evaluative judgements, often of a pejorative kind, filled by reference to some idealized, now usually textual, standard, such as 'pure Christanity', or 'the incontrovertibly Christian'.

Perhaps the most pressing hazard, past which the essays negotiate, comes from the rising tide of high modernity. This foregrounds cultural hybrids on the assumption that what cultural and social intercommunication produces virtually everywhere is the hybrid. On this assumption, also, comes the idealization of change as cross-cultural borrowing, copying, and mixing. It is as if such interaction is endemic in all social life: and to that, religious change cannot appear to be an exception. Hence, from such a starting point, what easily gets placed beyond discovery is the central relation of syncretism to anti-syncretism.

The editors themselves, having opened out a very broad field for exploration, are understandably reluctant to narrow it down – as it were, to commit themselves to anti-syncretism in advance – by a pre-emptive definition of syncretism. They leave no doubts about the focus of the essays' theoretical interests: 'The Politics of Religious Synthesis' is their subtitle. Nevertheless, only *in principle* do they agree that syncretism, both as a process and as a discourse, is of and about religion and ritual.

That agreement is the basis, in the editors' view, for no more than a provisional definition, one that is best left open, for the heuristic purposes of a truly comparative anthropology. The error would be to focus upon religion as if universally it were institutionalized and had a domain of its own, as it does among ourselves. The editors' aim is to avoid Eurocentrism. Hence, in their usage, syncretism is a broad term, much broader in scope than the relatively limited range of societies having institutionalized religion.

In commenting on this, the editors respond generously in order to take us beyond the limits of a suggestion which I myself first put as a discussant for the panel on syncretism at the 1992 American Anthropological meetings. On my first reading of the papers, I was struck by the diversity in hybridization – there was an evident potential for carrying the initial arguments a stage further by making a set of conceptual distinctions for understanding differences in the processes of hybridization and also in the related discourses. I recognize that, in the present edition, the development of the analysis of shifts in and between syncretism and anti-syncretism meets one part of this problem of conceptualization.

For another part, however, I still find it useful to make an analytic distinction between syncretism and bricolage. Very briefly, bricolage is the formation of fresh cultural forms from the ready-to-hand debris of old ones. By contrast, the contentious and distinctively ritual and/or religious hybridization is syncretism.

The distinction makes it possible to consider how and why the tendencies toward or against hybridization vary or are made to unfold in a whole set of actual situations. Included in this are some situations in which in practice it is difficult to distinguish bricolage from syncretism, and some others in which, over time and through the work of active agents upon the traces of cultural sedimentation, earlier syncretism becomes later bricolage, and conversely. This suggested usage has the further advantage of keying analysis to that semantic load of religious contestation and contentiousness which is so dominantly distinctive of syncretism.

In this Afterword, I have taken advantage of the editors' invitation to have the last word. It has given me the opportunity to express my sense of excitement in being a party to the rediscovery of syncretism/anti-syncretism as a fit subject for anthropological argument. On the evidence of this collection, the editors' are right, for sure: syncretism, as term and as concept, along with anti-syncretism, now joins fetishism in a major revival. It links the anthropology of religion and politics to the widest debates about socio-cultural hybridization as an outstanding contemporary transformation of our time.

Name index

Subject index